# Concrete Technology
## (Theory and Practice)

**AUTHORS**

**Prof. Sasankasekhar Mandal**
*Professor,*
Department of Civil Engineering,
IIT (BHU), Varanasi, India

**Dr. Vishwajit Anand**
*Assistant Professor,*
Department of Civil Engineering,
IIT (BHU), Varanasi, India

**Prof. Sushil Kumar Agarwala**
*Former Professor,*
Department of Civil Engineering,
IIT Roorkee, India

**REVIEWER**

**Dr. M. L. Waikar**
*Adjunct faculty (Former Professor),*
Department of Civil Engineering
Shri Guru Gobind Singhji Institute of Engineering and
Technology, Nanded, Maharashtra, Indirsity), Bengaluru

**KHANNA BOOK PUBLISHING CO. (P) Ltd.**
4C/4344, Ansari Road, Darya Ganj,
New Delhi, India

**All India Council for Technical Education**
Nelson Mandela Marg, Vasant Kunj,
New Delhi, India

Dear Readers,

To prevent the piracy, this book is secured with HIGH SECURITY HOLOGRAM on the front title cover. In case you don't find the hologram on the front cover title, please write us to at contact@khannabooks.com or whatsapp us at +91-99109 09320 and avail special gift voucher for yourself.

Specimen of Hologram on front Cover title:

Moreover, there is a SPECIAL DISCOUNT COUPON for you with EVERY HOLOGRAM.

How to avail this SPECIAL DISCOUNT:

Step 1: Scratch the hologram

Step 2: Under the scratch area, your "coupon code" is available

Step 3: Logon to www.khannabooks.com

Step 4: Use your "coupon code" in the shopping cart and get your copy at a special discount

Step 5: Enjoy your reading!


**ISBN:** 978-93-5538-265-8

**Book Code:** DIP437EN


**Concrete Technology (Theory and Practice)**

*by* Prof. Sasankasekhar Mandal, Dr. Vishwajit Anand and Prof. Sushil Kumar Agarwala


**First Edition:** 2025

*Originally Published by:*

**All India Council for Technical Education, Ministry of Education, GOI**

*Exclusively Published & Distributed by:*

**Khanna Book Publishing Co. (P) Ltd.**

4C/4344, Ansari Road, Daryaganj,
New Delhi (INDIA)

Visit us at: **www.khannabooks.com**

Write us at: **contact@khannabooks.com**

To view complete list of books, Please scan the QR Code:

KPH

*Printed in Bharat.*

प्रो. टी. जी. सीताराम
अध्यक्ष
Prof. T. G. Sitharam
Chairman

सत्यमेव जयते

आज़ादी का अमृत महोत्सव

अखिल भारतीय तकनीकी शिक्षा परिषद्
(भारत सरकार का एक सांविधिक निकाय)
(शिक्षा मंत्रालय, भारत सरकार)
नेल्सन मंडेला मार्ग, वसंत कुंज, नई दिल्ली–110070
दूरभाष : 011–26131498
ई–मेल : chairman@aicte-india.org

ALL INDIA COUNCIL FOR TECHNICAL EDUCATION
(A STATUTORY BODY OF THE GOVT. OF INDIA)
(Ministry of Education, Govt. of India)
Nelson Mandela Marg, Vasant Kunj, New Delhi-110070
Phone : 011-26131498
E-mail : chairman@aicte-india.org

# FOREWORD

Engineers are the backbone of any modern society. They are the ones responsible for the marvels as well as the improved quality of life across the world. Engineers have driven humanity towards greater heights in a more evolved and unprecedented manner.

The All India Council for Technical Education (AICTE), have spared no efforts towards the strengthening of the technical education in the country. AICTE is always committed towards promoting quality Technical Education to make India a modern developed nation emphasizing on the overall welfare of mankind.

An array of initiatives has been taken by AICTE in last decade which have been accelerated now by the National Education Policy (NEP) 2020. The implementation of NEP under the visionary leadership of Hon'ble Prime Minister of India envisages the provision for education in regional languages to all, thereby ensuring that every graduate becomes competent enough and is in a position to contribute towards the national growth and development through innovation & entrepreneurship.

One of the spheres where AICTE had been relentlessly working since past couple of years is providing high quality original technical contents at Under Graduate & Diploma level prepared and translated by eminent educators in various Indian languages to its aspirants. For students pursuing 2nd year of their Engineering education, AICTE has identified 87 books, which shall be translated into 12 Indian languages - Hindi, Tamil, Gujarati, Odia, Bengali, Kannada, Urdu, Punjabi, Telugu, Marathi, Assamese & Malayalam. In addition to the English medium, books in different Indian Languages are going to support the students to understand the concepts in their respective mother tongue.

On behalf of AICTE, I express sincere gratitude to all distinguished authors, reviewers and translators from the renowned institutions of high repute for their admirable contribution in a record span of time.

AICTE is confident that these outcomes based original contents shall help aspirants to master the subject with comprehension and greater ease.

(Prof. T. G. Sitharam)

## ACKNOWLEDGEMENT

We extend their gratitude to All India Council for Technical Education (AICTE) for providing an opportunity to ink this book on *Concrete Technology: Theory and Practice* for Diploma students. We are thankful for their meticulous planning and execution, right from providing relevant syllabus to publication of the book.

We sincerely acknowledge the contributions of the reviewer of the book Prof. Waikar Milind Laxmanrao, Adjunct faculty, Shri Guru Gobind Singhji Institute of Engineering and Technology, Nanded. His valuable suggestions proved instrumental in enhancing the quality of the book and making it friendly for students. We are also thankful to Dr. Amit Kumar Srivastava, Director, Faculty Development Cell, AICTE for facilitating the entire process and being available with prompt responses.

We sincerely acknowledge various authors and experts, whose books, articles, footnotes and other valuable information enriched us at the time of writing the book. We also thank Bureau of Indian Standards (BIS) and Indian Institute of Technology (Banaras Hindu University) for making Indian Standards available to us.

We are thankful to efforts from our postgraduate students at IIT (BHU), Amarendra Nath Shandilya, Ashish Singh, Karri Srinivas, Mangeshkumar Rajkumar Shendkar, Shreesh Shrivastav, Subhajit Mondal and Vijay Kumar. We acknowledge Akhilesh Kumar Jaiswar, Technical Assistant, IIT BHU. The book could be possible only with their support in drafting and drawing of sketches.

We extend our gratitude to our family members to be with us always during this noble journey.

**Prof. Sasankasekhar Mandal**

**Dr. Vishwajit Anand**

**Prof. Sushil Kumar Agarwala**

# PREFACE

Concrete is the most versatile building material. Its property to get moulded in any shape easily makes it widely used in infrastructure projects including buildings, bridges, dams, silos and pavements. Durability of these structures depends on quality production, testing and maintenance of concrete.

This book is intended to provide students and professionals, a deep understanding of concrete technology. It explains the fundamental concepts, material characteristics and related laboratory experiments on concrete and its ingredients. It also includes relevant provisions of Indian Standards such as IS 456, IS 10262, IS 383, IS 2386 and IS 516.

Unit 1 details properties of ingredients of concrete, viz., cement, aggregates and water.

Unit 2 describes the different grades of concrete and properties of fresh concrete.

Unit 3 outlines the procedure to obtain concrete mix design as per IS 10262. It also explains destructive and non-destructive tests on hardened concrete.

Unit 4 provides details of quality control during various concreting operations. It also details formwork for concreting, waterproofing and joints in concrete construction.

Unit 5 discusses chemical admixtures, special concrete and extreme weather concreting.

Unit 6 details laboratory and field experiments to determine properties of concrete and its ingredients.

The book provides latest scientific advances in concrete technology. We hope that students will find it easy to comprehend, and concrete technology fraternity at large will get benefitted. Comments and suggestions to further improve the book are always welcome, and can be sent to *smandal.civ@iitbhu.ac.in, anand.civ@iitbhu.ac.in, sushilkumar39@gmail.com.*

**Prof. Sasankasekhar Mandal**
**Dr. Vishwajit Anand**
**Prof. Sushil Kumar Agarwala**

# OUTCOME BASED EDUCATION

For the implementation of an outcome based education the first requirement is to develop an outcome based curriculum and incorporate an outcome based assessment in the education system. By going through outcome based assessments evaluators will be able to evaluate whether the students have achieved the outlined standard, specific and measurable outcomes. With the proper incorporation of outcome based education there will be a definite commitment to achieve a minimum standard for all learners without giving up at any level. At the end of the program running with the aid of outcome based education, a student will be able to arrive at the following outcomes:

**PO-1.** **Engineering knowledge:** Apply the knowledge of mathematics, science, engineering fundamentals, and an engineering specialization to the solution of complex engineering problems.

**PO-2.** **Problem analysis:** Identify, formulate, review research literature, and analyze complex engineering problems reaching substantiated conclusions using first principles of mathematics, natural sciences, and engineering sciences.

**PO-3.** **Design / development of solutions:** Design solutions for complex engineering problems and design system components or processes that meet the specified needs with appropriate consideration for the public health and safety, and the cultural, societal, and environmental considerations.

**PO-4.** **Conduct investigations of complex problems:** Use research-based knowledge and research methods including design of experiments, analysis and interpretation of data, and synthesis of the information to provide valid conclusions.

**PO-5.** **Modern tool usage:** Create, select, and apply appropriate techniques, resources, and modern engineering and IT tools including prediction and modeling to complex engineering activities with an understanding of the limitations.

**PO-6.** **The engineer and society:** Apply reasoning informed by the contextual knowledge to assess societal, health, safety, legal and cultural issues and the consequent responsibilities relevant to the professional engineering practice.

**PO-7.** **Environment and sustainability:** Understand the impact of the professional engineering solutions in societal and environmental contexts, and demonstrate the knowledge of, and need for sustainable development.

**PO-8.** **Ethics:** Apply ethical principles and commit to professional ethics and responsibilities and norms of the engineering practice.

**PO-9.** **Individual and team work:** Function effectively as an individual, and as a member or leader in diverse teams, and in multidisciplinary settings.

**PO-10.** **Communication:** Communicate effectively on complex engineering activities with the engineering community and with society at large, such as, being able to comprehend and write effective reports and design documentation, make effective presentations, and give and receive clear instructions.

**PO-11. Project management and finance:** Demonstrate knowledge and understanding of the engineering and management principles and apply these to one's own work, as a member and leader in a team, to manage projects and in multidisciplinary environments.

**PO-12. Life-long learning:** Recognize the need for, and have the preparation and ability to engage in independent and life-long learning in the broadest context of technological change.

# COURSE OUTCOMES

After completion of the course the students will be able to:

**CO-1:** Use different types of cement and aggregates in concrete

**CO-2:** Prepare concrete of desired compressive strength.

**CO-3:** Prepare concrete of required specification.

**CO-4:** Maintain quality of concrete under different conditions.

**CO-5:** Apply relevant admixtures for concreting.

Mapping of Course Outcomes with Programme Outcomes to be done according to the matrix given below:

| Course Outcomes | Expected Mapping with Programme Outcomes (1- Weak Correlation; 2- Medium correlation; 3- Strong Correlation) | | | | | | | | | | | |
|---|---|---|---|---|---|---|---|---|---|---|---|---|
| | PO-1 | PO-2 | PO-3 | PO-4 | PO-5 | PO-6 | PO-7 | PO-8 | PO-9 | PO-10 | PO-11 | PO-12 |
| CO-1 | 2 | - | - | - | 3 | 2 | 3 | - | - | - | - | 1 |
| CO-2 | 3 | 3 | 3 | - | 3 | - | 3 | - | 2 | - | 2 | 2 |
| CO-3 | 2 | 3 | 3 | - | 3 | - | 3 | - | 2 | - | 2 | 2 |
| CO-4 | 2 | 2 | 2 | - | 3 | 2 | 3 | 3 | 3 | 2 | 3 | 2 |
| CO-5 | 2 | - | - | 2 | 2 | 2 | 3 | 1 | 1 | - | 1 | 1 |

## GUIDELINES FOR TEACHERS

To implement Outcome Based Education (OBE) knowledge level and skill set of the students should be enhanced. Teachers should take a major responsibility for the proper implementation of OBE. Some of the responsibilities (not limited to) for the teachers in OBE system may be as follows:

- Within reasonable constraint, they should manoeuvre time to the best advantage of all students.
- They should assess the students only upon certain defined criterion without considering any other potential ineligibility to discriminate them.
- They should try to grow the learning abilities of the students to a certain level before they leave the institute.
- They should try to ensure that all the students are equipped with the quality knowledge as well as competence after they finish their education.
- They should always encourage the students to develop their ultimate performance capabilities.
- They should facilitate and encourage group work and team work to consolidate newer approach.
- They should follow Blooms taxonomy in every part of the assessment.

### Bloom's Taxonomy

| Level | Teacher should Check | Student should be able to | Possible Mode of Assessment |
|---|---|---|---|
| Creating | Students ability to create | Design or Create | Mini project |
| Evaluating | Students ability to Justify | Argue or Defend | Assignment |
| Analysing | Students ability to distinguish | Differentiate or Distinguish | Project/Lab Methodology |
| Applying | Students ability to use information | Operate or Demonstrate | Technical Presentation/ Demonstration |
| Understanding | Students ability to explain the ideas | Explain or Classify | Presentation/Seminar |
| Remembering | Students ability to recall (or remember) | Define or Recall | Quiz |

## GUIDELINES FOR STUDENTS

Students should take equal responsibility for implementing the OBE. Some of the responsibilities (not limited to) for the students in OBE system are as follows:

- Students should be well aware of each UO before the start of a unit in each and every course.
- Students should be well aware of each CO before the start of the course.
- Students should be well aware of each PO before the start of the programme.
- Students should think critically and reasonably with proper reflection and action.
- Learning of the students should be connected and integrated with practical and real life consequences.
- Students should be well aware of their competency at every level of OBE.

# LIST OF FIGURES

# AICTE'S LIST OF PRESCRIBED TEXTBOOKS

As Per Model Curriculum & Outcome Based Education

*aligned with*

**NATIONAL EDUCATION POLICY 2020**

## UNDERGRADUATE COURSE BOOKS

| S.No. | ISBN | Book Name | Author |
|---|---|---|---|
| 1 | 9789355382160 | Advanced Electrical Machines: Theory and Practicals | Bharat Singh Rajpurohit |
| 2 | 9789355382139 | Analog Electronic Circuits: Theory and Practical | Venu Sonti, Sachin Jain |
| 3 | 9789355383808 | Analog Electronic Devices: Theory and Practicals | N. B Balamurugan |
| 4 | 9789391505158 | Basic Electrical Engineering (with Lab Manual) | S.K. Sahdev |
| 5 | 9789355388087 | Basic of Electronics | Brijesh Iyer |
| 6 | 9789355387127 | Basics of Electrical Machines: Theory and Practicals | D. K. Palwalia, U. K. Kalla, R. K. Kumawat |
| 7 | 9789355389381 | Basics of Mechanics | Shubhankar Bhowmick, N. Venkata Swamy Naidu |
| 8 | 9789355386250 | Basics of Thermodynamics | Parmod Kumar, Atul Dhar |
| 9 | 9789355386984 | Biology for Engineers | Annamma Odaneth |
| 10 | 9789391505141 | Chemistry-I | Manisha Agarwal |
| 11 | 9789355384843 | Civil Engineering Societal and Global Impact | Shakuntala Acharya |
| 12 | 9789355382184 | Computer Aided Civil Engineering Drawing | D. Chandra Mouli, B. Swathi |
| 13 | 9789355382580 | Computer Aided Design & Analysis | Hari Kumar Voruganti |
| 14 | 9789355387592 | Computer Architecture | D. Vaithiyanathan |
| 15 | 9789355385093 | Computer Networks | Hari Prabhat Gupta |
| 16 | 9789355385307 | Construction Engineering & Management | Sparsh Johari |
| 17 | 9789355388728 | Control Systems | S.N. Deepa |
| 18 | 9789355385420 | Data Structure and Algorithms | Ranbir Singh Sanasam |
| 19 | 9789355386700 | Design and Analysis of Algorithms | Hari P. Gupta, Rahul Mishra |
| 20 | 9789355388872 | Digital Electronics and System | Abhishek Bhatt |
| 21 | 9789355386571 | Digital Signal Processing | Sanjeev Sharma |
| 22 | 9789355383396 | Disaster management | Pradeep K. Goyal, Anil K. Gupta |
| 23 | 9789355385222 | Discrete Mathematical Structures | Narendra S. Chaudhari, Sharmila S. P. |
| 24 | 9789355387868 | Effective Technical Communication | Pritee Sharma, Sanchita Verma |
| 25 | 9789355383389 | Electrical Circuit Analysis and Network Theory | Shouri Chatterjee |
| 26 | 9789355388957 | Electromagnetic Waves | Uttam M. Pal, Srijith K. |
| 27 | 9789355384652 | Electronic Communication | Vimal Bhatia |
| 28 | 9789355388711 | Embedded Systems | Santanu Chattopadhyay |
| 29 | 9789355385147 | Energy Science and Engineering | M. Rizwan, Majid Jamil |
| 30 | 9789355387929 | Engineering Economics, Estimation & Costing | Yogesh C. Joshi |
| 31 | 9789355384669 | Engineering Geology | R. N. Khare, Ketan Chourasia |
| 32 | 9789391505066 | Engineering Graphics & Design | Pradeep Jain |
| 33 | 9789391505097 | English (with Lab Manual) | Kulbhushan Kumar |
| 34 | 9789355385963 | Environmental Engineering | Chandra Sekhar Matli |
| 35 | 9789355388117 | Fluid Mechanics | Shreenivas N. Londhe, Pradnya R. Dixit |
| 36 | 9789355388377 | Fluid Mechanics & Fluid Machines | R.P. Saini |
| 37 | 9789355387103 | Geotechnical Engineering | Paramita Bhattacharya |

## UNDERGRADUATE COURSE BOOKS

| S.No. | ISBN | Book Name | Author |
|---|---|---|---|
| 38 | 9789355385130 | Hydraulic Engineering | Sayantan Ganguly |
| 39 | 9789355385550 | Hydrology & Water Resources Engineering | Mitthan Lal Kansal, P.K. Agarwal |
| 40 | 9789355389688 | Information Technology Workshop in MATLAB | Hari Prabhat Gupta |
| 41 | 9789355383235 | Instrumentation for Civil Engineering Applications | Ashim Kanti Dey, Manita Das |
| 42 | 9789355387042 | Introduction to Civil Engineering | Manabendra Saharia, Nagendra R. Velaga |
| 43 | 9789355384805 | Introduction to Database Systems | Vikram Singh |
| 44 | 9789355387509 | Machine Element & System Design | Sabah Khan |
| 45 | 9789355385383 | Machine Learning | Himanshu Mittal |
| 46 | 9789355388414 | Manufacturing Automation | Chitragupt Swaroop Chitransh |
| 47 | 9789355387233 | Manufacturing Processes | Dheerendra Kumar Dwivedi |
| 48 | 9789355389886 | Materials Engineering | Dheerendra Kumar Dwivedi |
| 49 | 9789391505172 | Mathematics - I Calculus and Linear Algebra [For Non-Computer Science Engineering Branches] | Reena Garg |
| 50 | 9789391505271 | Mathematics - I Calculus and Linear Algebra [For Computer Science Engineering Branches] | Reena Garg |
| 51 | 9789355384607 | Measurements & Metrology | V.P. Chandramohan |
| 52 | 9789355383730 | Mechanics of Materials | Arvind Vyavahare |
| 53 | 9789355383358 | Mechatronics, Robotics & Control | J. Srinivas |
| 54 | 9789355385116 | Microprocessor and Microcontroller | Saurabh Chaudhury, Risha Mal |
| 55 | 9789355386083 | Microprocessors | Yogendra Kumar Gupta |
| 56 | 9789355389169 | Mobile Communication and Networks | Vimal Bhatia |
| 57 | 9789355385475 | Operating Systems | Sukomal Pal |
| 58 | 9789355385604 | Operating Systems | Sanjaya Kumar Panda |
| 59 | 9789391505134 | Physics ( Oscillations, Waves and Optics) With lab manual | A.B. Bhattacharya, Atanu Nag |
| 60 | 9789391505257 | Physics ( Quantum Mechanics for Engineers) With lab manual | A.B. Bhattacharya, Atanu Nag |
| 61 | 9789391505165 | Physics (Introduction to Electromagnetic Theory) (with Lab Manual) | A.B. Bhattacharya, Atanu Nag |
| 62 | 9789391505059 | Physics (Introduction to Mechanics) (with Lab Manual) | A.B. Bhattacharya, Atanu Nag |
| 63 | 9789355385956 | Power Electronics: Theory and Practicals | Lalit Chandra Saikia |
| 64 | 9789355384942 | Power Systems-I | Suresh Mikkili |
| 65 | 9789355386236 | Power Systems-II | Arun Rahul S, Manas K. Jena |
| 66 | 9789355383754 | Product Innovation & Entrepreneurship | Vigneswaran C |
| 67 | 9789355384584 | Production & Operation Management | Navin Kumar Dev |
| 68 | 9789391505219 | Programming for Problem Solving (with Lab Manual) | R.S. Salaria |
| 69 | 9789355385451 | Signals and Systems | Sanjay L. Nalbalwar |
| 70 | 9789355386021 | Strength of Materials | Uday Shanker Dixit, Nelson Muthu, S. M. Kamal |
| 71 | 9789355383792 | Structural Engineering | T.D. Gunneswara Rao, D. Ravi Prasad |
| 72 | 9789355387004 | Surveying and Geomatics | P. K. Garg |
| 73 | 9789355384317 | Testing & Evaluation of Civil Engineering Materials | Sandeep Chaudhary, Kashyap A Patel |
| 74 | 9789355382306 | Theory of Computation | Debi Prasanna Acharjya |
| 75 | 9789355384928 | Transportation Engineering | A.K. Raji |
| 76 | 9789355385208 | VLSI Design | Mahendra Sakare, Shonal Chouksey |
| 77 | 9789391505332 | Workshop / Manufacturing Practices (with Lab Manual) | Veeranna D.K. |

## DIPLOMA COURSE BOOKS

| S.No. | ISBN | Book Name | Author |
|---|---|---|---|
| 1 | 9789355382481 | Aanandam An Act of Community Service | Shuchi Sharma |
| 2 | 9789355385567 | Advanced Manufacturing Processes | Ranjeet Kumar Sahu, Devendra Laxman Kamble |
| 3 | 9789355385109 | Advanced Surveying: Theory & Practice | Ramakant Agrawal, Parshottam Sarathe |
| 4 | 9789355384546 | Algorithms | Piyoosh P, Arnab Sarkar |
| 5 | 9789391505448 | Applied Chemistry (with Lab Manual) | Anju Rawlley, Devdatta Vinayakrao Saraf |
| 6 | 9789391505431 | Applied Physics-I (with Lab Manual) | Vinod Kumar Yadav, Mina Talati |
| 7 | 9789391505578 | Applied Physics-II (with Lab Manual) | Hussain Jeevakhan |
| 8 | 9789355387530 | Basic Mechanical Engineering | Dharmendra Singh, Chandra Shekhar Rajoria |
| 9 | 9789355387394 | Building Construction | Rinku Kumar, Sandeep Panchal |
| 10 | 9789355383280 | Building Electrification | Arnab Ghosh |
| 11 | 9789355384379 | Building Planning and Drawing | Aparna Dwivedi |
| 12 | 9789391505493 | Communication Skills in English | Anjana Tiwari |
| 13 | 9789355383570 | Computer Aided Machine Drawing Practice | Kanak Kalita |
| 14 | 9789355388964 | Computer Networking and Data Communication | Sanjaya Shankar Tripathy |
| 15 | 9789355382986 | Computer Networks: Theory & Practicals | Brijendra Pratap Singh, Manoj Madhava Gore |
| 16 | 9789355382672 | Computer Programming: Theory and Practicals | Satyendra Singh Chouhan |
| 17 | 9789355387714 | Computer System Organization | Sonal Yadav |
| 18 | 9789355382658 | Concrete Technology: Theory and Practice | Sasankasekhar Mandal, Vishwajit Anand, Sushil K. Agarwala |
| 19 | 9789355383334 | Construction Materials and Testing | Vanita Aggarwal |
| 20 | 9789355383501 | Consumer Electronics | Amit M. Joshi, Maulin M. Joshi, Urvashi Prakash Shukla |
| 21 | 9789355387684 | Data Structures: Theory & Practicals | NB Venkateswarlu |
| 22 | 9789355388513 | Design of Machine Elements | A. Kumaravel, M. Kathirselvam |
| 23 | 9789355388360 | Design of Steel and RCC Structure | Sparsh Johari |
| 24 | 9789355383303 | Digital Communication | Muralidhar Kulkarni, K. S. Shivaprakasha |
| 25 | 9789355387295 | Digital Electronics | Menka Yadav |
| 26 | 9789355389435 | Electric Circuits and Networks | Jamuna K., Nilanjan Tewari |
| 27 | 9789355388452 | Electric Motors and Transformers (Theory and Practicals) | Sanjay B. Bodkhe |
| 28 | 9789355385901 | Electric Power Transmission and Distribution | Sudhir Sharma |
| 29 | 9789355389466 | Electrical & Electronics Measurements and Instrumentation | Sudarsan Sahoo, Vipin Chandra Pal, Sudipta Chakraborty |
| 30 | 9789355382696 | Electronic Communication | M. D. Selvaraj, P. Nagaradjane |
| 31 | 9789355387202 | Electronic Devices and Circuits | Ankesh Jain |
| 32 | 9789355386373 | Electronic Equipment Maintenance | Chanchal Sharma |
| 33 | 9789355384690 | Embedded Systems | Deepa M, G. Santhanamari, Susithra. N |
| 34 | 9789355384867 | Energy Conservation and Audit | M. Rizwan, Majid Jamil |
| 35 | 9789391505509 | Engineering Graphics | Sharad K. Pradhan, K.K. Jain |
| 36 | 9789391505608 | Engineering Mechanics (with Lab Manual) | Bhankhar Bharat, Gokaldas Vandana Somkuwar |

## DIPLOMA COURSE BOOKS

| S.No. | ISBN | Book Name | Author |
|---|---|---|---|
| 37 | 9789391505516 | Engineering Workshop Practice | A. K. Sarathe |
| 38 | 9789391505653 | Environmental Science | Subrat Roy |
| 39 | 9789355384966 | Estimating, Costing and valuation | Sandeep Panchal |
| 40 | 9789355389510 | Fluid Mechanics & Hydraulic Machinery | Suman Chakraborty, Sourav Mitra, Aditya Bandopadhyay |
| 41 | 9789391505592 | Fundamentals of Electrical and Electronics Engineering (with Lab Manual) | Susan S. Mathew, Saji T. Chacko |
| 42 | 9789355387240 | Fundamentals of Power Electronics | Soumitra Kumar Mandal |
| 43 | 9789355389602 | Geotechnical Engineering (Theory & Practicals) | Neelima Satyam |
| 44 | 9789355386137 | Induction, Synchronous, and Special Electrical Machines | K. Selvajyothi, S. Tamilselvi, Sarat Kumar Sahoo |
| 45 | 9789355382290 | Industrial Engineering & Management | A. Manimaran |
| 46 | 9789355384959 | Internet of Things | Sujata Pal |
| 47 | 9789355388650 | Introduction to DBMS: Theory & Practicals | Myneni Madhu Bala |
| 48 | 9789355384294 | Introduction to e-Governance | Kamal Kant Verma |
| 49 | 9789355386564 | Introduction to Electric Generation Systems | Lalit Chandra Saikia, Nalin Behari, Deb Choudhury |
| 50 | 9789391505585 | Introduction to IT Systems (with Lab Manual) | Prashant Joshi |
| 51 | 9789355382900 | Linear Integrated Circuit | B. T. Krishna |
| 52 | 9789355388148 | Manufacturing Engineering | Santosh Kumar |
| 53 | 9789355383877 | Material Science & Engineering | Vinod Kumar, Nisheeth k. Prasad |
| 54 | 9789391505424 | Mathematics-I | Deepak Singh |
| 55 | 9789391505523 | Mathematics-II | Garima Singh |
| 56 | 9789355385994 | Measurements and Metrology | A. Gnanavelbabu, M. Santhana kumar, R. Saranraj |
| 57 | 9789355388131 | Mechanics of Materials and their Testing | R. Velmurugan, Pragathi |
| 58 | 9789355385048 | Microcontroller Applications | Ritula Thakur |
| 59 | 9789355385062 | Microcontrollers and Applications | Santanu Chattopadhyay |
| 60 | 9789355388100 | Mobile and Wireless Communication | Maulin Joshi, Urvashi P. Shukla |
| 61 | 9789355387790 | Production & Operations Management | Mayank Kumar Agrawal |
| 62 | 9789355388704 | Public Health Engineering | Rinku Kumar |
| 63 | 9789355387455 | Python Programming | Rupesh Nasre |
| 64 | 9789355387189 | Renewable Energy Technologies | Sanjay Agrawal, Rajeev K. Mishra |
| 65 | 9789355387479 | Software Engineering | Salman Abdul Moiz |
| 66 | 9789355389749 | Theory of Machines & Mechanisms | G. C. Mohan Kumar |
| 67 | 9789355387332 | Theory of Structures | Arunachalam Subramanian Balu |
| 68 | 9789355389015 | Thermal Engineering - I | V. Raghavan |
| 69 | 9789355389831 | Thermal Engineering - II | Parvesh Antil |
| 70 | 9789355386779 | Transportation Engineering (Theory & Practice) | A.K. Raji, K.K. Babu |
| 71 | 9789355384287 | Water Resource Engineering (Theory & Practice) | Prakash C. Swain, Dillip K. Ghose |
| 72 | 9789355383051 | Web Technologies: Theory & Practical | Raman Dugyala |

## LIST OF TABLES

## CONTENTS

# 1 Cement Aggregate and Water

## UNIT SPECIFICS

Through this unit we have discussed the following aspects:

- Different types of cement, their physical and chemical properties have been discussed.
- The methods to test the acceptability of cements by various laboratory experiments have been described.
- BIS specifications and field applications of different types of cements have been given briefly.
- Types and properties of fine and coarse aggregates have been described in detail.
- Quality of water used for concreting has been discussed as per IS 456-2000.

The practical applications of the topics are discussed for generating further curiosity and creativity as well as improving the basic understanding of the concepts.

Besides giving a large number of multiple-choice questions as well as questions of short and long answer types marked in two categories following lower and higher order of Bloom's taxonomy, a list of references and suggested readings are given in the unit so that one can go through them for practice. It is important to note that for getting more information on various topics of interest some QR codes have been provided in different sections which can be scanned for relevant supportive knowledge.

## RATIONALE

This unit on fundamental constituents of concrete will help students to get a primary idea about the physical and chemical properties of cement, aggregate and water. The unit explains the IS specifications and different laboratory experiments to be conducted on these constituent materials of concrete. All these basic aspects are relevant to understand the basics of producing a durable concrete.

## PRE-REQUISITES

Chemistry: Chemical reactions (Class XII)

## UNIT OUTCOMES

List of outcomes of this unit is as follows:

**U1-O1:** To understand the physical and chemical properties of cement

**U1-O2:** To know about the properties of coarse and fine aggregates

**U1-O3:** To learn about laboratory experiments on cement, aggregate, and water

**U1-O4:** To realize the role of water in concrete production as per IS specifications

| Unit-1 Outcome | EXPECTED MAPPING WITH COURSE OUTCOMES (1 - Weak Correlation; 2 - Medium Correlation; 3 - Strong Correlation) | | | | |
|---|---|---|---|---|---|
| | CO-1 | CO-2 | CO-3 | CO-4 | CO-5 |
| U1-01 | 3 | 2 | 1 | 2 | 1 |
| U1-02 | 3 | 2 | 1 | 1 | 1 |
| U1-03 | 3 | 2 | 1 | 2 | 1 |
| U1-04 | 1 | 3 | 2 | 2 | 2 |

# 1. CEMENT, AGGREGATES AND WATER

Concrete consists of mixed ingredients such as cement, water, sand, coarse aggregate, chemical admixtures, and supplementary cementitious materials. All the components are bound together by cement and other cementitious materials. In order to understand behaviour of concrete, we need to understand properties of these constituents. This unit introduces properties of cement, sand, coarse aggregates and water. Different laboratory experiments related to these properties are discussed in detail in Unit VI.

## 1.1 PHYSICAL PROPERTIES OF OPC AND PPC

Currently in construction practices, Ordinary Portland Cement (OPC) and Pozzolana Portland Cement (PPC) are most commonly used. Cement is the most important constituent in concrete. Cement consists of various oxides such as calcium oxide, silicon dioxide, and other oxides. The Bogue's equation for percentage of main compounds in cement has been popularly used in the assessment of their amounts as:

$$C_3S = 4.07(CaO) - 7.60(SiO_2) - 6.72(Al_2O_3) - 1.43(Fe_2O_3) - 2.85(SO_3)$$
$$C_2S = 2.87(SiO_2) - 0.754(3CaO.SiO_2)$$
$$C_3A = 2.65(Al_2O_3) - 1.69(Fe_2O_3)$$
$$C_4AF = 3.04(Fe_2O_3)$$

The cement mainly consists of the above four compounds popularly known as Bogue's compounds. He provided, for the first time, the detailed procedure of calculating the amount of these compounds in a typical cement. The terms, shown in brackets in above expressions, are the percentages of the corresponding oxide compounds in the total mass of cement. The other names of these compounds are Alite ($C_3S$), Belite ($C_2S$), Aluminate ($C_3A$) and ferrite ($C_4AF$).

Typical oxide composition of OPC

| Name of the oxide | Percentage | Average |
|---|---|---|
| Lime (CaO) | 60-65 | 63 |
| Silica ($SiO_2$) | 17-25 | 20 |
| Alumina ($Al_2O_3$) | 3.5-9 | 6.3 |
| Iron Oxide ($Fe_2O_3$) | 0.5-6 | 3.3 |
| Magnesia (MgO) | 0.5-4 | 2.4 |

| Name of the oxide | Percentage | Average |
|---|---|---|
| Sulfur trioxide ($SO_3$) | 1-2 | 1.5 |
| Alkalis ($Na_2O$ and $K_2O$) | 0.5-1.3 | 1.0 |

**Manufacturing of Portland cement**

The OPC is manufactured by burning proportionately mixed argillaceous (having alumina) and calcareous (having lime) materials at 1450°C. To note the amount of coal burnt per tonne of cement ranges between 200-350 kg. Burnt material is called clinker, usually of diameter as 5-25 mm. The same is cooled and ground to the desired fineness. Raw rock like material is passed through jaw crusher to reduce the size to about 150 mm. The same is passed through the crusher mill to further make it to about 40 mm size. The same is stored in stacks. From here, the material is pushed into a vertical ball mill along with clay or crushed shale in suitable proportion. The product is called raw meal.

The process of manufacturing cement can be classified as dry process and wet process. For wet process, the material is then mixed with water and blended to slurry. In tanks the slurry is stirred constantly for obtaining uniformity. After that the same is passed through huge firebrick lined rotary kilns.

In dry process, the raw meal is homogeneously mixed and passed through a set of five or six stage pre-calcining units and fed to the inclined kilns in the dry state. The temperature of the material is progressively increased. At 425°C, water is completely driven out. At 875°C, limestone gives out $CO_2$ and CaO powder remains. At about 1450°C, also called the initial melting stage, the point of incipient fusion is reached. At this time sintering, a thermal process of converting loose fine particles into a solid coherent mass, occurs and clinker is formed. A typical flow diagram of manufacturing of concrete is provided in Fig. 1.1.

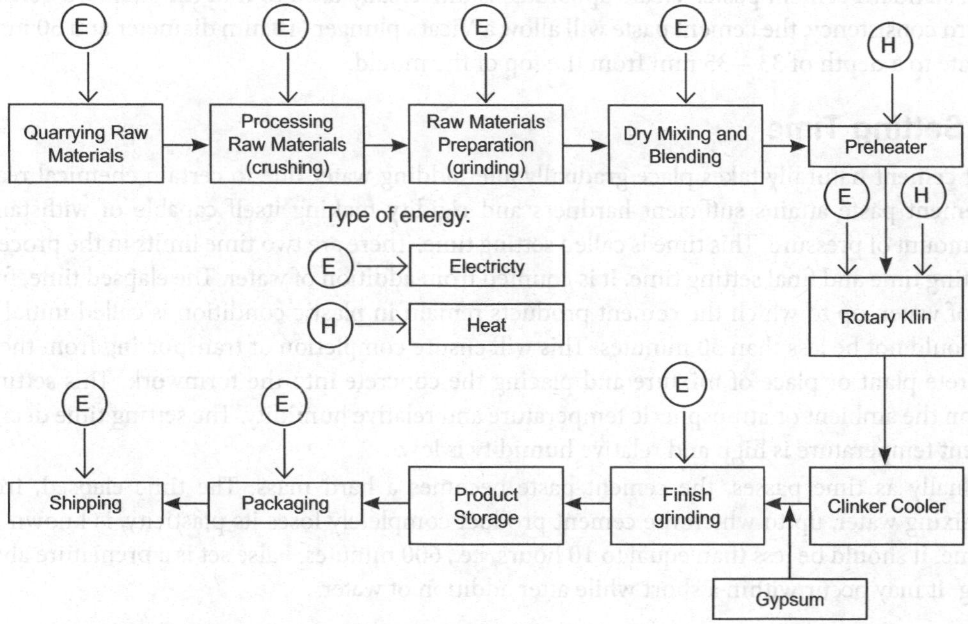


**Fig. 1.1:** Flow diagram of cement manufacturing (Golewski, 2020)

**Hydration of cement**

Anhydrous cement powder acquires adhesive property after mixing water. The chemical reaction between water and cement is called hydration of cement. Hydration of cement is an exothermic reaction. The rate of heat energy liberation is maximum at the instant of adding water to cement. This rate slows down and reaches its local minimum at about 2 seconds. Beyond this, the rate increases again to reach local maximum at about 6 to 8 seconds, and thereafter it reduces continuously with time.

The products of hydration of $C_2S$ and $C_3S$ are calcium silicate hydrates (usually called C-S-H gel) and calcium hydroxide ($Ca(OH)_2$). Hydration of $C_3A$ produces calcium aluminate hydrates which remains stable up to a temperature of 225°C. Bogue's compounds can be arranged in descending order of their contribution to strength development of cement as: $C_3S$, $C_2S$, $C_3A$ and $C_4AF$.

Among various Bogue's compounds, $C_2S$ reacts slower than $C_3S$. On the other hand, $C_3A$ reacts very fast. Presence of $C_3A$ in larger quantities in cement may lead to flash set. Gypsum is added to the cement clinkers while grinding to avoid flash set. Faster rate of hydration implies higher heat of hydration.

### 1.1.1 Fineness

Fineness of cement indicates the average size of cement particles. It increases with specific surface area of cement. Finer cement has higher specific surface area and it gives higher rate of hydration and early gain of strength. Nowadays, using latest equipment and tools, the grinding efficiency has effectively increased. There are disadvantages of excessively fine cements. If the cement is too fine, there is a probability of air setting and quality of cement may deteriorate faster during storage.

### 1.1.2 Standard Consistency

It is also called as normal consistency. It refers to a particular percentage of water by weight of cement to produce a standard cement paste. Vicat's apparatus is universally used to find the standard consistency. At standard consistency, the cement paste will allow a Vicat's plunger (10 mm diameter and 50 mm long) to penetrate to a depth of 33 – 35 mm from the top of the mould.

### 1.1.3 Setting Time

Setting of cement naturally takes place gradually after adding water due to certain chemical reactions. Plastic cement paste attains sufficient hardness and rigidity making itself capable of withstanding a definite amount of pressure. This time is called setting time. There are two time limits in the process, viz., initial setting time and final setting time. It is counted from addition of water. The elapsed time, from the addition of water, up to which the cement products remain in plastic condition is called initial setting time. It should not be less than 30 minutes. This will ensure completion of transporting from the ready-mix concrete plant or place of mixture and placing the concrete into the formwork. This setting time depends on the ambient or atmospheric temperature and relative humidity. The setting time decreases if the ambient temperature is high and relative humidity is low.

Gradually as time passes, the cement paste becomes a hard mass. The time elapsed, from the time of mixing water, up to which the cement product completely loses its plasticity, is known as final setting time. It should be less than equal to 10 hours, i.e., 600 minutes. False set is a premature abnormal hardening. It may occur within a short while after addition of water.

### 1.1.4 Soundness

It refers to any expansion in volume of hydrated cement after setting. It occurs due to the presence of lime, magnesia and calcium sulphates. They may cause large expansion in volume of cement paste. This is because of hydration of free lime after setting of cement. As the slaked lime ($Ca(OH)_2$) has larger volume, severe cracking and disruption of hardened cement paste may occur. To reduce, the effect of unsoundness, the magnesia content is limited to 0.5%. Fine grinding may reduce the unsoundness. The cement should be allowed to aerate for a longer time and mixing should be thorough so that proper hydration is achieved.

### 1.1.5 Compressive Strength

For structural use, the compressive strength of cement is mostly evaluated, and it depends on the chemical constituents of the cement. Typical combinations of oxides form Bogue's compounds. Each of these compounds has a specific contribution to the strength of cement. The development of strength is mainly contributed by the tri-calcium silicate followed by di-calcium silicate. The tri-calcium aluminate and tetra-calcium alumino-ferrite have relatively low contributions to the strength of cement. The rate of gain of compressive strength depends on the type of cement. For example, rapid hardening Portland cement (RHPC) develops the compressive strength at a much faster rate than Ordinary Portland Cement (OPC).

Latest research findings have pointed out that the strength properties of cement are predominantly a function of the cooling rate of the clinker. The moderate cooling rate has provided a marginally higher strength of cement than that provided by a slower cooling rate. Generally, it refers a cooling, in which the temperature is lowered from 1200°C to 500°C in 15 minutes and thereafter to ambient temperature in 10 minutes. Basically, this cooling rate characterizes the crystal size of cement and degree of crystallization.

High-strength cement pastes are made by improving their micro-structure by several means such as: (i) by mixing ultrafine silica fume, the particle mass packed per unit volume may be increased, (ii) by applying heat and pressure on the cement paste, (iii) by removing the entrapped air.

### 1.1.6 Different Grades of OPC and Relevant IS Codes

IS 269-2015 describes the requirements of different types of OPC. Depending upon the compressive strength of cement, they are identified as OPC 53 grade, OPC 43 grade, and OPC 33 grade. Here, the grade indicates the compressive strength of cement, i.e., 53 grade of cement indicates that the compressive strength of cement cube after 28 days of curing will be 53 N/mm$^2$ (MPa). The new version of the code included two railway sleeper grade cements, viz., OPC 43S and OPC 53S. Some performance improvers, also known as mineral admixtures, could be added to OPC. They are rice husk ash, fly ash, silica fume, blast furnace slag. In such cases, the cement is known by an entirely different name according to the mineral admixture used. Their specific properties and applications are shown in section 1.3. Certain specifications as per IS 269 are given in Table 1.1.

**Table 1.1:** Chemical requirements of Ordinary Portland Cement

| Characteristic | OPC 33 | OPC 43 | OPC43S | OPC53 | OPC53S |
|---|---|---|---|---|---|
| Lime-silica ratio | 0.66-1.02 | 0.66-1.02 | 0.80-1.02 | 0.80-1.02 | 0.80-1.02 |
| Insoluble residue, percent by mass, Maximum | 5 | 5 | 2 | 5 | 2 |

| Characteristic | OPC 33 | OPC 43 | OPC43S | OPC53 | OPC53S |
|---|---|---|---|---|---|
| Magnesia, percent by mass, Maximum | 6 | 6 | 5 | 6 | 5 |
| Loss on ignition, percent by mass, maximum | 5 | 5 | 4 | 4 | 4 |
| Chloride content, percent by mass, maximum | 0.1 | 0.1 | 0.1 | 0.1 | 0.1 |

Cement used for railway sleepers should have a maximum content of $C_3A$ and $C_3S$ as 10% and 45% by mass of cement respectively.

## 1.2 TESTING OF CEMENT: LABORATORY TESTS

Detailed laboratory tests are conducted to determine various properties of cement. The individual experiments have been described in detail in Unit VI.

### 1.2.1 Fineness

Fineness of cement influences the rate of hydration as well as total amount of heat of hydration. Strength development of concrete is the result of the chemical reaction of water with cement particles. Larger the specific surface area, i.e., the surface area per gram of the cement, available for reaction, higher is the rate of hydration. Rapid strength development of cement requires greater degree of fineness. Rapid Hardening Cement, therefore, requires greater fineness. However, too much fineness is also undesirable, because the cost of grinding is high for higher fineness. Finer cement deteriorates more quickly when exposed to air and cause more shrinkage, but less prone to bleeding. Greater fineness also requires relatively higher amount of gypsum for proper retardation. Also, water required for the paste of standard consistency is greater.

### 1.2.2 Standard Consistency

The standard consistency is used for determination of initial setting time, final setting time and soundness. It is determined by Vicat's apparatus. A standard paste is said to be formed when the plunger, 10 mm ± 0.05 mm diameter, in its own weight penetrates to a certain value. The test is repeated with different water contents until it produces a distance of 6 ± 1 mm between the plunger tip and the base plate. In other words, the plunger of Vicat's apparatus should stop between 5 to 7 mm from the bottom.

About 400 grams of cement is weighed and mixed with 30% of potable water with the help of spatula for 30 seconds. After about 30 seconds, it is thoroughly mixed with hand for about 1 minute. The mould is filled completely with the paste and the excess paste is removed by single stroke of the trowel making it level with the top of the mould. Shaking of mould is done to expel the air. The mould is placed together with the glass plate, under the plunger. The details of the test procedure are provided in Unit VI.

### 1.2.3 Setting Time, Soundness, Compressive Strength

These tests have been described in detail in Unit VI. These tests are performed as per guidelines prescribed in Parts 5, 3 and 2 of IS 4031 respectively.

### 1.2.4 Storage of Cement and Effect of Storage on Properties of Cement

As per the IS 269-2013, the cement shall be stored in such a manner as to permit easy access for proper inspection and identification. A suitable water-tight building should be used to store to protect the cement from dampness and to minimize warehouse deterioration. Based on the storage time, the strength deterioration is of the order of the data as shown in the Table 1.2.

Table 1.2: Deterioration of cement strength over time

| Period of storage | Fresh cement | 3 months | 6 months | One year | 5 year |
|---|---|---|---|---|---|
| Percentage decrease in strength when tested at 28 days | 0% | 20% | 30% | 40% | 50% |

## 1.3 BIS SPECIFICATIONS AND FIELD APPLICATIONS OF DIFFERENT TYPES OF CEMENT

In recent times, due to advancements in research and latest equipment, several chemically different types of cements are manufactured. Each type of cement caters to a specific purpose. This section describes the specific properties of different types of cement as per relevant IS codes.

### 1.3.1 Rapid Hardening Cement

Specification of RHPC cement is covered in the IS 8041-1990. Some of the properties of RHPC are the same as that of OPC. The composition of the RHPC differs from OPC only in the relative ratio of $C_3S$ and $C_2S$. Compared to OPC, the RHPC cement contains higher $C_3S$ and lower $C_2S$. RHPC is different from that of quick setting cement. It is because RHPC not only sets but also hardens much earlier than OPC. Usually, the three day strength of RHPC is of the order of the strength of seven day strength of OPC. The specific surface area of RHPC is always more than 3250 sq. cm. per gram. This is about 1.5 times higher than that of OPC, however, it is lesser than quick setting cement (4000 sq. cm./gram). For mass concreting RHPC should not be used, as rate of evolution of heat of hydration is very high.

RHPC is used for (i) Precast and prefabricated concrete construction, (ii) Structural elements having requirement of early removal of formwork (iii) Repair of rigid pavements, and (iv) cold weather concreting.

As per BIS specification, if cement exhibits false set, the ratio of final penetration measured after 5 min of completion of mixing period to the initial penetration prepared exactly after 20 s of completion of mixing period, expressed as percent, shall be not less than 50 when tested by the method described in IS 4031 (Part 14): 1989.

### 1.3.2 Low Heat Cement

In 1930, low heat cement was developed in USA for concreting of dams. IS 12600-1989 specifies the physical and chemical requirements of low heat cement. Hydration of cement is an exothermic process. Large heat of hydration may weaken the crystal structure of the hydrated cement paste. In large concrete dams, mass concreting is done. The temperature inside the concrete mass reaches excessively higher value. To avoid it, low heat cement is used for such mass concreting. In such cement $C_3S$ and $C_3A$ content is lower. Instead, relative amount of $C_2S$ is increased. Thus, the heat of hydration is lower and hydration process gets prolonged for a longer time. The rate of gain of strength is also lower. The final strength, setting time and soundness of low heat cement is the same as that of OPC.

### 1.3.3 Portland Pozzolana Cement

IS 1489- 1991 allows the use of reactive pozzolanic material between 15-35% by mass of cement. The pozzolanic material is ground with OPC clinker. Pozzolanic materials may be siliceous (if originates from bituminous coals) or aluminous in composition. They will react with $Ca(OH)_2$ liberated during hydration of cement. At ordinary temperature, they combine together to form a cementitious compound. The pozzolanic material must be finely ground. Fly ash, also called pulverized fuel ash, is such an artificial pozzolanic material. Flue gases of coal fired thermal power stations are passed through electrostatic precipitators (ESPs) fitted before the chimney. The fly ash is collected at these ESPs. Latest thermal power plants have the latest ESPs to collect high quality fly ash. This fly ash is also used as a mineral admixture to augment the durability of the concrete.

As PPC produce low heat cements, mass concrete constructions use such cements. They are used in marine and other hydraulic structures. Strength development using PPC cement is slower than OPC. However, the ultimate strength in both cases are generally identical. The prolonged curing is essential for concrete using PPC. Inert or non-reactive type pozzolana may not be as effective as reactive pozzolanic material.

The merits of PPC are:

(i) They are economical as a waste material such as fly ash are used to replace 15-35% of OPC.
(ii) Calcium hydroxide is converted to a cementitious material in combination with fly ash.
(iii) It can reduce the micro-cracks in concrete by improving pore size distribution in concrete.
(iv) The permeability of concrete using PPC is lesser, and PPC gives more volume of mortar.
(v) For sufficient curing of PPC, the long-term strength of PPC may be more than OPC.

The demerits of PPC are:

(i) The removal of formwork takes longer time as rate of strength development is slow, and setting time is longer in case of such cements.
(ii) The $Ca(OH)_2$ is absorbed by pozzolanic material, thereby the alkalinity of hydrated cement paste is reduced. This may increase the risk of corrosion.

Various other types of pozzolans are volcanic ash (also known as original pozzolans), pumicite, Opaline cherts and shales, calcined diatomaceous earth, burnt clay. It is important to ensure uniformity in properties of pozzolans.

### 1.3.4 Sulphate Resisiting Cement

IS 12330-1988 gives detailed requirements of this cement. Magnesium sulphate combines with free $Ca(OH)_2$ in set cement to form Calcium sulphate as

$$Ca(OH)_2 + MgSO_4 = CaSO_4 + Mg(OH)_2$$

It also combines with calcium aluminates hydrate to for Calcium sulphoaluminate. The volume of this product is 2.27 times more than the initial volume. This results in cracking of the set hydrated cement paste. Hydrated silicate gels may also be chemically converted to sulphates. This is also known as sulphate attack which takes place only with sulphates in solution form. In case of a concrete experiencing alternate drying and wetting frequently, the probability of formation of sulphate compounds is higher.

Cement with low $C_3A$ is sulphate attack resistant. So, a sulphate resistant cement has lower $C_3A$ (less than 5%) and $C_4AF$. The total amount of $2C_3A + C_4AF$ should be less than equal to 25%.

The use of sulphate resistant cement is desirable in following situations: (i) Concrete to be used in marine environment, (ii) In basement and foundations located in a sulphate rich surroundings, (iii) Concrete pipes used in marshy or sulphate rich soils, and (iv) Concrete used in sewage treatment plants.

### 1.3.5 Blast Furnace Slag Cement

IS 455-1989 describes the requirements of the blast furnace slag cement. It is obtained by thorough mixing and grinding of OPC clinker, gypsum and granulated blast furnace slag in suitable proportion. When gypsum is added, the IS 455 specifies that the sulphur trioxide content should not be more than 3%. This cement has low heat of hydration, therefore can be used for mass concreting. The rate of hardening is slower than that of OPC. At 28 days the strength is lower than OPC, however, at one year the strength is same as that of OPC. The slag fraction improves the strength at later stages. It also has improved pore structure and reduced permeability. Thus, it possesses inherent improved potential towards better resistance to chloride, and sulphate attack, alkali metals, acidic environment. This cement uses the waste product from blast furnaces. The amount of blast furnace varies from 25 – 70% by mass of cement. The maximum quantity upto 85% has been used in some countries. The fineness, setting time, soundness and strength is similar to OPC. Use of right quality of slag is important.

The crystal structure of the slag is improved by chilling the slag very rapidly. This prevents crystallization and promotes glassification.

### 1.3.6 High Alumina Cement

High Alumina cement should satisfy the requirements of IS 6452-1989 for structural use and IS 15895-2018 for refractory use. Alumina (bauxite) and calcareous (limestone, consisting essentially carbonates) materials are fused together at high temperature (1550 – 1600°C), and the fused mixture is ground to a fine powder. At such a high temperature, cement remains in a liquid state. Thereafter, it is run into moulds and cooled to form pigs, a dark compact rocklike mass. These pigs are crushed and ground to 3000 sq.cm/gms. The minimum total alumina content should be 32% by mass. The expansion of HAC should not be more than 5 mm when tested by the Le-Chatelier method described in IS 4031 (Part 3). Also, as per IS 15895-2011, the final setting time for refractory use high alumina cement should be not more than 400 minutes. This code has classified the high alumina cement as high purity and medium purity grade. The high purity grade cement has higher fineness, and lower $SiO_2$ content. The value of final setting time for HAC used for structural use should be less than 10 hours, same as OPC.

Hydration of high alumina cement produces monocalcium aluminate decahydrate ($CAH_{10}$), dicalcium aluminate octahydrate ($C_2AH_8$), and alumina gel ($AH_n$). These compounds impart high strengths to concrete. But as they are metastable compounds, i.e., they deteriorate with time and convert to weaker crystals with compounds like tricalcium aluminate hexahydrate ($C_3AH_6$) and gibbsite. This is known as conversion or retrogression of strength. This is accompanied by reduction in volume of solids, resulting into increase in porosity of the concrete. Initially at Stepney in UK in 1974, failure of two roof beams in a school occurred due to this conversion, and detailed research was undertaken, leading to the understanding of the detailed chemical process involved.

This cement is used for making refractory concrete, which can withstand high temperature. It is also preferred where high early strength development is essential.

### 1.3.7 White Cement

This cement is used for architectural purposes. IS 8042- 1999 prescribes requirements for such cements. It contains low content of soluble alkalis. Thus, steining is avoidable, while such a cement is used. White cement is derived from china clay. It has lowest quantity of iron oxide and manganese oxides. It is difficult to make the cement free from contaminations. A special kind of pure limestones (having more than 96% $CaCO_3$) are used as raw material. As per IS 8042, dolomite, marble are also used as raw material. However, their addition shall not be more than 8%. Also, it should satisfy the two conditions as per IS 8042 as total of CaO and MgO shall not be less than 50 percent by mass of performance improver, when tested as per IS 1760 (Part 3). Whiteness shall not be less than 70 percent when tested as per Annex B of the code. The reflectivity of the compact white cement surface is compared with standard magnesium oxide blocks of certified reflectivity on absolute scale with the help of a suitable apparatus, for example, a reflectometer or reflectance spectrophotometer.

To comply with the above requirements, the cost of manufacturing white cement is double than that of OPC. Fuel used are refined furnace Oil (RFO) or gas. Different colours can be obtained by mixing suitable pigments (5-10% by mass) to white cements. The compatibility of pigments should be thoroughly checked. They should not adversely affect the strength of the white cement. Another important aspect of pigments is their long-term durability.

The properties of white cement are same as OPC. Fineness is higher than that of OPC. It leads to higher strength of white cements than OPC. Hunter scale is used for measuring whiteness of white cement. The value of whiteness should be larger than 90%.

## 1.4 AGGREGATES

Aggregates are important ingredients of concrete. They comprise 70-80 % volume of the concrete and form skeleton of concrete, and therefore significantly affect properties and economy of the mix.

Aggregates are usually obtained by crushing igneous, sedimentary and metamorphic rocks. Gravel and sand obtained from natural deposits such as river beds are also widely used in concrete. Apart from these aggregates obtained from natural sources, synthetic aggregates produced in industries are also being used these days.

### 1.4.1 Requirements of Good Aggregate

As mentioned above, aggregates significantly affect properties of concrete. Therefore, good concrete would require good aggregates. Good aggregates have following requirements:

- Since aggregates form skeleton of concrete, they should be strong and have sufficient impact, crushing and abrasive strength. These different types of strength are discussed in Section 1.6.
- In order to achieve good packing in concrete, the aggregates used should comprise of different sizes. Such aggregates are called well-graded aggregates. They should further satisfy IS 383 stipulations.
- Aggregate particles should be angular in shape and rough in texture to have a good bond with the cement paste.
- Aggregates should be inert so that they do not react with other constituents of concrete.
- Aggregates should be free from organic impurities. If organic impurities are present, they will decay with time leaving behind large voids.

### 1.4.2 Classification According to Size and Shape

On the basis of size, aggregates are usually classified as coarse and fine aggregates. Sieve analyses are used to ascertain whether the given aggregates are coarse or fine.

Coarse Aggregates: These are the aggregates that are retained on 4.75 mm sieve (Fig. 1.2). Coarse aggregates are characterized by nominal maximum size of aggregates (MSA) which is defined as sieve size through which most of the particles (typically 95%) should pass. MSA of aggregates to be used is determined based on practical requirements such as thickness of concrete section, clear cover and spacing between steel reinforcement bars. For example, regular building construction uses coarse aggregates with MSA of 20 mm. On the other hand, large concrete structures such as dams use coarse aggregates with MSA of 40 mm. Coarse aggregates are usually obtained by artificial crushing of rocks in quarries.

Fine Aggregates: These are the aggregates that pass through 4.75 mm sieve and are retained on 600 μm sieve (Fig. 1.3). Natural sand deposited by rivers are often used as fine aggregates. However, stone dust obtained by crushing stones are also sometimes used. Fine aggregates are further classified into four different zones depending on particle size distribution which is discussed in Section 1.5.

On the basis of particle size distribution, aggregates can also be classified as well-graded, poorly graded, uniformly graded and gap graded. Well-graded aggregates contain particles of all relevant sizes. Therefore, use of well-graded aggregates lead to better packing resulting in good quality concrete.

On the basis of shape, aggregates are classified into rounded, partly rounded, angular, flaky and elongated. General description for these aggregate types is outlined in Table 1.3. The shape of aggregates primarily depends on parent rock material and type of crusher used in the process. For example, aggregates obtained from schists, shales and slates are usually flaky in shape. On the other hand, aggregates obtained from quartzite and basalt are either rounded or partly rounded.

**Table 1.3:** General description for different types of aggregates based on shape of particles

| Classification | Description |
|---|---|
| Rounded | Fully water worn or completely shaped due to attrition by water |
| Partly rounded | Partly shaped due to attrition by water; having rounded edges |
| Angular | Well defined edges at intersection of roughly planar faces |
| Flaky | Angular particles with thickness very small relative to length and/or width |
| Elongated | Particles with width and thickness very small relative to length |

Shape of aggregate particles affect the workability of concrete. Workability of concrete means ease in handling, placing and compacting the concrete, and is elaborately discussed in Chapter 2. For a given water-cement ratio, rounded aggregates can lead to a reduction in cement requirement in concrete. This is because rounded aggregates have least surface area per unit volume (also known as specific surface area) leading to low water absorption. This leads to reduced water requirement implying lower cement requirement for a given water-cement ratio. However, angular aggregates lead to higher strength and improved durability of concrete due to better bond and interlocking with the cement paste. Flaky and elongated aggregates are not used as they lead to poor bond with the cement paste resulting into poor durability of the structure.

Aggregates can also be classified into smooth and rough depending on texture of particles. While smooth aggregates lead to improved workability, rough aggregates often lead to higher strength.

From the above discussion, it is clear that choice of aggregates is very important to achieve desired result in construction. The next two sections describe fine and coarse aggregates respectively.

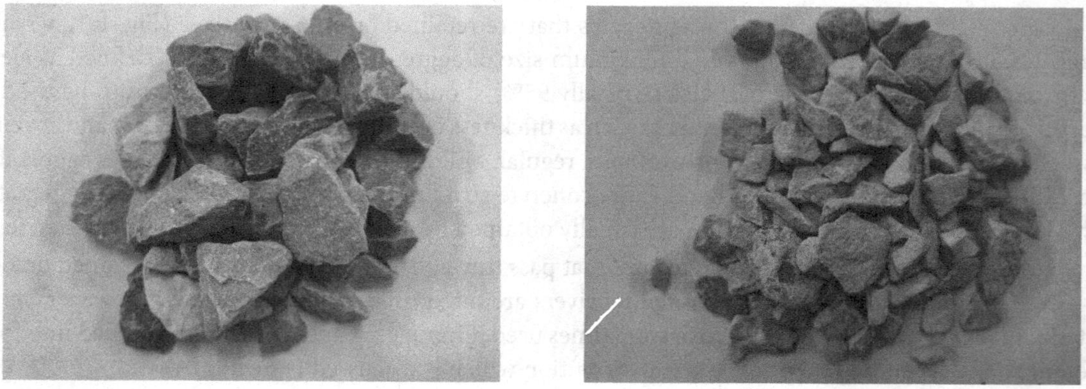

(a) (b)

**Fig. 1.2:** Coarse aggregates: (a) CA20 mm and (b) CA10 mm

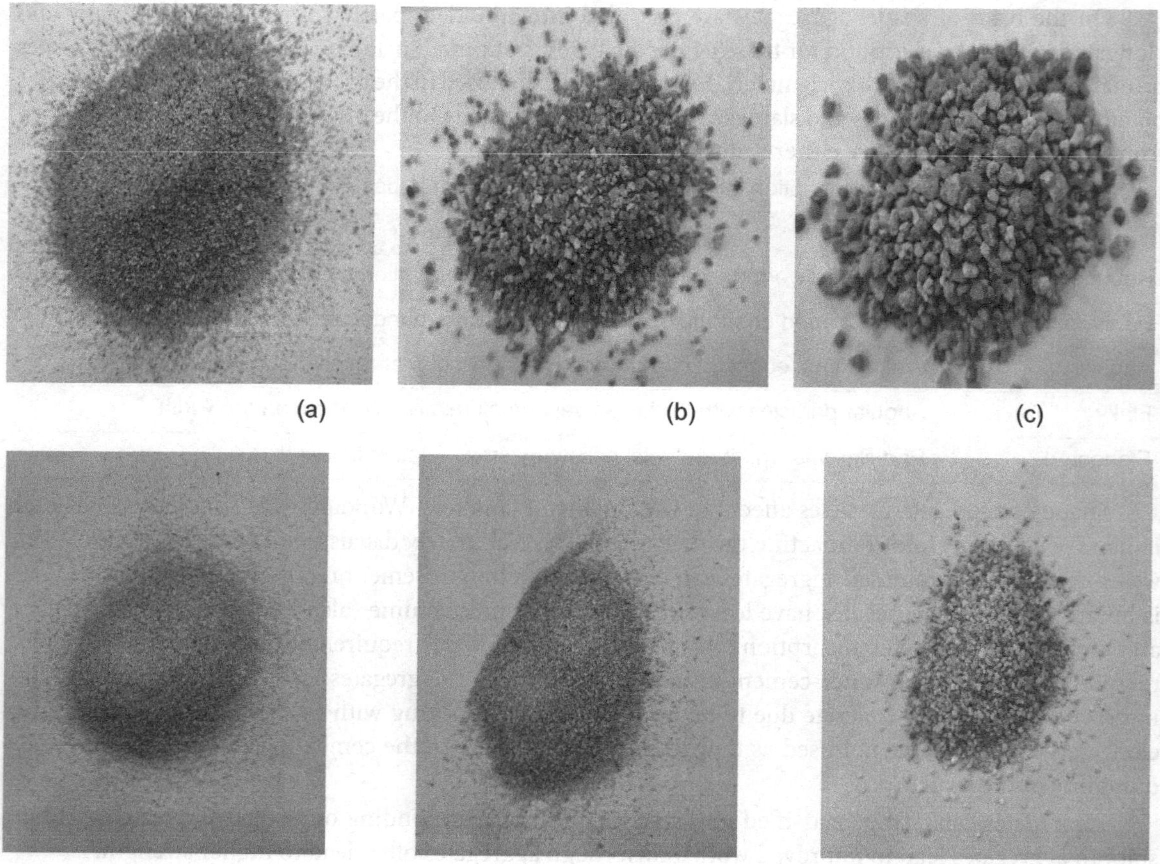

(a) (b) (c)

(d) (e) (f)

**Fig. 1.3:** Fine aggregates: Local sand (a) Grade III (b) Grade II (c) Grade I Standard Ennore sand (d) Grade III (e) Grade II (f) Grade I

## 1.5 FINE AGGREGATES

**Introduction**

Fine aggregates comprise of particles finer than 4.75 mm in mean diameter. They form a part of the cement mortar and also act as fillers between the coarse aggregates. Sand obtained from river beds is commonly used as fine aggregates in concrete. Due to environmental concerns, there has been limitations on sand quarrying. Therefore, crushed sand is also being used in larger projects where large quantities of fine aggregates are required.

### 1.5.1 Properties

Since fine aggregates form an important part of concrete mix, its properties determine whether the mix will be able to deliver required properties. Fine aggregates are usually characterized by size, particle size distribution, specific gravity, bulk density, fineness and water absorption. Some of the important properties of fine aggregates are outlined in following sections.

### 1.5.2 Size

Fine aggregates pass through 4.75 mm sieve and are typically retained on 600 μm sieve. However, some quantity of particles may pass through 600 μm sieve. Sieve analysis is performed to understand particle size distribution in a given sample. The sieve sizes used are 4.75 mm, 2.36 mm, 1.18 mm, 600 μm, 300 μm, 150 μm and 75 μm, along with a pan. The procedure to conduct sieve analysis on fine aggregates is elaborated in the section on laboratory tests.

A certain sample of fine aggregates is weighed and then added to the sieve assembly with 4.75 mm sieve at the top. Upon sieve analysis, the mass of fine aggregate particles retained on each sieve is measured. Percentage mass retained on each sieve is then calculated. Cumulative percentage mass retained for a sieve size is then obtained by adding percentage mass retained on that sieve as well as larger sieves. Subtracting this cumulative percentage mass retained from 100 yields cumulative percentage passing through that respective sieve. This cumulative percentage passing is plotted against sieve size where sieve size is represented using a log scale. This is called a grading curve for fine aggregates. Table 1.4 and Fig. 1.4 outline the calculations involved in sieve analysis and the obtained grading curve using an example.

**Table 1.4:** Example of sieve analysis performed on a given sample of fine aggregates

| Sieve Size | Mass retained (grams) | Percentage mass retained | Cumulative percentage mass retained | Cumulative percentage mass passing |
|---|---|---|---|---|
| 4.75 mm | 7.54 | 1.44 | 1.44 | 98.56 |
| 2.36 mm | 3.25 | 0.62 | 2.06 | 97.94 |
| 1.18 mm | 34.84 | 6.67 | 8.73 | 91.27 |
| 600 μm | 182.86 | 34.98 | 43.71 | 56.29 |
| 300 μm | 202.75 | 38.79 | 82.50 | 17.50 |
| 150 μm | 84.43 | 16.15 | 98.65 | 1.35 |
| Pan | 7.06 | 1.35 | 100.00 | 0 |
| Total | 522.72 | | | |

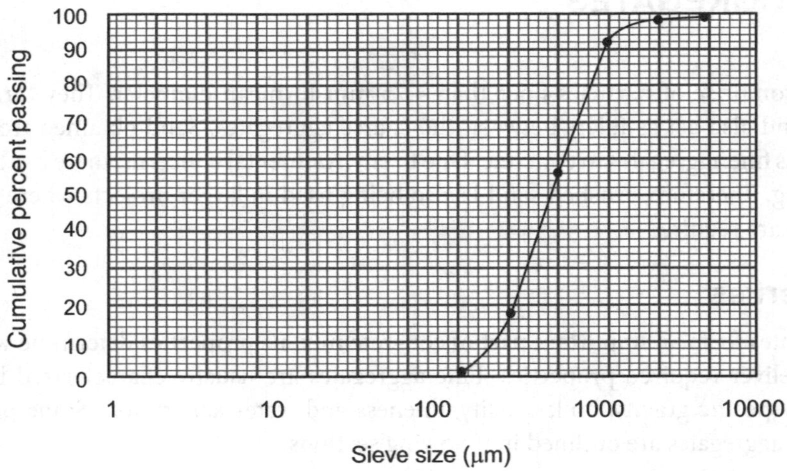


**Fig. 1.4:** Grading curve obtained from sieve analysis example in Table 1.4

### 1.5.3 Specific Gravity

Specific gravity of a material is defined as ratio of its density to that of a given reference material at the same temperature. The reference material is usually taken as water. Therefore, specific gravity can be understood as the ratio of mass of a material in a given volume to that of water in the same volume at the same temperature. Since aggregate particles contain voids and may be either permeable or impermeable, specific gravity can be estimated in a number of ways.

Absolute specific gravity is defined as ratio of mass of solid material to that of mass of water in the volume of solid material excluding all pores/voids. Impermeable voids are totally enclosed and do not allow ingress of water. It is not possible to trace volume occupied by such voids in natural state of aggregates. Aggregate particles are therefore pulverized to eliminate these impermeable voids and thereby obtain absolute specific gravity. The process to estimate absolute specific gravity is cumbersome and therefore absolute specific gravity is not often used in practice.

On the other hand, if only permeable voids are eliminated, apparent specific gravity is obtained. Apparent specific gravity for fine aggregates is usually obtained using pycnometer. Pycnometer is a jar with a water-tight brass conical screw-top with a hole at apex. Most widely used pycnometers have a volume of 1 litre (IS 2386). Mass of empty pycnometer is recorded as $M_1$. A sample of fine aggregate is put in oven for 24 hours at temperature of 100°C to 110°C. The oven-dried sample is then transferred to pycnometer and the total mass of pycnometer with sample is measured as $M_2$. The pycnometer is then filled with water up to the hole in brass cap. The contents are shaken and stirred during the process so that all the permeable voids get saturated with water. The mass of pycnometer with oven-dried sample and water is measured as $M_3$. Finally, the pycnometer is cleaned, wiped from outside and filled with water. The mass of pycnometer filled with water is recorded as $M_4$. The apparent specific gravity ($G_a$) is then calculated using the following relation. On a careful observation, the denominator can be understood as mass of water in the same volume of fine aggregates considering only impermeable voids.

$$G_a = \frac{(M_2 - M_1)}{(M_2 - M_1) - (M_3 - M_4)}$$

The specific gravity of fine aggregates depends on the parent rock, the formation process and the attrition by water. Typical range lies between 2.60 and 2.70, with most values around 2.65 to 2.67.

### 1.5.4 Bulk Density

Bulk density is defined as mass of a given sample of a material divided by its total volume. Bulk density depends on a number of factors: (i) particle shape, (ii) particle size distribution, and (iii) quality of packing of particles in the aggregate sample. Well-graded aggregates comprising of particles of all sizes exhibit good packing with little voids, and therefore show high bulk density.

### 1.5.5 Water Absorption

As outlined in Section 1.5.3, aggregate particles have pores/voids. Some of these pores are permeable while others are impermeable. While permeable pores tend to absorb water, impermeable pores cannot be accessed by water. Porosity and water absorption influence the amount of water available for hydration of cement and for provision of workability. For example, aggregates with very high water absorption capacity tend to absorb a lot of water resulting in less free water available in the concrete mix. This leads to reduced workability of the mix. Further, porosity of aggregates also affects durability of concrete when it is exposed to freeze-thaw cycles and/or aggressive chemicals.

Water absorption of aggregate is obtained by measuring increase in weight of oven-dry sample when immersed in water for 24 hours. The increase in weight expressed as percent of weight of the oven-dry sample is called water absorption.

Fine aggregates obtained from river beds usually contain a lot of surface moisture. When it is brought to site and stored in heaps, the outer portions gradually become dry while the inner portions remain moist. Dry aggregates tend to absorb water from the mixing water and lowers workability of the mix. On the other hand, moist aggregates contribute additional water to the mix and thereby increases water-cement ratio resulting in poor strength development. Both of these conditions are harmful for the concrete. While obtaining proportions of different ingredients in a concrete mix, we assume that the aggregates are in saturated surface dry (SSD) condition. SSD condition implies that the permeable pores in the aggregate particles are saturated and the surfaces of particles are dry. In a later section on concrete mix design, corrective measures to be taken for water absorption as well as excess of free water will be discussed. These measures will ensure that design mix possesses desired properties.

### 1.5.6 Bulking

Excess of free water in fine aggregates leads to bulking of its volume. Total moisture in aggregates comprises of absorbed and free moisture. While absorbed moisture is present in pores/voids of aggregate particles, free moisture is retained on the surface of these particles in form of films. Due to surface tension in these films, aggregate particles tend to repel each other and the particles are no longer in contact with each other. This leads to an increase in volume which is called bulking of sand.

The extent of bulking depends on moisture content and particle size of fine aggregates. It is observed that bulking increases with increase in moisture content up to a certain limit. Beyond this limit, an increase in moisture content leads to reduction in volume. The moisture content at which volume of sand becomes equal to that under dry conditions is called saturation point. Since fine sand has high specific surface area (surface area per unit mass), surface tension effects are significant. This implies that fine sand shows more bulking compared to coarse sand. Further, coarse aggregates exhibit little bulking which can be neglected. Crushed sand discussed in a later section usually has particles finer than 15 μm. This makes crush sand highly susceptible to bulking with bulking as high as 40%.

Bulking is measured as increase in volume due to free water expressed as a percent of volume of fine aggregates in SSD conditions. A simple field test is conducted to measure bulking. A sample of moist fine aggregate is placed into a measuring cylinder and the height ($h_1$) is noted. Water is then poured into the cylinder so as to submerge the sand. The cylinder is shaken so that the sand sample gets completely saturated. Since volume of fully saturated sand is same as that of SSD sand, the recorded height ($h_2$) refers to volume of sand under SSD conditions. Percentage of bulking is then calculated as follows:

$$Percentage\ of\ bulking = \frac{h_1 - h_2}{h_2} * 100$$

Bulking can significantly affect volume of the aggregates. Therefore, volume batching, i.e. mixing ingredients of concrete by measuring their volumes, is not recommended. Weight batching is mandatory for mixing quality concrete, and corrections related to water absorption and excess of free water are used.

### 1.5.7 Fineness Modulus

As the name suggests, fineness modulus is a measure of overall size and grading of fine aggregates. It is obtained by dividing a sum of cumulative percentage mass retained for various sieves by 100. For instance, fineness modulus for the sample of fine aggregates illustrated in Table 1.4 is found to be 2.37, as calculated below.

$$Fineness\ modulus = \frac{1.44 + 2.06 + 8.73 + 43.71 + 82.5 + 98.65}{100} = 2.37$$

It should be noted that cumulative percentage retained on pan (100%) is not considered in this calculation. Typical range for fineness modulus of fine aggregates is 2.3 to 3.2. Higher value of fineness modulus means coarser sand. Lower value of fineness modulus means finer sand. Fineness modulus for fine, medium and coarse sand typically lies between 2.3 to 2.6, 2.6 to 2.9 and 2.9 to 3.2 respectively.

### 1.5.8 Grading Zone of Sand

Based on cumulative percentage passing through different sieves, IS 383 classifies fine aggregates into four zones, I, II, III and IV. The grading limits for the four zones are presented in Table 1.5. It should be noted that the limits overlap for every sieve except for 600 μm. Therefore, the limits pertaining to 600 μm sieve are considered while determining the grading zone of sand. However, the cumulative percentage passing values for other sieve sizes should not lie outside the prescribed limits by more than a total of 5 percent. For instance, Zone II sand should have cumulative percent passing between 50% and 95% for 1.18 mm sieve.

**Table 1.5:** Grading zones of sand as per IS: 383-1970

| Sieve Size | Cumulative percentage passing | | | |
|---|---|---|---|---|
| | Zone I | Zone II | Zone III | Zone IV |
| 10 mm | 100 | 100 | 100 | 100 |
| 4.75 mm | 90-100 | 90-100 | 90-100 | 95-100 |
| 2.36 mm | 60-95 | 75-100 | 85-100 | 95-100 |
| 1.18 mm | 30-70 | 55-90 | 75-100 | 90-100 |

| Sieve Size | Cumulative percentage passing | | | |
|---|---|---|---|---|
| | Zone I | Zone II | Zone III | Zone IV |
| 600 µm | 15-34 | 35-59 | 60-79 | 80-100 |
| 300 µm | 5-20 | 8-30 | 12-40 | 15-50 |
| 150 µm | 0-10 | 0-10 | 0-10 | 0-15 |
| Fineness modulus | 4.00 – 2.71 | 3.37 – 2.10 | 2.78 – 1.71 | 2.25 – 1.35 |

While Zone I sand is the coarsest, Zone IV sand is the finest. Fine aggregates conforming to zones II and III are typically used in construction.

Based on the size, Indian standard sand, also known as Ennore sand, are classified into three grades such as Grade I (the coarsest one, size smaller than 2 mm and greater than 1 mm), Grade II (the medium size, smaller than 1 mm and greater than 500 µm), Grade III (finer size, below 500 µm but greater than 90 µm).

### 1.5.9 Silt Content

Impurities finer than fine aggregates such as silt and crusher dust can be present in the fine aggregates. Usually, these are present as surface coatings. If present in excess, as specific surface area increases, they tend to absorb a significant portion of mixing water affecting workability of the mix. In order to achieve the desired workability, water-cement ratio is increased which can lead to poor strength development. Further, silt and dust create hindrance to good bond between aggregate particles and cement paste, resulting in poor quality concrete. As per IS 383, silt content in sand should be limited to 8%.

### 1.5.10 Concept of Crushed Sand

Our country is undergoing infrastructure building at a very fast pace. A number of expressways, bridges, dams and industries are being built in addition to regular buildings. Natural sand deposited by rivers is becoming scarce day by day. Due to scarcity of natural sand and environmental impacts of excessive sand mining from river beds, many state governments have restricted mining of natural sand from river beds. As a result, crushed sand or manufactured sand is making its way to civil engineering projects.

Natural sand particles are mostly rounded with smooth surface due to attrition with water. Such particles impart good workability to the concrete mix. On the other hand, crushed sand particles are usually flaky, poorly graded and rough leading to poor workability of the concrete mix. Crushed sand also contains a lot of dust which further lowers the workability. In order to achieve similar workability while using crushed sand, one needs to add super-plasticizers which makes the concrete mix expensive. Super-plasticizers are admixtures that improve the workability of the concrete mix. Therefore, crushed sand has not been widely accepted in construction in India.

However, over the last decade, the methods of manufacturing crushed sand have been revamped. Modern crushers are able to produce crushed sand with cubic-rounded, smooth-textured and well-graded particles. These crushers use both imported and indigenously devised technology. Some of the common trade names for these modern crushers are Jaw master crusher and Barmac Rock on Rock VSI crusher. Due to desirable properties exhibited by crushed sand manufactured in these crushers, mega projects such as Mumbai-Pune Expressway and Yamuna Expressway have used crushed sand instead of natural sand.

Presence of dust in fine aggregates is undesirable as it tends to absorb a lot of water. The increased water absorption implies less water available for hydration of cement. This will lead to poor strength development in concrete. Therefore, dust with particle size finer than 75 μm should be restricted to 15% in case of fine aggregates. Modern crushers have mechanisms to control dust in crushed sand.

## 1.6 COARSE AGGREGATES

**Introduction**

Coarse aggregates comprise of particles coarser than 4.75 mm in mean diameter. They form the skeleton of concrete and therefore their properties influence the properties of concrete. Coarse aggregates are usually obtained by crushing rocks in quarries.

### 1.6.1 Properties

Since coarse aggregates form 50% of concrete mix by weight, they significantly affect properties and economy of the concrete mix. Therefore, the properties of coarse aggregates determine whether the mix will be able to deliver required properties. Coarse aggregates are usually characterized by shape, size, particle size distribution, surface texture, specific gravity, bulk density, soundness, fineness and water absorption. Since coarse aggregates form skeleton of the concrete mix, it is important to understand its performance under crushing, abrasive and impact loadings. Some of the important properties of coarse aggregates are outlined in following sections.

### 1.6.2 Size

Coarse aggregates comprise of particles with mean diameter larger than 4.75 mm. However, some quantity of particles may pass through 4.75 mm sieve. Sieve analysis is performed to understand particle size distribution in a given sample. The sieve sizes used are 20 mm, 16 mm, 12.5 mm, 10 mm, 4.75 mm, along with a pan. The procedure to conduct sieve analysis on coarse aggregates is elaborated in the section on laboratory tests.

A certain sample of coarse aggregates is weighed and then added to the sieve assembly with 20 mm sieve at the top. Upon sieve analysis, the mass of coarse aggregate particles retained on each sieve is measured. Percentage mass retained on each sieve is then calculated. Cumulative percentage mass retained for a sieve size is then obtained by adding percentage mass retained on that sieve as well as larger sieves. Subtracting this cumulative percentage mass retained from 100 yields cumulative percentage passing through that respective sieve. This cumulative percentage passing is plotted against sieve size where sieve size is represented using a log scale. This is called a grading curve for coarse aggregates. Table 1.6 and Fig. 1.5 outline the calculations involved in sieve analysis and the obtained grading curve using an example.

**Table 1.6:** Example of sieve analysis performed on a given sample of coarse aggregates

| Sieve Size | Mass retained (grams) | Percentage mass retained | Cumulative percentage mass retained | Cumulative percentage mass passing |
|---|---|---|---|---|
| 20 mm | 0 | 0 | 0 | 100.00 |
| 16 mm | 47.3 | 4.73 | 4.73 | 95.27 |
| 12.5 mm | 494.0 | 49.40 | 54.13 | 45.87 |
| 10 mm | 374.7 | 37.47 | 91.60 | 8.40 |

| Sieve Size | Mass retained (grams) | Percentage mass retained | Cumulative percentage mass retained | Cumulative percentage mass passing |
|---|---|---|---|---|
| 4.75 mm | 76.0 | 7.60 | 99.20 | 0.80 |
| Pan | 8.0 | 0.80 | 100.00 | 0 |
| Total | 1000.0 | | | |

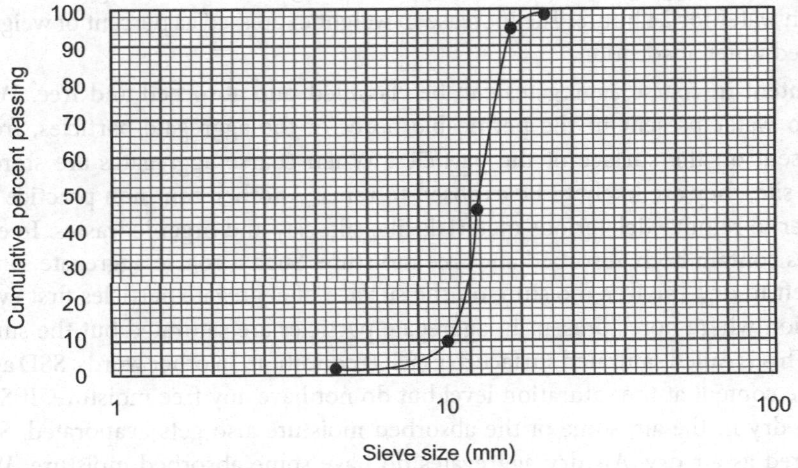


**Fig. 1.5:** Grading curve obtained from sieve analysis example in Table 1.6

## 1.6.3 Shape

Most coarse aggregate particles are irregular in shape. However, depending on general particle shape, coarse aggregates can be classified as rounded, partly rounded, angular, flaky and elongated. The general description of these aggregate types is outlined in Table 1.3. Shape of aggregate particles affect properties of fresh concrete more than those of hardened concrete.

## 1.6.4 Surface Texture

Surface texture measures how smooth or rough aggregate particles are. It also hints about imperfections and flaws on the surface of particles. Depending on visual inspection and touch, coarse aggregates can be classified as glassy, smooth, granular, rough, crystalline, porous and honeycombed.

Surface texture affects bond between aggregate particles and cement paste. Aggregate particles with rough and porous surface texture results in good bond development and is therefore preferred. Selecting aggregates with suitable surface texture can enhance aggregate-cement bond by 75% leading to 20% increase in compressive and flexural strength of concrete.

## 1.6.5 Water Absorption

Similar to fine aggregate particles, coarse aggregate particles also have permeable and impermeable pores/voids. While permeable pores tend to absorb water, impermeable pores cannot be accessed by water.

The effect of porosity and water absorption is similar to that in case of fine aggregates. They influence how much water is available for hydration of cement and for workability of the fresh mix. For example, aggregates with very high water absorption capacity tend to absorb a lot of water resulting in less free water available in the concrete mix. This leads to reduced workability of the mix. Further, porosity of aggregates also affects durability of concrete when it is exposed to freeze-thaw cycles and/or aggressive chemicals. However, some amounts of surface pores help in development of bond between aggregate particles and cement paste.

Water absorption of aggregate is obtained by measuring increase in weight of oven-dry sample when immersed in water for 24 hours. The increase in weight expressed as percent of weight of the oven-dry sample is called water absorption.

Moisture content in coarse aggregates can be classified into absorbed and free. While absorbed moisture refers to water present in the permeable pores of the aggregate particles, free moisture is the moisture present on the surface of the particles. When coarse aggregates are stored in outdoor environments on site, they are likely to be exposed to rains. Another common practice is to wash the aggregates in order to remove deleterious materials like silt, clay and organic wastes. In either case, the aggregate particles contain both absorbed and free moisture. Such a coarse aggregate sample is termed as moist. When left to dry, the free moisture on the surface of aggregate particles first evaporates. This results in a situation where pores present in aggregate particles are saturated but the surfaces of these particles are dry. This is called saturated surface dry (SSD) condition. In other words, SSD aggregates have absorbed moisture content at the saturation level but do not have any free moisture. If SSD aggregates are further left to dry in the air, some of the absorbed moisture also gets evaporated. Such aggregate samples are referred as air dry. Air dry aggregates do have some absorbed moisture. When a coarse aggregate is placed in an oven for 24 hours at a temperature of 100°C to 110°C, this absorbed moisture is also lost. Such a sample is called oven dry or bone dry, and does not contain any form of moisture. To summarize, coarse aggregates can be under moist, SSD, air dry or oven dry conditions depending on moisture content.

Concrete mixes are designed assuming that the aggregates are in SSD condition. While dry aggregates tend to absorb water from the mixing water and lowers workability of the mix, moist aggregates contribute additional water to the mix and thereby increases effective water-cement ratio resulting in poor strength development. Both of these conditions are harmful for the concrete. Corrective measures, needed to be applied while obtaining the proportion of different ingredients of concrete, are discussed in a later section on concrete mix design.

It is common to come across dry coarse aggregates and moist fine aggregates on most sites. Typical water absorption capacity for coarse aggregates ranges between 0.5 and 1 % by weight of oven dry aggregates. However, coarse aggregates obtained from porous and/or laminar parent rocks such as sandstone can have water absorption capacity as high as 4%.

### 1.6.6 Soundness

Soundness is the ability of aggregates to resist excessive volume changes when exposed to environmental changes. These environmental changes include temperature variations, freeze-thaw cycles, wetting-drying cycles under normal and marine conditions. Porous and weak aggregates undergo excessive volume changes when they are exposed to these variations. Presence of impurities including clay, silt and organic materials makes aggregates more prone to such changes in volume. Aggregates which exhibit such excessive volume changes are termed as unsound. Use of unsound aggregates affect durability of the hardened concrete and is therefore undesirable.

Soundness of aggregates is estimated in laboratory by exposing the sample to alternative wetting and drying. However, the sample is immersed in a solution of sodium sulphate or magnesium sulphate instead of water. This is because accumulation of these salt crystals imparts similar stresses in the aggregate particles as freezing of water in freeze-thaw cycles. Some portions of these particles tend to disintegrate with these wetting-drying cycles leading to a loss of weight of the aggregate sample. As per IS 2386 Part V, the loss in weight over 10 wetting-drying cycles should not exceed 12% and 18% when aggregates are immersed in sodium sulphate and magnesium sulphate solutions respectively. However, the test is not reliable. The aggregate samples which withstand the test, i.e., undergo loss in weight within the specified limits, are necessarily potent to produce durable concrete. However, the samples which exhibit loss in weight more than specified limits need not be rejected.

### 1.6.7 Specific Gravity

Specific gravity has earlier been defined in Section 1.5.3, in the context of fine aggregates. Similar to fine aggregates, apparent specific gravity is usually measured for coarse aggregates also. The measurement principle remains similar. However, large cylindrical measures of volume either 3 litres or 15 litres are used instead of pycnometer. For coarse aggregates with lower MSA, pycnometer can also be used. Typical values for specific gravity of coarse aggregates lie between 2.6 and 2.8.

### 1.6.8 Bulk Density

Bulk density of coarse aggregate is also defined similar to that of fine aggregates, as mass of a given sample of a material divided by its total volume. Factors influencing bulk density have been mentioned in Section 1.5.4. Well-graded aggregates comprising of particles of all sizes exhibit good packing with little voids, and therefore show high bulk density. It is therefore common to use coarse aggregates with MSA 20 mm as well as 10 mm while mixing concrete, to obtain improved packing (Fig. 1.2).

### 1.6.9 Fineness Modulus of Coarse Aggregate

Similar to fine aggregates, fineness modulus of coarse aggregates is obtained by dividing a sum of cumulative percentage mass retained for various sieves by 100. The sieve sizes used in case of coarse aggregates are 20 mm, 16 mm, 12.5 mm, 10 mm, 4.75 mm, along with a pan. Fineness modulus is a measure of overall size and grading of coarse aggregates.

Typical range for fineness modulus of coarse aggregates is 5.5 to 8.0. Higher value of fineness modulus means sample with coarser particles. For all-in aggregates, fineness modulus varies in the range of 3.5 to 6.5.

### 1.6.10 Grading of Coarse Aggregates

The process of obtaining grading curve for coarse aggregates is illustrated in Section 1.6.2 using an example. Depending on nature of the grading curve, coarse aggregates can be classified as well-graded, poorly graded, uniformly graded and gap graded.

Well-graded aggregates comprise of particles of all different sizes in right proportions over a size range. Availability of particles of different sizes in right proportions ensures proper packing of aggregates leading to good quality concrete. Poorly graded aggregates do contain particles of different sizes but not in right proportions. Such aggregates do not lead to required packing and therefore concrete is not of good quality. While most particles of uniformly graded aggregates are of similar size, gap graded aggregates are characterized by sample not having particles of a certain size. Uniformly graded and gap graded aggregates also lead to poor packing and therefore not preferred.

### 1.6.11 Crushing Value

Since concrete comprises of aggregate particles bound together by cement paste, strength of concrete primarily depends on strength of the cement paste and quality of the bond between aggregate particles and cement paste. This means that if either the cement paste or the bond exhibits low strength (or poor quality), the concrete will not attain its target strength even if the aggregates have a very high strength. However, if good quality cement paste and strong bond between aggregate particles and cement paste are ensured, the strength of concrete depends on the mechanical properties of aggregates. In simple words, good quality aggregates are necessary but not sufficient for producing good quality concrete.

Mechanical properties of aggregates represent its strength under different types of loads. Strength of parent rock can be estimated by testing its cylindrical specimen with 25 mm diameter and 25 mm height under compression. Compressive strengths of these rock samples vary significantly from 45 to 545 MPa. However, strength of aggregates is not well represented by strength of parent rock because it depends on method of crushing as well. Therefore, mechanical properties of aggregates are usually characterized by aggregate crushing value, aggregate impact value and aggregate abrasion value.

Aggregate crushing value is a relative measure of its resistance to crushing under gradually applied compressive load. The test is performed on a sample of coarse aggregates comprising of particles with relatively similar size. The particles usually pass through 12.5 mm sieve and are retained on 10 mm sieve. The sample is placed in a cylindrical mould where it is subjected to 40 ton load through a plunger. The sample is then sieved through 2.36 mm sieve. The weight of material that passes through 2.36 mm sieve is measured. When this weight is expressed as a percentage of the weight of original sample used in the test, aggregate crushing value is obtained. For ascertaining good quality of aggregates, aggregate crushing value should be less than 30%.

In case of weaker aggregates, the particles get crushed and compacted very soon. Due to compaction, further crushing does not take place. In such situations, the standard aggregate crushing value test described above is not accurate. A simple test called "10 percent fines value" is therefore performed for weaker aggregates, i.e., if aggregate crushing value is higher than 30%.

### 1.6.12 Impact Value

Since concrete is also used in pavements for roads and runways, it is necessary to know the response of aggregates when they are subjected to impact and abrasive loads. Aggregates with good response to impact loads are called tough, and their ability to withstand large impact loads is called toughness.

A sample of standard sized coarse aggregates is placed in a mould and subjected to 15 blows, by dropping a metal hammer weighing 14 kilograms from a height of 38 cm. Standard sized sample usually comprises of particles that pass through 12.5 mm sieve but are retained on 10 mm sieve. The sample is then sieved through 2.36 mm sieve. The ratio of weight of material that passes through 2.36 mm sieve to the weight of original sample expressed as percentage is called aggregate impact value.

IS 383-2016 specifies that aggregate impact value should not be more than 45% for concrete to be used in non-wearing applications. For concrete used in wearing applications, it should be restricted to 30%. Wearing applications include pavements, roads and runways.

### 1.6.13 Abrasion Value

Coarse aggregates to be used in concrete for wearing applications need to be tested for their resistance to wear or abrasive loads. The most common test for aggregate abrasion value is Los Angeles Abrasion Test. A specified quantity of standard sized coarse aggregate sample is added to a standard cylinder along with specified number of abrasive charges. The cylinder is then revolved for certain number of revolutions. The particles which become smaller than 1.7 mm are separated out. The ratio of mass of particles smaller than 1.7 mm to that of the original sample expressed as percentage gives aggregate abrasion value. The aggregate abrasion value should not exceed 30% for use in wearing surfaces, and 50% for use in other applications.

## 1.7 WATER

Water is the most common ingredient of concrete. Water used for mixing, and curing shall be clean and free from injurious amounts of oils, acids, alkalis, salts, sugar, organic materials or other substances that may be deleterious to concrete or steel. Potable water is generally considered satisfactory for mixing of concrete.

### 1.7.1 Quality of Water

IS 456-2000 describes the requirements of water in detail. Permissible limits for solids shall be strictly adhered to the codal provisions. The suitability of water for concreting shall be ascertained by the compressive strength and initial setting time tests specified. The sample of water taken for testing shall represent the water proposed to be used for concreting, due account being paid to seasonal variation.

The pH value of water, shall be not less than 6. Sea Water Mixing or curing of concrete, especially reinforced concrete, with sea water is not recommended because of harmful salts in sea water.

Regarding quality of water the following set of guidelines have been prescribed by IS 456-2000.

(i) Neutralization of sample water of 100 ml quantity with phenolphthalein indicator. The sample should not require 0.02 normal sodium hydroxide solution more than 5 ml

(ii) Neutralization of sample water of 100 ml quantity with another mixed indicator. The sample should not require 0.02 normal Sulphuric acid more than 25 ml.

### 1.7.2 Impurities in Mixing Water and Permissible Limits for Solids as Per IS 456:2000

In case of any doubt whether the water is suitable or not, it is better to cast concrete with it and separately with distilled water. Then compare the 7 day and 28 day strength of both the concrete. If the strength of concrete using the doubtful water is up to 90% of the concrete with distilled water, then the doubtful water is acceptable for concreting.

Carbonates and bi-carbonates of sodium (cause quick setting) and potassium affect the setting time of cement. Brackish water containing chlorides and sulphates is harmful to concreting. Water having salts of manganese, tin, zinc, copper and lead cause marked reduction in strength of concrete. Sodium sulphide contents of more than 100 ppm is harmful. Water containing silt and suspended particles are undesirable. A turbidity limit of 2000 ppm has been suggested. For detailed quantitative description of impurities, the IS 456-2000 tables are to be referred.

| Impurities | IS code to be referred | Maximum permissible limits |
|---|---|---|
| Organic | IS 3025 (Part 18) | 200 mg/L |
| Inorganic | IS 3025 (Part 18) | 3000 mg/L |
| Sulphates as $SO_3$ | IS 3025 (Part 24) | 400 mg/L |
| Chlorides as Cl | IS 3025 (Part 32) | 2000 mg/L for concrete without embedded steel, and 500 mg/L for reinforced concrete |
| Suspended particulate matter | IS 3025 (Part 17) | 2000 mg/L |

Recycled water can be used as mixing water for concrete, provided such water meet all the requirements specified by the IS 456. The recycled water should not adversely affect the setting time and compressive strength of concrete. The hydrated cement and calcium hydroxide present in wash water accelerate the setting time of concrete.

## UNIT SUMMARY

This Unit introduced different types of cement, their physical and chemical properties. The methods to experimentally determine the acceptability of cements have been discussed. BIS specifications and field applications of some widely used cements have been given briefly. Types and properties of fine and coarse aggregates have been described in detail. Quality of water used for concreting has been discussed as per IS 456-2000. The understanding of this properties described in this unit will form the foundation of students towards gaining detailed knowledge of concrete technology.

## EXERCISES

**Multiple Choice Questions**

**1.** Which of the following is not a grade of Ordinary Portland Cement as per IS269

(a) OPC 33 (b) OPC 33S

(c) OPC 43 (d) OPC 43S

**2.** Select incorrect statement for OPC

(a) Maximum 5% loss on ignition by mass

(b) Maximum 6% magnesia by mass

(c) Maximum 5% Insoluble residue by mass

(d) Maximum 1% Chloride content by mass

**3.** Select incorrect statement for fineness test of OPC

(a) Fineness is measured by air permeability test as per IS 4031 part 2

(b) Fineness of OPC 43 and OPC 53 is 225 $m^2/kg$

(c) Fineness of OPC 43S and OPC 53S is 370 $m^2/kg$

(d) None of above

**4.** Select correct statement for OPC

(a) Maximum initial setting time is 30 minutes

(b) Minimum final setting time is 600 minutes

(c) Le-Chatelier apparatus is used for determining setting time test of OPC
(d) Increase in size of any side must not exceed 0.8% in autoclave test

5. Select incorrect statement for Sand
(a) Fineness modulus of fine sand is less as compared to coarse sand
(b) Size of zone IV sand is greater than Zone II sand
(c) Fineness modulus of fine sand lies between 2.2 to 2.6
(d) Sand is an inert material

6. If the fineness modulus of a sample of the fine aggregates is 4.5, the mean size of the particles in the sample is between
(a) 150 µm and 300 µm
(b) 2.36 mm and 4.75 mm
(c) 300µm and 600 µm
(d) 1.18 mm and 2.36 mm

7. Who invented Portland cement and in which year?
(a) Joseph Aspdin, 1824
(b) William Aspdin, 1840
(c) Joseph Aspdin, 1840
(d) William Aspdin, 1824

8. Flakiness index and elongation index tests are not applicable to aggregate sizes smaller than
(a) 10 mm
(b) 6.3 mm
(c) 2.36 mm
(d) 1.70 mm

9 .The test intended to study the resistance of aggregates to weathering action is
(a) Abrasion test
(b) Crushing test
(c) Soundness test
(d) Impact test

10. Which of the following aggregates gives maximum strength in concrete?
(a) Rounded aggregate
(b) Elongated aggregate
(c) Flaky aggregate
(d) Cubical aggregate

11. An aggregate which passes through 25 mm I.S. sieve and is retained on 20 mm sieve, is said to be flaky if its least dimension is less than
(a) 22.5 mm
(b) 18.5 mm
(c) 16.5 mm
(d) 13.5 mm

12. The specific gravity of particles of ordinary Portland cement is
(a) 3.15
(b) 2.55
(c) 2.65
(d) 1

**13 to 1.22 contain questions to match from List I & List II**

13. List I (Methods of Test for Cement) — List II (Name of IS Code)

| List I (Methods of Test for Cement) | List II (Name of IS Code) |
|---|---|
| (A) Fineness by Blaine air permeability method | (1) IS: 4031 Part 1 |
| (B) Fineness by dry sieving | (2) IS: 4031 Part 2 |
| (C) Initial and final setting times | (3) IS: 4031 Part 4 |
| (D) Consistency of standard cement paste | (4) IS: 4031 Part 5 |

14. List I (Name of IS Code) — List II (Method of Test of Aggregate)

| List I (Name of IS Code) | List II (Method of Test of Aggregate) |
|---|---|
| (A) IS 2386 Part1 | (1) Specific Gravity & Bulking of Sand |
| (B) IS 2386 Part 3 | (2) Flakiness index and Elongation index |

(C) IS 2386 Part 4 — (3) Soundness of Aggregate
(D) IS 2386 Part 5 — (4) Aggregate Impact & Aggregate Crushing Values

15. List I (Test) — List II (Apparatus used)
(A) Specific gravity test — (1) Le-Chatelier apparatus
(B) Consistency test — (2) Air Permeability method
(C) Soundness test — (3) Le-Chatelier's flask
(D) Fineness test — (4) Vicat's apparatus

16. List I (Test of Cement) — List II (Amount of water required)
(A) Initial or Final setting time test — (1) 0.85P
(B) Compressive strength test — (2) P/5+2.5
(C) Soundness test — (3) P/4+3
(D) Tensile strength test — (4) 0.78P
(P = Standard Consistency of Cement)

17. List I (Type of Cement) — List II (Specific Surface area)
(A) Ordinary Portland Cement — (1) 225 $m^2/kg$
(B) Rapid Hardening Cement — (2) 300 $m^2/kg$
(C) Portland Pozzolana Cement — (3) 325 $m^2/kg$

18. List I (Constituents of Portland Cement) — List II (Average Composition in %)
(A) Silica, $SiO_2$ — (1) 60 to 65
(B) Lime, CaO — (2) 17 to 25
(C) Iron Oxide, $Fe_2O_3$ — (3) 3 to 8
(D) Alumina, $Al_2O_3$ — (4) 0.5 to 6

19. List I (Apparatus) — List II (Purpose )
(A) Le-chatelier — (1) Workability of concrete
(B) Vicat's needle with annular collar — (2) Soundness of cement
(C) Vee-Bee — (3) Tensile strength of cement
(D) Briquettes test machine — (4) Final setting time of cement

20. List I (Job requirement) — List II (Type of Cement )
(A) High early strength — (1) Pozzolanic cement
(B) Lining for canals — (2) Rapid hardening cement
(C) Frost and acid resistance — (3) Sulphate resisting cement
(D) Marine structures — (4) High alumina cement

21. List I (Bogue compounds) — List II (Composition %)
(A) Alite ($C_3S$) — (1) 6 to 10
(B) Belite ($C_2S$) — (2) 8 to 12
(C) Celite ($C_3A$) — (3) 20 to 45
(D) Felite ($C_4AF$) — (4) 30 to 50

22. List I (Type of Portland Cement) — List II (IS Code)
(A) Ordinary Portland Cement — (1) 1489

(B) White Portland Cement (2) 8041
(C) Portland Pozzolana Cement (3) 8042
(D) Rapid Hardening Portland Cement (4) 269

**23.** Plaster of Paris is obtained by calcining the
(a) Bauxite (b) Gypsum
(c) Kankar (d) Lime stone

**24.** Cement is an important ingredient of concrete because
(a) It is a binding medium for discrete ingredients
(b) It is the only scientifically controlled ingredient
(c) It is an active ingredient
(d) It is a delicate link of the chain
(e) All of the above

**25.** In the manufacturing of cement, definite proportions of argillacious and calcareous materials are burnt at a temperature of
(a) 425°C (b) 875°C
(c) 1450°C (d) 1650°C

**26.** During the manufacturing process of Port land cement, gypsum or Plaster of Paris is added
(a) To increase the strength of cement
(b) To modify the color of cement
(c) To adjust setting time of cement
(d) To reduce heat of hydration

**27.** The percentage of gypsum added to the clinker during manufacturing process is
(a) 0.25 to 1 % (b) 1 to 2 %
(c) 2.5 to 3.5 % (d) 5 to 10 %

**28.** The tricalcium aluminate compound present in cement
(a) provides weak resistance against sulphate attack
(b) is responsible for highest heat of hydration
(c) characteristically fast reacting with water
(d) All of above

**29.** The constituents of cement which act as binders are
(a) tricalcium silicate, dicalcium silicate and sulfur trioxide
(b) tricalcium silicate and tetracalciumalumino-ferrite
(c) tricalcium silicate, dicalciumsili cate and tricalcium aluminate
(d) dicalcium silicate, tetracalcium al umino-ferrite, and tricalciumaluminate.

**30.** Which of the contribution of constituents of cement to the strength of cement is in decreasing order?
(a) $C_3S$, $C_2S$, $C_3A$ and $C_4AF$
(b) $C_2S$, $C_3S$, $C_3A$ and $C_4AF$
(c) $C_2S$, $C_4AF$, $C_3A$ and $C_3S$
(d) $C_3S$, $C_3A$, $C_2S$ and $C_4AF$

31. The time taken by dicalcium silicate (CS) to add to the strength of cement is
(a) 1-5 days (b) 5-7 days
(c) 7-14 days (d) 14-28 days
32. The heat generated during the setting and hardening of cement is called
(a) sensible heat (b) heat of evaporation
(c) latent heat (d) heat of hydration
(e) Slacking
33. Heat of hydration is determinated by an apparatus called
(a) hydrometer (b) photometer
(c) calorimeter (d) hygrometer
34. The hydration of concrete ceases at the temperature of
(a) 0°F (b) 0°C
(c) 11°F (d) 11°C
35. The average specific surface of cement is closer to
(a) 200,000 $mm^2/g$ (b) 300,000 $mm^2/g$
(c) 400,000 $mm^2/g$ (d) 500,000 $mm^2/g$
36. Which of the following statement(s) is/are incorrect?
(a) Calcium chloride should not be used in prestressed concrete
(b) Strength of concrete increases below freezing point of water
(c) Hardening of concrete takes place rapidly in hot weather
(d) The ingredients of concrete should be mixed within three minutes
(e) All of the above
37. For Ordinary Portland Cement, the maximum expansion by Le Chatelier's method should not exceed
(a) 2 mm (b) 5 mm
(c) 8 mm (d) 10 mm
38. Autoclave method is used to determine
(a) residue (b) expansion
(c) heat of hydration (d) sulphur content
(e) None of the above
39. Le Chatelier's method can be used to determine
(a) unsoundness of cement (b) soundness of cement
(c) fineness of aggregate (d) sulphur content
(e) All of the above
40. The specific surface of OPC is determined by
(a) Le Chatelier's apparatus (b) air-permeability method
(c) autoclave method (d) sieve analysis
41. What are the colours of Ordinary Portland Cement and Portland Pozzolana Cement
(a) white, black (b) brown, gray

(c) gray, light gray (d) white, gray
(e) gray, black

42. During the test of OPC for loss on ignition, the loss in weight occurs due to
(a) decomposition of silicates
(b) chemical reaction
(c) burning of constituents
(d) melting of tricalcium aluminate
(e) evaporation of moisture and carbon dioxide

43. Total heat of hydration of cement is independent of
(a) ambient temperature (b) composition of cement
(c) fineness of cement (d) All of the above

44. The insoluble residue in cement should be
(a) between 10% and 15% (b) less than 10%
(c) between 5% and 10% (d) between 1.5% and 5%
(e) less than 0.85%

45. The cyclopan aggregate has a size more than
(a) 4.75 mm (b) 20 mm
(c) 55 mm (d) 75 mm

46. If the fineness modulus of sand is 2.5, it is graded as
(a) very coarse sand (b) coarse sand
(c) medium sand (d) fine sand
(e) very fine sand

47. Grading of the aggregate
(a) affects the workability
(b) affects the strength of concrete
(c) is dependent on the shape and texture of the particles of the aggregate
(d) affects the water-cement ratio
(e) All of the above is true

## Answers for Multiple Choice Questions

1. b, 2. d, 3. d, 4. d, 5. b, 6. d, 7. a, 8. b, 9. c, 10. d, 11. d, 12. a,
13. A-2, B-1, C-4, D-3
14. A-2, B-1, C-4, D-3
15. A-3, B-4, C-1, D-2
16. A-1, B-3, C-4, D-2
17. A-1, B-3, C-2
18. A-1, B-2, C-4, D-3
19. A-2, B-4, C-1, D-3
20. A-2, B-3, C-4, D-1
21. A-4, B-3, C-2, D-1

22. A-4, B-3, C-1, D-2

23. b, 24. e, 25. c, 26. c, 27. c, 28. d, 29. c, 30. a, 31. d, 32. d, 33. c, 34. c, 35. b,
36. b, 37. d, 38. b, 39. b, 40. b, 41. c, 42. e, 43. c, 44. e, 45. d, 46. d, 47. a

## Short and Long Answer Type Questions

1. Describe the Le Chatelier's test for unsoundness of cement test.
2. Describe the role of $C_3A$ in cement.
3. How does gypsum affect the hydration process of cement?
4. What are the main products of hydration of high alumina cement? What do you mean by conversion of high alumina cement?
5. What are the initial and final setting time of cement? Why is a minimum of 30 minute prescribed for initial setting time of cement?
6. What are the typical oxide components in cement?
7. What compounds are known as Bogue's compounds?
8. Under what site conditions, rapid hardening Portland cements are used?
9. Describe the precautions required in manufacturing of white cement?
10. What are the alkalis present in cement?
11. What type of cement is used in refractory concrete?
12. What do you mean by pozzolans? What are the different types of pozzolans used in manufacturing of PPC?
13. What are the merits of using pozzolans in cement?

## KNOW MORE

Did you know, who is the inventor of modern cement and why the name Portland has been given? Joseph Aspdin, a builder from Leeds, invented cement after lot of experiment based research by burning finely ground chalk and clay in a kiln until the carbon dioxide was removed. His father Thomas Aspdin was bricklayer. He joined the job of his father in 1817. He experimented a lot and got the British patent in 1824. The patent number was BP 5022. The title of the patent was an improvement in the mode of producing an artificial stone. He called the new material Portland as it had the properties similar to Portland stone.

The first cement factory was built in Porbandar, Gujarat, in 1904. However, the first cement production started in a factory established by a company called South India Industrial Ltd. in Madras in the same year.

In ancient India also, ancient knowledge of many binding materials were used for construction of grand temple structures. The Indians, Egyptians used **calcined gypsum** ***as a binding material and the Greeks and Romans used lime.*** In India a binding material like cement used to be made by mixing calcined clay, limestone surkhi mix, eggs, thick sugarcane jiggery like materials. The same were used at the joints of stones to build structures such as temples, forts and palaces.

Can you imagine the number of particles in cement per kilogram? In One kilogram of cement, there are about $1.1x10^{12}$ particles.

## REFERENCES AND SUGGESTED READINGS

1. Gambhir, M.L., *Concrete Technology*, Tata McGraw Hill Publishing Co. Ltd., Delhi.
2. Shetty, M.S., Concrete Technology, S. Chand and Co. Pvt. Ltd., Ram Nagar, Delhi.
3. Santhakumar, A. R., *Concrete Technology*, Oxford University Press, New Delhi.
4. Neville, A. M. and Brooks, J.J., *Concrete Technology*, Pearson Education Pvt. Ltd.
5. Neville, A. M., *Concrete Technology*, Pearson Education Pvt. Ltd., New Delhi.
6. Sood, H., Kulkarni P. D., Mittal L. N., *Laboratory Manual in Concrete Technology*, CBS Publishers, New Delhi.
7. Golewski, G. L. (2020). *Energy Savings Associated with the Use of Fly Ash and Nano-additives in the Cement Composition*." Energies, 13, 2184; doi: 10.3390/ en13092184.

# 2 Concrete

## UNIT SPECIFICS

Through this unit we have discussed the following aspects:

- Different grades of concrete and related provisions of IS 456-2000 have been discussed.
- Duff Abram water cement (w/c) ratio law and interdependence of w/c ratio and compressive strength of concrete have been explained.
- Appropriate approach to select of w/c ratio to obtain different grades of concrete has been outlined.
- Based on exposure conditions, maximum w/c ratio and minimum cement content for different grades of concrete have been discussed.
- Workability of fresh concrete, factors affecting it, and various methods to determine workability of concrete by slump cone, compaction factor, Vee-Bee time have been detailed.
- The methods to avoid segregation, bleeding and preventive measures have been described.
- Important properties of Hardened concrete such as strength, durability, and impermeability have been described.

The aspects of producing good quality concrete, related quality control of fresh concrete have been discussed for generating further understanding of the state-of-the-art concepts of acceptable quality concrete has been introduced.

A large number of multiple-choice questions as well as questions of short and long answer types marked in two categories following lower and higher order of Bloom's taxonomy, a list of references and suggested readings are given in the unit so that one can go through them for practice. It is important to note that for getting more information on various topics of interest some QR codes have been provided in different sections which can be scanned for relevant supportive knowledge.

## RATIONALE

The fundamentals discussed in this Unit will help students to get a primary idea about the physical properties of fresh concrete as well as properties of hardened concrete. The unit explains the IS specifications on different grades of concrete, the laboratory experiments to be conducted to assess the workability of fresh concrete. All these basic aspects are relevant to understand the basics of producing a strong, durable and impermeable concrete.

## PRE-REQUISITES

Basics of good quality aggregates and other ingredients of concrete

## UNIT OUTCOMES

List of outcomes of this unit is as follows:

**U2-O1:** To understand the procedure to produce different grades of concrete based on appropriate selection of water ratio.

**U2-O2:** To learn the requirements of maximum w/c ratio and minimum cement content for different grades of concrete on the basis of exposure conditions.

**U2-O3:** To understand the factors affecting workability and their measurement techniques.

**U2-O4:** To learn the preventive measures to avoid segregation and bleeding in order to obtain good quality concrete.

**U2-O5:** To understand important properties of hardened concrete such as strength, durability, and impermeability.

| Unit-2 Outcome | EXPECTED MAPPING WITH COURSE OUTCOMES (1 - Weak Correlation; 2 - Medium Correlation; 3 - Strong Correlation) | | | | |
|---|---|---|---|---|---|
| | CO-1 | CO-2 | CO-3 | CO-4 | CO-5 |
| U2-O1 | 1 | 3 | 3 | 2 | 1 |
| U2-O2 | 1 | 3 | 3 | 3 | 1 |
| U2-O3 | 1 | 1 | 3 | 2 | 2 |
| U2-O4 | 1 | 1 | 3 | 3 | 2 |
| U2-O5 | 1 | 3 | 3 | 3 | 1 |

## 2.1 CONCRETE

**Introduction**

The concrete is the man-made artificial stone and the basic building material in the modern times. The strength and durability properties can be varied widely by changing the relative composition of its constituents. As the fresh concrete is plastic in nature, it can be moulded to any desired shape. This chapter will introduce the properties of fresh concrete as well as hardened concrete. As per IS 10262, the basic principles which underline the proportioning of mixes are Abram's law for strength development and Lyse's rule for making mix with adequate workability for placement in a dense state so as to enable the strength development as contemplated.

This chapter aims to describe how to produce different grades of concrete based on appropriate selection of water ratio. The requirements of maximum w/c ratio and minimum cement content for different grades of concrete based on different exposure conditions are also described. Factors affecting fresh concrete properties such as workability are described. Different techniques to measure workability are also outlined. Fresh concrete can be prone to segregation and bleeding which can be detrimental for a durable concrete. Different preventive measures to avoid segregation and bleeding are mentioned. Important properties of hardened concrete such as strength, durability, and impermeability are described in detail.

### 2.1.1 Different Grades of Concrete

The different grades of concrete vary from M15 to M80 as per IS 456. Here the designation number implies the characteristic strength in N/mm$^2$ at 28 days. The characteristic strength is strength value of the material below which not more than 5 percent of all possible test results are expected to fall. Based on specified characteristic compressive strength, the IS 456 has grouped the concrete in three groups, viz., Ordinary concrete (strength ranging from 15-20 N/mm$^2$), standard concrete (25-55 N/mm$^2$) and high strength concrete (60-80 N/mm$^2$). Varying the water cement ratio and using well graded aggregate and certain admixtures, the higher grades of concrete are obtained.

### 2.1.2 Provisions of IS 456

Is 456:2000 describes various requirements of concrete in terms of materials, workmanship, inspection and testing. The salient points of these provisions are:

(i) Concretes of grades up to M15 are normally used in plain concrete constructions, lean concrete, simple foundations, foundation for masonry walls and temporary constructions.

(ii) Depending upon the grade of concrete, type of cement, duration of curing, and environmental exposure conditions, the requirements of mix design changes.

(iii) Direct tensile strength of concrete is tested by split cylinder test as per IS 5816. The flexural tensile strength is obtained by testing concrete beams as per IS 516. Flexural tensile strength ($f_{cr}$) may be related to the characteristic compressive strength ($f_{ck}$) as

$$f_{cr} = 0.7 * \sqrt{f_{ck}}$$

(iv) The elastic deformation of concrete is calculated by assuming the modulus of elasticity as

$$E = 5000 * \sqrt{f_{ck}}$$

The actual value may vary ±20% from the values as per the above equation. Also, the actual modulus of elasticity depends on the reasons outlined in point (ii) above.

(v) Shrinkage of concrete depends on cement and water content as well properties of constituents of concrete. For a given humidity and temperature, shrinkage of concrete is more influenced by the water content. For higher water cement ratio, generally shrinkage is higher. Lower the alkali ($Na_2O$, $K_2O$) content, lower is shrinkage. Higher the loss on ignition of cement, the greater is the shrinkage. Concretes with well graded aggregate possess lesser pores, higher density, so results in lesser shrinkage. Larger the maximum size of aggregate, lower is the shrinkage.

(vi) In absence of appropriate test data, for design purposes, shrinkage strain may be adopted as 0.0003. IS 1343 gives a detailed procedure to account for shrinkage effect of concrete. To note, the shrinkage of sand mortar is 2 to 3 times as great as 20 mm aggregate concrete, and it is 3 to 4 times as great as 40 mm aggregate concrete. The reason for the same is that as the aggregate size is larger, the specific surface area is lower, so mortar required to be taken is lower. This in turn results in lower shrinkage for higher aggregate size. Also, higher modulus of elasticity of aggregate gives lesser shrinkage values.

(vii) As per IS 456, creep of concrete depends upon factors such as (a) the level of stress in the concrete (b) age of concrete (i.e., time elapsed after casting the concrete up to the time when load is being applied) at loading and (c) duration of loading.

As long as the applied stress is less than $f_{ck}/3$, then creep is linearly proportional to stress. Creep coefficient is defined as

$$\frac{\text{Ultimate creep strain}}{\text{Elastic creep strain at the age of loading}}$$

Also, a detailed procedure for calculation of deflection due to shrinkage and creep are provided in annexure C of IS 456.

For long span structures, it is advisable to determine the actual creep strain. However, as a guide, the following values of creep coefficients are suggested in IS 456 as

| Age of Loading | 7 days | 28 days | 1 year |
|---|---|---|---|
| Creep Coefficient | 2.2 | 1.6 | 1.1 |

(viii) Thermal expansion: The thermal expansion of concrete depends upon the nature of cement, the aggregate, the cement content, the relative humidity and the size of the sections.

## 2.2 EFFECT OF WATER CEMENT RATIO ON CONCRETE

**Introduction**

The water cement ratio and the aggregate cement ratio both play important role in the strength of the hardened concrete. When supplementary cementitious materials (SCM) are used, the effective water cement ratio should also take the contribution of these additional materials. Let us assume that F grams of SCM is used with cement of C grams for water of W grams. If the cementing efficiency of the SCM is k, then effective water cement ratio is W/(C+kF). Cementing efficiency is said to be k, where 100 grams of SCM is producing equivalent strength of k grams of cement. Effective water cement ratio is also called water-binder ratio.

Also, the effective water cement ratio should be carefully maintained on site during casting of structural elements. For a hot dry weather, when rich mixes (i.e., mixes of higher grade concrete) are produced, the hot coarse aggregates surface is quickly coated by the cement paste, and it becomes dry immediately. This dry layer prevents further ingress of water and absorption by the aggregate. Thus, the effective water ratio becomes higher resulting into lower strength of the concrete mix. The absorption of water by aggregates results into progressive loss of workability. To avoid this, aggregates are recommended to be in saturated surface dry condition.

At times on site, due to rains during casting, the aggregates may have excess water. To generate equivalent SSD condition, the water to be mixed should be adjusted as per the moisture content of these aggregates.

### 2.2.1 Duff Abram Water Cement (W/C) Ratio Law

During the evolution of concrete, many theories have been propounded by many researchers. Some of them held valid for some time and then underwent some changes while others did not stand the test of time and hence slowly disappeared. But Abrams water/cement ratio law stood the test of time and is held valid even today as a fundamental truth in concrete-making practices.

**Abrams water/cement ratio** law was proposed in 1918-1919. The law states that the strength of concrete at a given age and at a normal temperature is inversely proportional to the water cement ratio (Fig. 2.1), provided the mix is workable. The law can be expressed as

$$S = \frac{A}{B^x}$$

Where, S = strength of the concrete, A & B are empirical constants. In SI units, A = 96 N/mm2 and B = 7, and theses constants are valid for strength of concrete at the age of 28 days, and x is the effective water cement ratio.

Feret, in 1897, formulated a general rule defining the strength of concrete paste and concrete in terms of volume fractions of the constituents by the equation:

$$S = K\left(\frac{c}{c+e+a}\right)^2$$

Where, S = Strength of concrete, c, e and a = volume of cement, water and air respectively and K = a constant. In this expression the volume of air is also included because it is not only the water/cement ratio but also the degree of compaction, which indirectly means the volume of air-filled voids in the concrete is taken into account in estimating the strength of concrete.

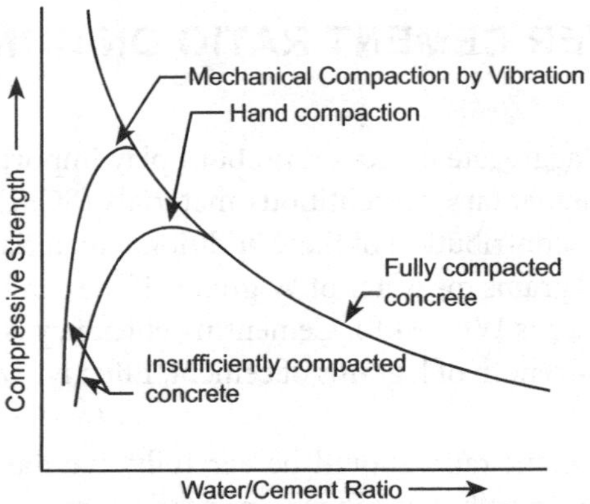


**Fig. 2.1:** Effect of water-cement ratio on compressive strength of concrete

## 2.2.2 Significance of W/C Ratio

It has been found that water required for chemical reaction is about 23% by mass of ordinary Portland cement. This water is known as bound water. Gel water, approximately 15% by mass of cement, is additionally required to fill the gel-pores. So, water in excess of 38% by mass of cement, will cause the undesirable capillary pores. For larger water cement ratio, the capillary pores formed, give a porous concrete. Therefore, for normal concrete, water cement ratio is preferably kept between 0.4 and 0.5. Lower the water cement ratio ensures lower permeability and higher strength.

The ratio of the amount of water to the amount of cement by weight is termed as water-cement ratio. The strength and quality of concrete depend on this ratio. The quantity of water is usually expressed in litre per bag of cement. The water-cement ratio should be such that it should impart a reasonable degree of workability to concrete, excess water affects the durability and strength of the concrete. A lesser water-cement ratio makes the concrete unworkable while concrete with excess water-cement ratio is liable to segregation.

The volume change in concrete results in cracks, and cracks are responsible for the disintegration of concrete. The low water-cement ratio concretes are less sensitive to carbonation, external chemical attack and other detrimental effects that cause a lack of durability of concrete. A low water-cement ratio and adequate cover is the best way to protect reinforcing steel against corrosion.

## 2.2.3 Selection of W/C Ratio for Different Grades

The selection of water cement ratio for different grades should be done as per the Fig. 1 of IS 10262, which is shown here in Fig. 2.2.

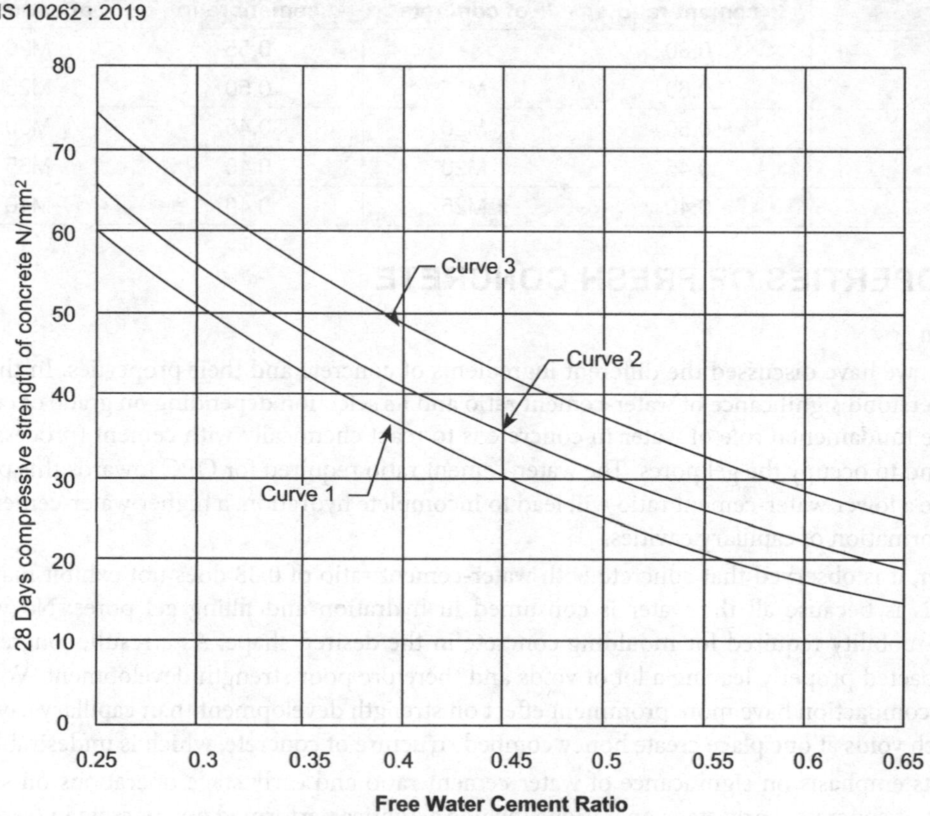


Curve 1: for expected 28 days compressive strength of 33 and < 43 $N/mm^2$.

Curve 2: for expected 28 days compressive strength of 43 and < 53 $N/mm^2$.

Curve 3: for expected 28 days compressive strength of 53 $N/mm^2$ and above.

**Notes:**

1. In the absence of data on actual 28 days compressive strength of cement, the curves 1, 2 and 3 may be used for OPC 33, OPC 43 and OPC 53, respectively.
2. While using PPC/PSC, the appropriate curve as per the actual strength may be utilized. In the absence of the actual 28 days compressive strength data, curve 2 may be utilized.

**Fig. 2.2:** Chart for selection of appropriate w/c ratio as per IS 10262-2019

## 2.2.4 Maximum W/C Ratio for Different Grades of Concrete for Different Exposure Conditions as per IS 456

Water-cement ratio for obtaining different grades of concrete should be restricted to values stipulated by IS 456. These values depend on different exposure conditions such as mild, moderate, severe, very severe and extreme, and are shown in Table 2.1.

**Table 2.1:** Maximum water-cement ratio for different grades of concrete as per IS: 456

| Exposure Conditions | Plain Concrete | | Reinforced Concrete | |
|---|---|---|---|---|
| | Maximum water-cement ratio | Minimum grade of concrete | Maximum water-cement ratio | Minimum grade of concrete |
| Mild | 0.60 | - | 0.55 | M20 |
| Moderate | 0.60 | M15 | 0.50 | M25 |
| Severe | 0.50 | M20 | 0.45 | M30 |
| Very Severe | 0.45 | M20 | 0.45 | M35 |
| Extreme | 0.40 | M25 | 0.40 | M40 |

## 2.3 PROPERTIES OF FRESH CONCRETE

**Introduction**

In the Unit I, we have discussed the different ingredients of concrete and their properties. In this unit, we have understood significance of water-cement ratio and its selection depending on grade of concrete required. The fundamental role of water in concrete is to react chemically with cement (process called hydration) and to occupy the gel pores. The water-cement ratio required for OPC towards this purpose is 0.38. While a lower water-cement ratio will lead to incomplete hydration, a higher water-cement ratio will lead to formation of capillary cavities.

However, it is observed that concrete with water-cement ratio of 0.38 does not exhibit maximum strength. This is because all the water is consumed in hydration and filling gel pores. No water is available for mobility required for moulding concrete in the desired shape. As a result, concrete does not get compacted properly leaving a lot of voids and therefore poor strength development. Voids due to improper compaction have more prominent effect on strength development than capillary cavities. A cluster of such voids at one place create honey combed structure of concrete, which is undesirable.

This puts emphasis on significance of water-cement ratio and early stage operations on strength development of concrete. Early stage operations include activities performed on concrete in fresh stage, usually within the initial setting time. These include mixing, transporting, placing, compacting and finishing the fresh concrete.

**Outline of concreting operations**

Different ingredients of concrete, viz. cement, water, sand, coarse aggregates and admixtures (if any), are first weighed as per quantity calculations. Sand is taken in required quantity and laid evenly in a pan. Cement is weighed and put over the sand layer. Cement and sand are then thoroughly mixed using trowel. Coarse aggregates of different maximum size (CA10 and CA20) are weighed. It should be noted that larger size aggregates (CA20) are first evenly laid in another pan, which is followed by smaller size aggregates (CA10). The two coarse aggregates are mixed thoroughly using trowels. Therefore, we have two pans, the first carrying a dry mix of sand and cement, and the second carrying a mix of coarse aggregates with different sizes. Water is measured in a graduated cylinder in required quantity. The contents of pan with coarse aggregates are first fed into the rotating mixer. Some portion from the measured water is added to the mixer. Thereafter, mix of sand and cement is fed into the mixer. Upon thorough mixing, remaining water is also added to the mixer. The obtained mix is called green concrete, and is poured out on a pan. Certain portion of the mix is used for assessing workability (typically using slump cone test).

Green concrete can be easily moulded in desired shape and size. The moulds (usually called formwork) conforming to different structural elements are filled with fresh concrete. To assess strength of concrete, cubes and/or cylinders are cast and tested in laboratory at different ages such as 7 days and 28 days.

The concrete filled in formwork is adequately compacted using vibrators. The exposed surfaces are smoothened using straight edge bars and trowels. This smoothening operation is called finishing and should be completed within initial setting time. The formwork filled with concrete is left for 24 hours. After that, concrete elements are suitably cured. Curing ensures adequate moisture and ambient temperature requirements in the concrete, which is important for development of strength. Duration of curing should be strictly followed as per IS 456, IS 1199 and IS 9013. The stripping off formworks is performed as per IS 456 depending on the type of structural elements.

The properties of fresh concrete are best represented by workability which is a measure of ease of carrying out above mentioned concrete operations.

### 2.3.1 Workability

From the above discussion, it is clear that the role of water is not only hydration and occupation of gel pores. The function of water is also to lubricate the ingredients of concrete so that the concrete can be placed and compacted in the formwork with ease and without loss of homogeneity. Concrete having such property is called workable concrete. Therefore, workability can be defined as the ease with which early stage operations such as mixing, transporting, placing, compacting and finishing the concrete can be performed such that we achieve concrete with minimum voids and no honeycombing on the surface.

Workability is a composite property which includes two major properties: (i) consistency, and (ii) cohesiveness. Consistency, also termed as fluidity/mobility, enables concrete to flow and thereby achieve the desired shape. On the other hand, cohesiveness refers to the property related to stability of the concrete mix such that its ingredients do not get segregated. While an increase in water-cement ratio is likely to increase the consistency of concrete mix, cohesiveness might get affected. Therefore, workability of concrete is a very important parameter while obtaining the proportions of different ingredients in the concrete mix.

Workability of concrete mix depends on the application of the concrete. A workable concrete mix for mass concreting such as that in dams may not be workable for regular concreting in buildings. A workable concrete mix designed for compaction using vibrators may not be a good choice for manual compaction. Workability of concrete is further influenced by thickness of section and density of reinforcement steel. For instance, a workable concrete mix for slabs (less thickness and dense reinforcement) may not be equally workable for beams and columns. Apart from applications, there are a number of factors affecting workability. These factors and their effects on workability are outlined in the following section.

### 2.3.2 Factors Affecting Workability of Concrete

Workability of fresh concrete mix is mainly affected by (i) proportions of different ingredients of concrete, (ii) properties of those ingredients, and (iii) environmental conditions. The effects of some important factors among these are outlined below.

**Water content**

Higher water content per unit volume of concrete leads to improved consistency/fluidity of concrete. However, increasing water content while keeping quantities of other ingredients same may lead to a loss of cohesiveness of mix and inhibit proper strength development of concrete. Therefore, an increase in water content should be associated with an increase in cement content as well, so that all of the increased water is not free water. Some of the increased water will be consumed in hydration. A practical approach is to increase water and cement contents while keeping the water-cement ratio constant.

**Mix proportioning**

Aggregate-cement ratio is an important parameter influencing workability of the concrete mix. While aggregates form the skeleton of the concrete, cement paste acts as lubricant in the mix. Therefore, higher aggregate-cement ratio means that the mix has impaired mobility and cohesiveness, and therefore low workability. A lower aggregate-cement ratio means that more cement paste per unit surface area of aggregate particles is available for lubrication. This improves both consistency and cohesiveness of the mix resulting in high workability.

**Shape of aggregates**

As elaborated in Section 1.6, aggregates can be rounded, cubic, angular, flaky or elongated. Use of angular, flaky and elongated aggregates results in very harsh concrete mix which may not be workable. On the other hand, rounded and cubic aggregates lead to increase in workability. There are two important reasons for this effect. Firstly, rounded and cubic aggregates have low surface area per unit mass and low surface voids, leading to a lower lubrication requirement. Secondly, rounded and cubic aggregates offer lower frictional resistance, and the obtained mix is therefore highly workable. In practice, river sand and gravel provide enhanced workability to the fresh concrete compared to crushed sand and aggregates, as river sand and gravel comprise of particles rounded due to attrition by water.

**Size of aggregates**

Larger aggregate particles have lower surface area per unit mass. Therefore, use of larger size aggregates lowers the lubrication requirement and hence increases workability of the concrete mix. However, this is true up to a certain limit. If the size of aggregates is increased beyond a limit, the mix may not remain cohesive.

Since fine aggregates have much higher surface area to be lubricated as compared to coarse aggregates, gradation of fine aggregates is much more important than that of coarse aggregates. Another important factor to be looked is ratio of fine aggregates to coarse aggregates (IS 10262 provides a table of the ratio as a guideline). An optimal choice of fine to coarse aggregate ratio is needed for a suitably workable concrete mix. An unsuitable choice may lead to honeycombing or segregation in the concrete mix.

In Section 1.6, we mentioned that usually a mix of 10 mm and 20 mm MSA coarse aggregates are used in construction. An expert concrete mix designer should be able to suitably adjust this proportion to get the desired workability of the concrete mix.

**Texture of aggregates**

While use of rough textured aggregates result in concrete mix with poor workability, use of glassy or smooth textured aggregates improve workability of the mix. This is because rough aggregate particles have a lot of surface pores/voids which increase the lubrication requirement and therefore lead to poor workability. Rough particles also increase the frictional resistance leading to poor mobility of particles in the cement paste, further reducing the workability.

From above discussion, it can be observed that shape, size and texture of aggregate particles have significant effects on workability of the concrete mix. It should also be understood that all these effects are related to surface area per unit mass of aggregate particles. The effects explained above assume that water content is kept constant across mixes with different aggregate properties. The effects of shape, size and texture of aggregates become even more prominent in case of high strength concrete mixes where the water-cement ratio is in below 0.30.

**Grading of aggregates**

In Section 1.6, we discussed how aggregate samples can be classified as well-graded, poorly graded, uniformly graded and gap graded based on the gradation curve. Well-graded aggregates comprise of particles of different sizes in the right proportion. This leads to lesser voids and therefore better packing. If other factors are kept constant, concrete mix with lesser voids have an excess cement paste available for lubricating the aggregate particles. As a result, the mix becomes cohesive and shows no segregation. This implies that use of well-graded aggregates improves workability of the mix. On the other hand, use of poorly graded, uniformly graded or gap graded aggregates results into a mix with poor workability.

**Water absorption and free moisture in aggregates**

Different aggregates show different water absorption depending on properties of parent rock and method of crushing used. Aggregates with large number of surface pores tend to absorb more water. Higher water absorption by aggregates results into lesser water availability for hydration of cement, filling gel pores and mobility of aggregates. This leads to a mix with poor workability. Therefore, in order to obtain a mix with desired workability, it is important to determine the water absorption capacity of coarse and fine aggregates prior to obtaining concrete mix design. Further, aggregates with water absorption capacity exceeding 2% should not be used.

On the other hand, availability of free moisture in aggregates can lead to excess water available in the mix. Though it can enhance mobility of aggregates in the mix, it can also lead to loss of cohesiveness resulting in a poorly workable mix. It is therefore important to determine the free moisture content present in aggregates prior to designing a concrete mix.

It is common to find dry coarse aggregates and moist fine aggregates on construction sites. Therefore, water absorption capacity and free moisture content in coarse and fine aggregates should be determined, and necessary corrections should be made while obtaining the proportions of different ingredients in the mix. These corrections are outlined in the unit on mix design.

**Properties of cement**

Fineness of cement particles influence workability of the concrete mix. Rapid Hardening Portland Cement (RHPC) contains higher proportions of $C_3S$, $C_3A$ and $SO_3$ compared to Ordinary Portland Cement (OPC). These compounds have finer particles with higher surface area per unit mass compared to $C_2S$, and therefore need more water for lubrication. If water content is kept same, use of RHPC leads to a reduction in workability.

On the other hand, blended cements such as Portland Pozzolana Cement (PPC) and Portland Slag Cement (PSC) contain pozzolanic materials such as fly ash and slag, which result in secondary cementitious products. Water requirement for hydration of these cement types is lower compared to OPC. This makes additional free water available for lubrication and mobility of aggregates, leading to improved workability of the mix.

On a general note, the influence of cement on workability is lesser than those of properties and grading of aggregates.

**Use of mineral admixtures**

Admixtures are optional ingredients used in concrete which have ability to modify properties of fresh concrete mix. Different types of admixtures will be discussed in unit on admixtures. Admixtures can be broadly categorized as mineral admixtures and chemical admixtures depending on their composition. Fly ash, silica fume and slag are the most common mineral admixtures used in concrete. They form additional C-S-H gel through secondary cementitious reactions with $Ca(OH)_2$ which is a by-product of hydration reaction. Their effect on workability is very similar to the use of blended cements.

**Use of chemical admixtures**

Admixtures which affect workability of a fresh concrete mix are called Water Reducing Admixtures (WRAs) and High Range Water Reducing Admixtures (HRWRAs). They are also called plasticizers and superplasticizers respectively. As name suggests, use of WRAs and HRWRAs lead to reduction in water to be used in concrete mix in order to achieve same workability. The only difference is that HRWRAs are more effective than WRAs. Therefore, if same water content is used, the mix with WRA/HRWRA will show improved workability. These admixtures are used in very small quantities with typical range between 0.5% and 2% by weight of cement.

Use of air entraining admixtures also reduces internal friction between the particles to a certain extent. This can also improve workability of the concrete mix.

**Ambient temperature**

Higher ambient temperature increases water requirements of the concrete mix for different purposes. If water content is kept the same, higher ambient temperature will therefore lead to a loss in workability of the concrete mix.

**Wind velocity**

Higher wind velocity increases water evaporation rate and hence increases water demand. If water content is unaltered, high wind velocity leads to a loss in workability of the concrete mix.

**Relative humidity**

Relative humidity is an important characteristic for evaporation rate at a specified place and time. Lower relative humidity leads to faster evaporation of water, making lesser water available for providing mobility. Therefore, lower relative humidity leads to poorly workable concrete mix.

Concreting in hot and arid climate (high ambient temperature and low relative humidity) would require additional water to achieve same level of workability. If water content is kept unaltered, there will be a loss in workability of the concrete mix.

A number of factors, involving properties of ingredient of concrete, proportions of these ingredients in the mix and environmental conditions, affect workability of the fresh concrete mix. Workability is therefore an important quantity which should be known while obtaining the design concrete mix. Further, mix design should be preceded by determination of relevant properties of cement, sand and coarse aggregates.

### 2.3.3 Determination of Workability of Concrete

Workability is a composite property that comprises of consistency and cohesiveness. It is difficult to quantify workability of a concrete mix. Researchers have attempted to define different suitable measures for workability. Some of the important tests to estimate workability of concrete mix are outlined below.

**Slump cone method**

Slump cone test is the most commonly used method to obtain a measure of workability. However, the test measures consistency of the concrete mix alone. Cohesiveness of the mix cannot be assessed from slump cone test. Therefore, slump cone test is not suitable for very dry or wet mixes which are prone to segregation and bleeding respectively. Segregation and bleeding will be explained in an upcoming section.

The basic apparatus for slump cone test comprises of slump cone which is a metallic cone frustum with bottom diameter of 200 mm, top diameter of 100 mm and height of 300 mm as shown in Fig. 2.3a and 2.3b. The thickness of cone frustum is not less than 1.6 mm. Additional apparatus required for the test include tamping rod, trowel and scale. Tamping rod is made of steel, and has diameter of 16 mm and length of 600 mm. It has a bulleted end.

Prior to conducting the test, the slump cone is thoroughly cleaned to get rid of any concrete sticking from a previous test. Water from cleaning is also rinsed well so that the inner surface is dry. The slump cone is then placed on the base plate and concrete mix is poured in four layers. Each layer is tamped 25 times using the bulleted end of the tamping rod. The top surface of the concrete is levelled with the top edge of slump cone using travel and tamping rod.

The slump cone is removed immediately by lifting it slowly and gently in the vertical direction. When the slump cone is removed, the concrete cone tends to subside. This subsidence from the initial condition is measured using a scale, and is reported as slump value in millimeter. Higher the slump value, higher is the consistency of the concrete mix. Higher consistency is usually associated with better workability, provided the mix does not undergo segregation and/or bleeding. Typical value for slump is 50 mm to 100 mm in case of concrete mix without admixtures. With use of superplasticizers, the slump value can be easily increased up to 200 mm.

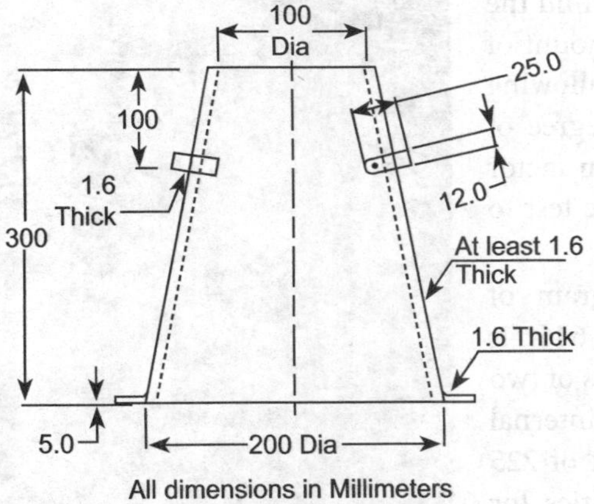


**Fig. 2.3 (a):** Schematic diagram of a slump cone

**Fig. 2.3 (b):** Slump Cone Test Apparatus in Laboratory

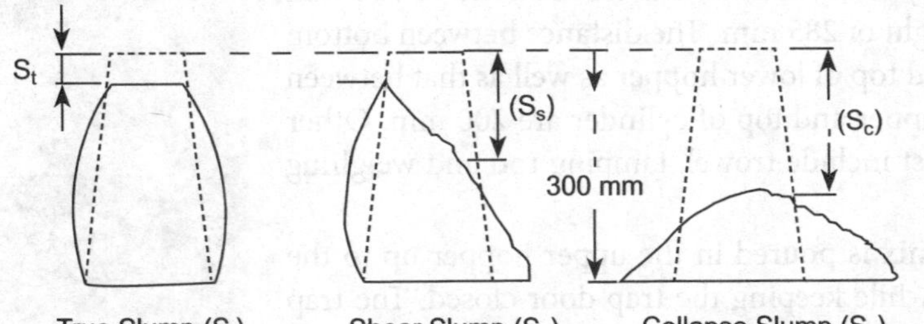


**Fig. 2.3 (c):** Different patterns of slump (Concrete Technology by M S Shetty)

In addition to slump value, slump pattern also indicates characteristics of concrete. Some common slump patterns, viz. true, shear and collapse, are shown in Fig. 2.3c. When the subsidence of concrete cone is even throughout, it is called true slump. When the subsidence is non-uniform with one side of cone sliding down, it is called shear slump. Slump value is measured as the difference between original level and average subsided level as shown. Shear slump indicates that the mix is not cohesive and is prone to segregation. This is usually observed in case of dry mixes with low water-cement ratio. In case of wet mixes with high water-cement ratio, the subsidence is very high as shown in Fig. 2.3c. Such subsidence is often referred as collapse slump.

Results of slump cone test are not sensitive to change in workability for dry concrete mixes. As a result, slump cone test is not a suitable test for very dry mixes. In case of very wet mixes, slump flow test is employed instead of slump cone test. The test procedure remains the same. Since very wet mixes are likely to undergo collapse slump, the diameter of the concrete mix on the base plate upon lifting the cone is measured. This diameter is called slump flow. A typical slump flow value is 500 to 700 mm.

Despite its limitations, slump cone test is the most widely used test for workability. This is because slump value is highly sensitive to change in consistency of concrete mix. Changes in important factors such as water-cement ratio and/or gradation of aggregates gets quickly reflected in slump value. Another reason for wide usage of this test is its simplicity. However, for certain applications like pavements where water-cement ratio is typically low (dry mix), compaction factor test is preferred over slump cone test.

**Compaction factor**

The underlying principle of compaction factor test is to find the degree of compaction achieved by doing a standard amount of work. This standard amount of work is performed by allowing the concrete to fall through a standard height. The degree of compaction achieved in the test is given by compaction factor which is the ratio of density of concrete achieved in the test to that of fully compacted concrete.

Fig. 2.4 (a): Compaction factor test apparatus

A laboratory photograph and a schematic diagram of the apparatus used in compaction factor test as per IS 6461 is shown in Fig. 2.4a and Fig. 2.4b. The apparatus comprises of two hoppers and a cylinder. While the upper hopper has top internal diameter, bottom internal diameter and internal height of 225 mm, 125 mm and 225 mm respectively, these quantities for lower hopper are 225 mm, 125 mm and 225 mm respectively. The two hoppers are equipped with trap doors at their respective bottom ends. The cylinder has an internal diameter of 150 mm and an internal height of 285 mm. The distance between bottom of upper hopper and top of lower hopper as well as that between bottom of lower hopper and top of cylinder are 200 mm. Other tools used in the test include trowel, tamping rod and weighing balance.

The concrete mix is poured in the upper hopper up to the brim using trowel while keeping the trap door closed. The trap door is then opened to allow the concrete to fall into the lower hopper. Then the trap door of the lower hopper is opened to allow the concrete to fall into the cylinder. In case of dry mixes, slight poking by tamping rod may be required for the concrete to fall through the trap doors.

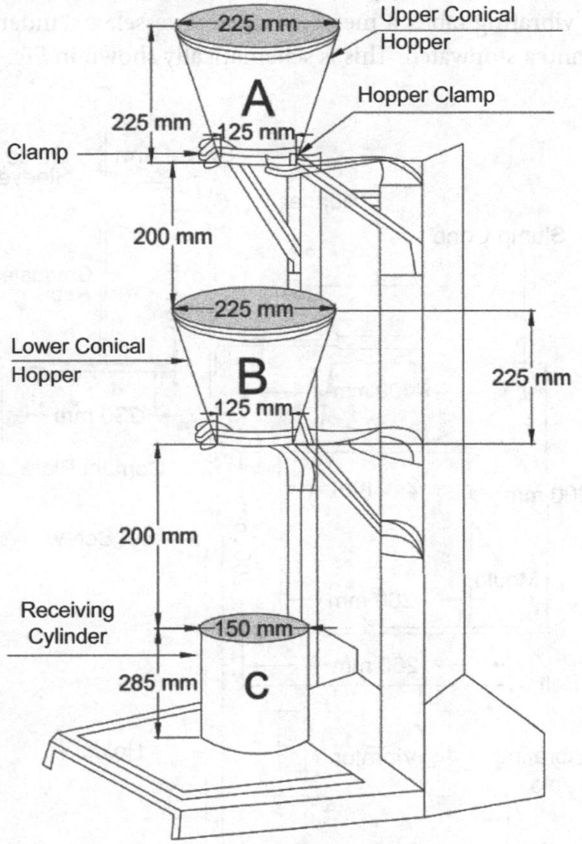


**Fig. 2.4 (b):** Schematic diagram of a typical compaction factor apparatus

The excess concrete above the brim of the cylinder is removed using tamping rod. The outside of the cylinder is cleaned by wiping any concrete sticking to it. The cylinder filled with concrete up to the brim is then weighed. The weight of concrete in the cylinder is then calculated by subtracting weight of empty cylinder from the weight of cylinder filled with concrete.

The cylinder is emptied and refilled with concrete from the same sample in 4 layers. Every layer is compacted by 25 blows using tamping rod. This leads to fully compacted concrete in the cylinder. The cylinder with fully compacted concrete is then weighed. The weight of fully compacted concrete is then obtained by subtracting weight of empty cylinder from the weight of cylinder with fully compacted concrete.

The weight of concrete in the cylinder obtained by passing through upper and lower hoppers is then divided by weight of fully compacted concrete. This gives a ratio of density obtained during test to that for fully compacted concrete. This density ratio is called compaction factor. Higher the compaction factor, higher is the workability of the concrete mix.

Compaction factor test is more precise and reliable than slump cone test. Moreover, the result of this test is quite sensitive to workability in case of dry mixes. Therefore, workability of dry mixes can be assessed using this test.

### Vee-Bee Consistometer

Vee-Bee consistometer test is a laboratory test used for indirect measurement of workability. The apparatus comprises of a vibrating table, a metal cylindrical vessel, a standard slump cone, a standard tamping rod, a glass disc and a stopwatch. This is schematically shown in Fig. 2.5.

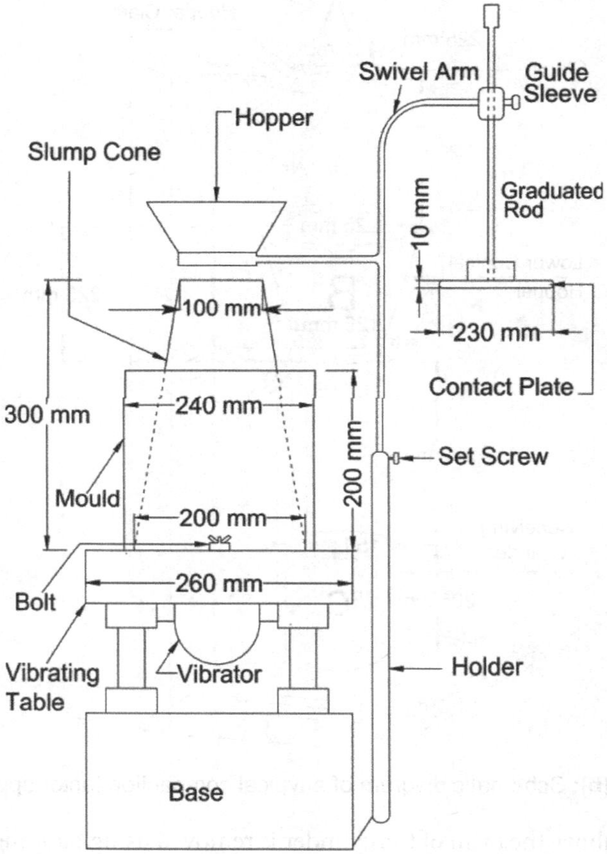


**Fig. 2.5:** Vee-Bee Consistometer

The cylindrical vessel is placed on the vibrating table. The standard slump cone (same as that used in slump cone test) is placed in the cylindrical vessel. The concrete mix is poured into the slump cone and the top surface is levelled up to the brim of the slump cone. The slump cone is then lifted vertically without disturbing the concrete. In simple words, slump cone test is performed within the cylinder placed on the vibrating table. Upon removing the slump cone, glass disk attached using a swivel is placed on the surface of concrete cone. The electrical vibrator is switched on and a stopwatch is started simultaneously. Due to vibrations, concrete gradually changes its shape from conical to cylindrical. The vibrations are continued till the time the concrete assumes a cylindrical shape and we can no longer observe transparency in the glass disc. At this instant, the vibrator is switched off and the stopwatch is also stopped. The time required for the concrete to change its shape from conical to cylindrical is known as Vee-Bee time.

Higher the Vee-Bee time, lower is the fluidity of the concrete mix. Therefore, workable concrete mixes have low Vee-Bee time. However, Vee-Bee time is not sensitive to workability of wet mixes as such mixes take very little time to change their shape from conical to cylindrical. Hence, this test is not suitable for wet mixes. On the other hand, this test offers great sensitivity towards workability of dry mixes and is preferred over other tests. Vee-Bee consistometer test is typically used for concrete mixes with slump value up to 50 mm.

Three most popular tests for assessing workability of a concrete mix have been discussed in this section, viz., slump cone test, compaction factor test and Vee-Bee consistometer test. There are other tests like K-slump test and Kelly ball test. However, they are not widely used in practice.

### 2.3.4 Value of Workability Requirement for Different Types of Concrete Works

In Section 2.3.1, it was briefly mentioned that workability depends on the nature of application. A concrete mix may be highly workable for a certain application, while being poorly workable for another application. Volume of concreting, density of reinforcement bars, method of compaction are prominent factors that dictate whether a prepared concrete mix is workable for the application at hand. Table 2.2 enlists workability requirements for different types of concrete works in terms of results obtained from different tests, viz. slump cone test, Vee-Bee consistometer test and compaction factor test.

**Table 2.2:** Workability requirements for different types of concrete works

| Placing Conditions | Degree of workability | Vee-Bee time (s) | Compaction factor | Slump (mm) |
|---|---|---|---|---|
| • Blinding concrete<br>• Shallow sections<br>• Pavements using pavers | Very low | 20-10 | 0.75-0.80 | Less than 25 mm; Determine workability as per IS 1199 |
| • Mass concrete<br>• Lightly reinforced sections in slabs, beams, walls, columns<br>• Hand placed pavements<br>• Canal linings<br>• Strip footings | Low | 10-5 | 0.80-0.85 | 25-75 |
| • Heavily reinforced sections in slabs, beams, walls, columns | Medium | 5-2 | 0.85-0.95 | 50-100 |
| • Slipform work<br>• Pumped concrete | Medium | 5-2 | 0.85-0.95 | 75-100 |
| • Trench fill<br>• In-situ piling | High | 5-2 | > 0.92 | 100-150 |
| • Tremie concrete | Very high | ≤ 2 | > 0.95 | Greater than 150 mm; Determine flow as per Annexure C of IS:9103 and IS:1199 |

### 2.3.5 Segregation, Bleeding and Preventive Measures

Segregation is defined as separation of different constituents of concrete. This leads to a loss of homogeneity of the concrete mix. In the next section on properties of hardened concrete, we will look how concrete derives its strength and durability from bond between matrix (paste of cement, sand and water) and coarse aggregates. Segregation leads to poor bond between aggregate particles and matrix, leading to poor strength and durability in the hardened state of concrete. Such concrete is undesirable, and therefore segregation need to be minimized if not avoided.

The principle underlying segregation is significantly different specific gravities of different constituents of concrete. When poured from a height, constituent materials of a composite material like concrete is likely to fall apart. Segregation can be seen in different forms. While coarse aggregates may tend to separate and settle down, matrix may tend to separate away from the coarse aggregates as well. Another form of segregation is when water separates from rest of the mix. When water moves to the surface of concrete upon separating from the rest of the mix, it is called bleeding.

Bleeding is generally observed in very wet mixes. During bleeding, movement of water to the concrete surface leads to formation of capillaries. This leads to increased permeability of concrete resulting in poor durability. In process of moving up, some of the bleeding water may be intercepted by aggregate particles. Accumulation of water on the underside of aggregate particles leads to poor bond between aggregate particles and matrix, resulting in a further loss of durability. Some matrix can also rise through the capillaries leading to formation of white patches on the surface of concrete. This is called laitance. Laitance makes concrete prone to shrinkage cracks.

Some of the conditions which are conducive for concrete mix to segregate are listed below.

i. **Use of poor-quality constituent materials**: If shape, size, surface texture and grading of aggregates are not desirable, the concrete mix may be prone to segregation. Presence of deleterious materials such as clay and organic wastes can also lead to separation of constituents.

ii. **Poorly proportioned concrete mix**: A concrete mix with coarse aggregates more than desired value will have insufficient matrix to bind the aggregate particles. This loss of bond is likely to result in coarse aggregate particles segregating out of the mix. If less coarse aggregates are used, excess quantity of matrix (paste of cement, sand and water) tends to separate. If water content in the concrete mix is too high, bleeding can be observed.

iii. **Insufficiently mixed concrete**: If different constituents of concrete are not sufficiently mixed, the concrete mix is highly prone to segregation. A mixer with worn out blades often leads to concrete mix which are susceptible to segregation and bleeding.

iv. **Careless transportation**: If proper care is not taken during transporting concrete from mixer plants to site, different constituent materials of concrete may tend to separate from each other.

v. **Too high drop**: Dropping concrete mix from greater heights, typically in case of columns, can promote segregate. Coarse aggregates tend to settle down because of high specific gravity.

vi. **Improper compaction**: Dry mixes must be compacted using vibrators to eliminate any form of segregation. On the other hand, excess use of vibrators in case of wet mixes can lead to segregation and/or bleeding.

vii. **Excessive working on concrete**: This problem is particularly important in case of slabs where the top surface is often excessively worked using straight edge and trowel to make it smooth and even. This can push aggregate particles downwards resulting in matrix occupying most of the top surface. This increased exposure of matrix to environmental conditions often leads to shrinkage cracks in slab.

From the above discussion, it is clear that segregation and bleeding can be minimized by wisely choosing constituent materials of concrete in right proportions and performing early stage operations (mixing, transporting, placing, compacting and levelling) appropriately. Some of the measures to prevent segregation and bleeding are listed below.

i. In case of very dry mixes, slump should be increased. In case of very wet mixes, slump needs to be reduced. However, change in slump should be considerate towards the concreting application at hand.
ii. Use of more fines can prevent segregation as more matrix can be available for binding with coarse aggregate particles. Depending on requirements, finer sand or pozzolanic materials such as fly ash, silica fume and slag can be used. One of the reasons behind popularity of blended cement is its ability to contain segregation.
iii. Since particle density of coarse aggregates is higher than bulk density of concrete, use of coarse aggregates with lower specific gravity can be helpful. Reducing content of coarse aggregates in the concrete can also minimize chances of segregation. Cleaning of coarse aggregates before use to get rid of deleterious materials should also be done.
iv. Use of air entraining admixtures can enhance cohesiveness of the concrete mix, and thereby making it resistant to segregation and bleeding.
v. Sufficient mixing of concrete in an appropriate concrete mixer must be performed.
vi. In order to achieve greater quality control, modern large construction sites use ready mix concrete (RMC) which are mixed in factory-controlled environments before being transported to the site. The transporting of RMC should be well-planned so that there is no significant delay. The concrete should also be continuously mixed by rotating the RMC drum.
vii. The concrete should be placed carefully into the formwork. Dropping from excessive heights should be avoided.
viii. Adequate compaction should be provided to the concrete mix. Too less or too much compaction can lead to problems of segregation and bleeding.
ix. Surface of any concreting work should be levelled with minimal vertical force in order to prevent coarse aggregates from getting pushed downwards.
x. If the concrete mix shows any form of segregation and/or bleeding prior to placing it in the formwork, remixing the concrete is likely to solve the problem.

## 2.4 PROPERTIES OF HARDENED CONCRETE

### Introduction

In last section, properties of fresh concrete has been discussed in detail. The most important one is workability which is a composite property comprising of consistency and cohesiveness. These properties are essential for ensuring ease in performing early stage operations, viz. mixing, transporting, placing, compacting and finishing. Over a certain time, the concrete sets, i.e., changes its state from plastic to solid. The time from addition of water to cement, sand and aggregates to the instant setting starts is called initial setting time. The time up to the completion of setting is called final setting time. The procedure to measure initial setting time and final setting time is presented in the section on laboratory tests. Once the concrete sets, it is said to be hardened. Therefore, for a structure to adequately perform its desired function, the concrete under hardened stage must have desirable properties. Some of the most important properties of hardened concrete are strength, durability and impermeability. While strength of concrete ensures the structure carries applied loads satisfactorily, durability enables the structure to perform its function for its entire design life. Impermeability is a necessary property for a durable concrete structure.

### 2.4.1 Strength

Different members of a structure are expected to carry loads differently. While beams carry transverse loads by developing bending moment and shear force, columns carry axial loads by developing compressive stresses. While the columns at the corners of a building may also be subjected to bending moments, some beams may also experience torsion moments. This exposes concrete in different members to compressive, tensile and shear stresses. However, as a material, concrete is extremely good in compression, fairly good in shear and poor in tension. Therefore, concrete is employed primarily to resist compressive stresses. Compressive strength of concrete is the most important property of hardened concrete. Other strength measures such as tensile and shear strength can be estimated from the compressive strength with reasonable accuracy. Many other hardened concrete properties such as flexural strength, modulus of elasticity, permeability, fire resistance, fatigue resistance and wear resistance can also be estimated from compressive strength with help of empirical expressions developed by different researchers. Therefore, compressive strength is the most widely tested property of hardened concrete.

Compressive strength of concrete is measured by testing cubes or cylinders using compression testing machine (CTM). The specimens are loaded till crushing of concrete is observed and the specimen can no longer take any additional stress. The crushing load is divided by cross-sectional area to obtain compressive strength of the specimen. In India, we use cubes with sides measuring either 150 mm or 100 mm. These cubes are tested at 3 days, 7 days and 28 days to monitor development of compressive strength. The laboratory procedure is outlined in the unit on laboratory tests. When compressive strength of concrete used in an existing structure is to be determined, cores are cut and brought to laboratory which are tested under compression. Though non-destructive tests can also be performed to assess the quality of concrete, compressive strength cannot be computed from their results.

Hardened concrete derives its compressive strength from matrix, coarse aggregate and interfacial transition zone (ITZ). ITZ refers to the boundary layer around the aggregate particles where mortar/matrix binds with the aggregate particles. Since the modulus of elasticity of matrix and aggregate particles are different, they are likely to have different strains. This leads to differential strains in ITZ leading to micro-cracks in ITZ prior to application of external loads. The compressive strength of concrete therefore depends on the quality of ITZ. The compressive load application up to crushing of concrete can be divided into four stages as shown in Table 2.3.

**Table 2.3:** Effects of load application till compressive strength of concrete

| Stage of load application | Stress (Percent of ultimate strength) | Description |
|---|---|---|
| I | 0 to 30 % | • Micro-cracks in ITZ remain stable.<br>• Stress-strain curve is linear. |
| II | 30 % to 50 % | • Micro-cracks in ITZ increase in length, width and number but system of micro-cracks remain stable. Matrix cracking is negligible.<br>• Stress-strain curve starts to deviate from linear. |
| III | 50 % to 75 % | • Cracks form in the matrix. Crack systems in ITZ as well as matrix become unstable; cracks start to propagate in the matrix.<br>• Stress-strain curve is nonlinear. |

| Stage of load application | Stress (Percent of ultimate strength) | Description |
|---|---|---|
| IV | 75 % to 100 % | • Cracks in ITZ and matrix propagate rapidly with crack systems becoming continuous.<br>• Stress-strain curve is nonlinear with development of very large strains. |

Compressive strength of concrete depends on properties and proportions of different constituents of concrete, viz. cement, water, sand, coarse aggregates and admixtures if used. Some of the important factors that affect compressive strength of concrete are outlined below.

**Water-cement ratio**

The most prominent factor influencing compressive strength is water-cement ratio. Compressive strength of concrete generally decreases with increasing water-cement ratio. The relationship between water-cement ratio and compressive strength of concrete is given by Abram's law and is explained in detail in Section 2.2.

**Type of cement**

Type of cement influences rate of strength development in concrete more than final compressive strength. Using blended cements like Portland Pozzolana Cement (PPC) and Portland Slag Cement (PSC) leads to slow strength development as the proportions of Bogue's compounds get reduced with addition of materials like fly ash and slag. However, the final compressive strength is slightly higher than that of concrete using Ordinary Portland Cement (OPC) because of secondary cementitious reactions possible with pozzolanic materials. The compressive strength development in concrete using OPC and PPC is shown in Fig. 2.6.

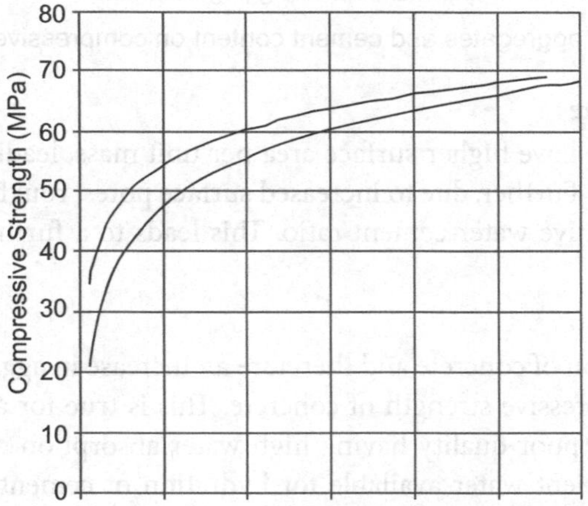


**Fig. 2.6:** Concrete compressive strength development with use of OPC and PPC (Amhudo et al. 2018)

On the other hand, Rapid Hardening Portland Cement (RHPC) contains higher proportions of $C_3S$ and $C_3A$ and lower proportion of $C_2S$ as compared to OPC. This increases the rate of hydration when RHPC is used, leading to faster strength development. Further, fineness of cement also affects rate of strength development. Finer the cement particles, faster is the hydration leading to rapid strength development.

### Maximum size of aggregates

It was earlier believed that larger aggregates with lower surface area per unit mass tend to reduce the water demand, and therefore concrete with larger aggregates has higher strength on account of reduced water-cement ratio.

However, larger aggregates also provide lower surface area for developing bond between cement matrix and aggregate particles. Further, the transition zone becomes weaker due to internal bleeding. These factors imply a loss of compressive strength if aggregates with larger MSA are used.

The overall effect of aggregate size on compressive strength of concrete is shown in Fig. 2.7. The compressive strength reaches its highest value for a given maximum size of aggregates. This is particularly true for high strength concrete where high cement content. For lean concrete mix with low cement content, increase in aggregate size leads to increase in compressive strength.

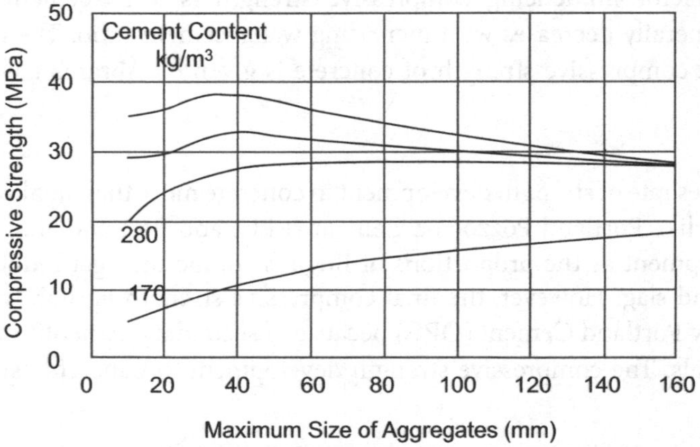


**Fig. 2.7:** Effect of size of aggregates and cement content on compressive strength of concrete

### Shape and texture of aggregates

Angular and rough aggregates have higher surface area per unit mass, leading to better bond between matrix and aggregate particles. Further, due to increased surface pores, rough angular aggregates absorb more water reducing the effective water-cement ratio. This leads to a further increase in compressive strength of concrete.

### Coarse aggregate-cement ratio

Coarse aggregates form skeleton of concrete and therefore an increase in aggregate-cement ratio usually results in an increase in compressive strength of concrete. This is true for a given water-cement ratio. Therefore, if aggregates are of poor quality having high water absorption capacity, they will absorb a lot of water and leave insufficient water available for hydration of cement. This can impair strength development and also lead to shrinkage cracks.

### Porosity of concrete

Porosity refers to the quantity of voids present in the concrete. Increased porosity leads to a reduction in compressive strength of concrete. In order to achieve desired strength, one needs to limit the porosity of concrete. This is possible by using well-graded aggregates and proper compaction of concrete. Use of blended cement may be further helpful as they contain finer particles like fly ash, silica fume and slag which lead to enhanced packing in the matrix.

## Curing of concrete

Curing is the process of maintaining ambient temperature and desired moisture content in concrete during its initial stages. It is usually performed by either immersing the concrete member in water, covering it with wet membranes, coating it with curing compounds or use of accelerated steam curing. It is initiated 24 hours after casting the structural member and is usually continued for 7 to 28 days.

Curing is very important for development of compressive strength in concrete. Loss of moisture from concrete due to evaporation particularly in hot and arid climate can lead to insufficient water available for hydration and occupying gel pores. Therefore, a concrete member which is not cured enough is likely to develop poor strength as compared to a continuously cured concrete member. This effect of curing reduces with age of concrete. Therefore, concrete structures need to be sufficiently cured during their initial stages, say 3 to 4 weeks. The effect of curing on strength development of concrete is shown in Fig. 2.8.

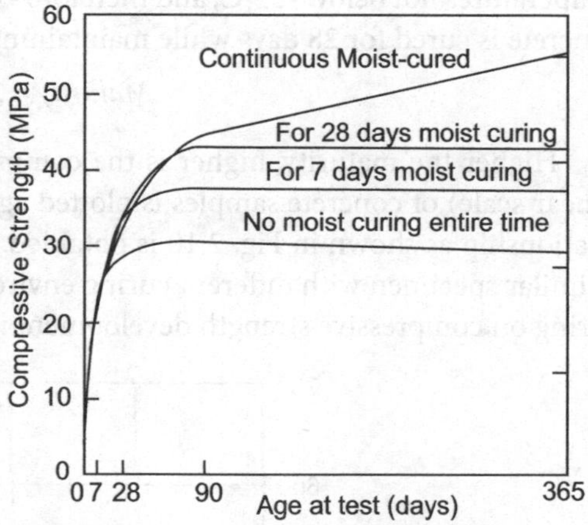


**Fig. 2.8:** Effect of curing duration on strength of concrete (Gonnerman and Shuman, 1928)

Temperature maintained during curing also affects strength development in concrete as shown in Fig. 2.9. If proper moisture contained is maintained, higher temperature during curing can lead to higher rate of strength development. Therefore, steam curing usually leads to faster strength development. However, the final compressive strength remains unaltered.

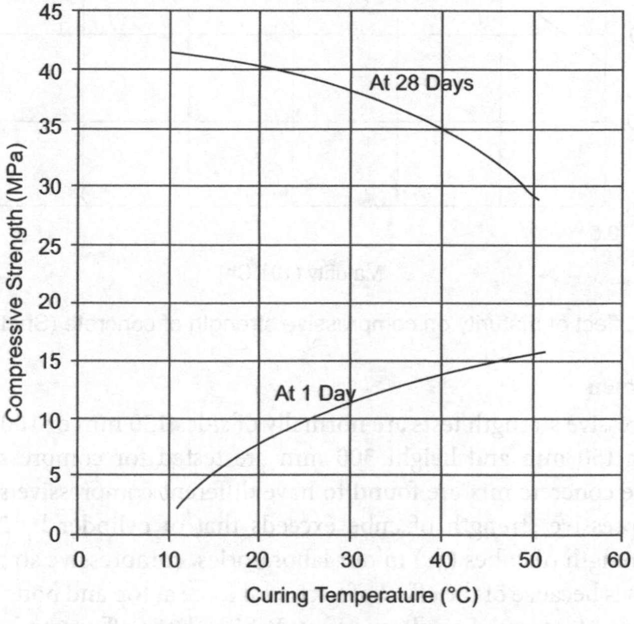


**Fig. 2.9:** Effect of curing temperature on strength of concrete

Since both curing time and temperature influences strength development in concrete, the two factors are usually included in one parameter termed maturity. Maturity of concrete is defined as summation of products of curing temperature (relative to a datum) and curing duration (in days). The sum is taken over all curing periods if there are multiple curing periods. Hydration of cement is found to happen at temperatures not below -11°C, and therefore -11°C is usually taken as datum. For instance, if a sample of concrete is cured for 28 days while maintaining a temperature of 18°C, maturity is calculated as below.

$$Maturity = 28 * \left(18 - \left(-11\right)\right) = 812°C.days$$

Higher the maturity, higher is the compressive strength of concrete. When compressive strength (linear scale) of concrete samples is plotted against their respective maturity values (log scale), a linear relationship as shown in Fig. 2.10 is obtained. This plot can be used to predict compressive strength of a similar specimen with different curing environments (curing duration and temperature). The effect of curing on compressive strength development is studied using accelerated curing test.

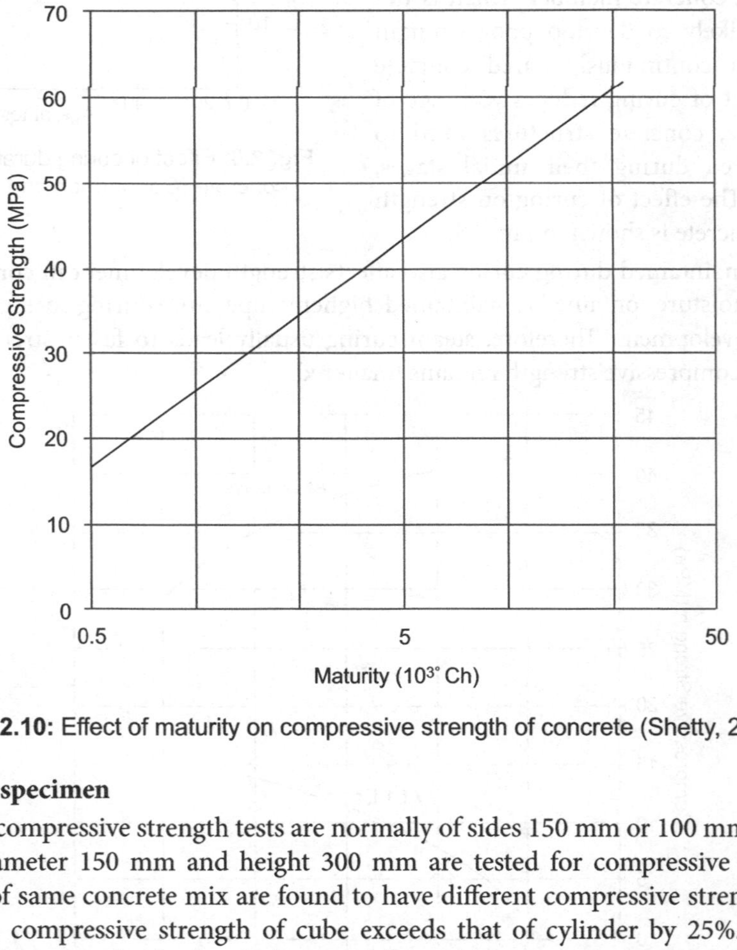


**Fig. 2.10:** Effect of maturity on compressive strength of concrete (Shetty, 2019)

### Shape and size of specimen

In India, cube for compressive strength tests are normally of sides 150 mm or 100 mm. In United States, cylinders with diameter 150 mm and height 300 mm are tested for compressive strength. The two specimens made of same concrete mix are found to have different compressive strengths. For medium strength concrete, compressive strength of cube exceeds that of cylinder by 25%. Since we usually measure compressive strength of cubes ($f_{ck}$) in our laboratories, compressive strength of cylinder ($f_c$) is obtained as 0.80*$f_{ck}$. This is because of the effect of frictional force at top and bottom platens used to hold the concrete specimen, usually termed as platen effect. While platen effect can be observed in concrete cube throughout its height, it is not present in the mid-section of the concrete cylinder. For high strength concrete, platen effect reduces and cube compressive strength exceeds cylinder compressive strength by 15%, and therefore $f_c$=0.87*$f_{ck}$.

The compressive strength of the concrete realized in practice is lower than that of the cube and/or cylinder specimen. This also happens due to platen effect as the supports in real structural members are placed at much larger distances than platens in laboratory tests. Compressive strength of practical members is estimated as 0.85 times of compressive strength of cylinder ($f_c$). Therefore, compressive strength of concrete in practice is considered as 0.85*0.80*$f_{ck}$, which computes roughly to 0.67*$f_{ck}$. While designing concrete structures, factor of safety considered is 1.5. Hence, the design compressive strength of concrete is taken as 0.446*$f_{ck}$.

**Other measures of strength of concrete**

Till now, we have seen how diverse factors ranging from properties and proportion of constituents of concrete to early stage operations including compaction and curing affect compressive strength of concrete. However, in certain applications such as slabs for pavements and airfields, we need to know strength of concrete subject to tension and shear.

**Tensile strength of concrete**

Though concrete with high compressive strength can be expected to have high tensile strength as well, there is no direct proportionality between compressive ($f_c$) and tensile ($f_t$) strengths. The ratio of tensile to compressive strength of concrete ($f_t/f_c$) reduces with increasing compressive strength ($f_c$) of concrete. It should be noted that tensile strength is being compared to compressive strength of cylindrical specimen.

Shape, size, texture and gradation of aggregates also affect ($f_t/f_c$) ratio. For instance, if rounded smooth aggregates are used, the tensile strength of concrete diminishes to almost zero.

Further, rate of tensile strength development diminishes with age of concrete, compared to rate of compressive strength development. As a result, ($f_t/f_c$) ratio decreases with time. This correlates well with the fact that ($f_t/f_c$) ratio reduces with increasing compressive strength ($f_c$).

While insufficient curing affects tensile strength more than compressive strength, air entrainment and inadequate compaction affects compressive strength more than tensile strength. This implies that ($f_t/f_c$) ratio will be lower for insufficiently cured concrete. On the other hand, air entrained concrete will have a higher ($f_t/f_c$) ratio. If concrete is not compacted well, ($f_t/f_c$) ratio will be higher as compressive strength is more harshly affected.

Many researchers have proposed empirical expressions relating compressive and tensile strengths of concrete. Most of them are of the following type, where *k* and *n* depend on concrete constituents and specimens.

Tensile strength of concrete is usually measured by either split cylinder test or flexure test as it is difficult to subject a concrete specimen to direct tension. However, values of tensile strength obtained from different tests show significant variations as the strength depends on shape and size of specimen. Therefore, the test conducted to obtain tensile strength must be specified while reporting the tensile strength of concrete. Some of these test procedures are elaborated in the unit on laboratory tests.

IS 456 specifies flexural strength (in MPa) as $0.7 * \sqrt{f_{ck}}$ where cube compressive strength ($f_{ck}$) is also measured in MPa. It also specifies elastic modulus of concrete as $5000 * \sqrt{f_{ck}}$ .

## 2.4.2 Durability

Durability of concrete deals with the aspects of satisfactory performance of concrete under anticipated exposure conditions during its service life span.

Durability of concrete may be defined as the ability of concrete to resist weathering action, chemical attack, and abrasion while maintaining its desired engineering properties. Different concretes require different degrees of durability depending on the exposure conditions of environment and properties desired. For example, concrete exposed to tidal seawater will have different requirements than an indoor concrete floor.

Failures of strong concrete pavement due to frost attack, saline water attack of pier of a jetty are the examples where durability is unsatisfactory. If a concrete is permeable, then water ingress takes place through the concrete. This increases the probability of volume change in the mass of concrete due to corrosion, alkali silica reaction. This volume change induces cracking and it results into increase in permeability. Thus, these three processes cause a dangerous cycle, in which one factor leads to increase in the other factor. The cyclic vicious circle in the long spoils the concrete. In other words, the durability of concrete is endangered. To prevent permeability, lowest possible water cement ratio must be recommended. Use of pozzolanic materials also helps to reduce permeability by filling capillary cavities.

High early strength development in steam cured concrete leads to durability problems in the long run. It also has lower modulus of elasticity leading to higher drying shrinkage. Similarly providing more reinforcement never stops cracking of concrete. Only it reduces the crack size from bigger to smaller. Therefore, the concrete mix designer should carefully consider the durability aspects.

Volume change in concrete: The volume change is induced in concrete by the following factors: (i) Larger heat of hydration causes volume change of the hydrated cement paste, (ii) The pozzolanic action also may cause volume change, (iii) Carbonation of concrete (iv) Moisture migration, (v) All types of shrinkage, (vi) Chloride attack induces increase in volume, (vii) rusting of reinforcement. One or more of these factors, when present in concrete, lowers the durability to a considerable extent. The durability of cement concrete is its ability to resist these processes of deterioration. This problem of durability causes huge loss of resources in both developed and developing countries.

One of the main characteristics influencing the durability of concrete is its permeability to the ingress of water, oxygen, carbon dioxide, chloride, sulphate and other potentially deleterious substances.

**Major Factors influencing durability**

The major factors affecting durability can be summarized as (i) the environmental factors (rain, heat, cold, fire, snow) (ii) The cover to the embedded steel (iii) The type and quality of constituent materials, (iv) The cement content and water/cement ratio of the concrete, (v) Workmanship, to obtain full compaction and efficient curing, (vi) The shape and size of the members (vii) Permeability and abrasion resistance

Effect of water cement ratio on durability: Higher water cement ratio for a concrete results in higher permeability of concrete. Thus volume change, crack formation and disintegration of such concretes take place faster. A concrete with lower water cement ratio, when properly compacted, results in lesser number of interconnected network of capillary pores. So, such concrete exhibits lower carbonation and chemical attacks.

**Physical Durability**

The ability of concrete to withstand environmental conditions is called its physical durability.

- **Abrasion**: Abrasion resistance defines the ability of a hardened concrete surface to remain intact without being worn away due to applied rubbing or friction. It is influenced by the exposure conditions, strength of concrete, aggregate properties, cementitious materials, curing methods and surface finish. Abrasion can completely wear away concrete from structural elements. Abrasion can reduce the concrete cover and increase the risk of corrosion as water and chlorides can easily come in contact with the reinforcing steel.

- **Freezing and Thawing**: Concrete in cold climates must possess adequate resistance to the expected freeze-thaw cycles. Ice occupies more volume than water, which causes micro-fractures in concrete and crack initiation occurs. De-icing chemicals in snowy environments worsen the cracking in concrete as they invariably contain chlorides. Air-entrainment increases the physical durability of concrete as it introduces microscopic air pockets to relieve internal pressure and provide tiny chambers for freezing water to expand.
- **Rain and Humidity**: Moisture and environmental conditions, to which concrete is exposed to, affect the pH levels of concrete. Quick and alternate drying and wetting may favour the initiation of Carbonation. It forms calcium carbonate leading to a reduction of alkaline concrete environment around rebars. This increases the probability of corrosion of reinforcing steel, which may result in damage to the structure.
- **Concrete cover:** Sufficient concrete 'cover' to the reinforcement should be included in the specifications in order to reduce moisture or salts penetrating to the rebar. Should the rebar corrode it will expand and the considerable forces involved cause the concrete to crack.

**Chemical Durability**

- **Alkali-Silica Reaction (ASR):** It is a reaction between chemicals where reactive silica ($SiO_2$) present in aggregates reacts with potassium and sodium alkalis in cement paste. It is also called alkali aggregate reaction. In aqueous solution, i.e., in presence of water, the following reactions take place:

$$SiO_2 + 2\,H_2O \rightleftharpoons Si(OH)_4$$

$$Si(OH)_4 + 2NaOH \rightarrow Na_2SiO_2.2H \text{ (Alkali-Silica gel)}$$

The product alkali-silica gel is expansive in nature. This causes internal bursting and cracks in concrete, spalling of joints, and movement of certain portions of a structure. The Rihand dam body experienced high scale ASR activity and large scale spalling of concrete from the body occurred. The retrofitting of the dam body was carried out using a concrete mix developed for under water applications (Kumar et al. 2005). To assess the alkali silica reactivity, IS 2386 Part VII provides a detailed procedure to evaluate the alkali silica reactivity of the cement and aggregates.

To reduce the ASR activity, it is recommended to use cement with less alkali content, non-reactive aggregates, pozzolanic materials like fly ash or slag cement, silica fume, volcanic ash, metakaoline. Also, it is essential to limit the other sources of salts from sea water or contaminated aggregates. Lithium hydroxide and various lithium salts have been known to ameliorate the effects of alkali silica reaction in concrete (Diamond, 1999). The relative humidity less than 75% in concrete mass will stop the ASR activity. Air entrained concrete also show lower damage as it allows expansion inside. Low permeable concrete by proper compaction shows lower ASR.

**Chemical aggression to concrete:**

- **Chloride induced corrosion of reinforcement:** Chlorides in de-icing chemicals or Chlorides present in subsoil and groundwater can make their way down to the reinforcing steel. A chemical reaction between the chlorides and the steel initiates the corrosion process which can create significant damage to structural concrete. Deck overlays, surface treatments, and especially coating reinforcing steel can help protect bridge concrete from corrosion due to chlorides.

Industrial effluents also contain sulphuric, hydrochloric, nitric, phosphoric, nitric and phenolic acids, ammonium compounds and sulphates that are injurious to concrete. The ground water should be used after thorough testing so that the risk of chemical attack is minimized. The concrete surface should be coated with a protective inert (thickness of coating more than 0.75 mm) as epoxy resin or polyester resin reinforced with fibre membrane.

- **Sulphates:** Sulphates in sea water, sewage (household waste), industrial waste, and salts in ground water or soil can combine with hydration products of concrete and cause damage. Formation of compounds such as Ettringite (calcium sulpho-aluminate) and gypsum takes place.

$$C_4AH_{10}+2CH+12H \rightarrow C_4AS_2H_{32} \text{ (ettringite)}$$

These sulphates can create pressure eventually leading to disintegration of concrete. Concrete used in heavy sulphate environments must be specially formulated to resist their effects. As mentioned in the previous chapter, section 1.3.4 stipulates the use of sulphate resisting cement.

## 2.4.3 Impermeability

Concrete possesses a porous structure. The capillary pore structure being interconnected allows for permeation of gases or liquids. The micro-structure of concrete consists of coarse and fine aggregates, hydrated cement paste, and entrapped air voids. The transition zone is the interface between the aggregate surface and hydrated cement paste. This zone is full of micro-cracks mainly caused by the shrinkage and thermal stresses. These cracks may create interconnected pores in the hardened concrete making it permeable. The gel pores, capillary pores and entrapped and entrained air voids contribute to the porosity of concrete.

The impermeability of concrete thus depends on its pore structure. In any case, concrete cannot be made fully impermeable. Factors influencing the permeability are (i) permeability characteristics of concrete constituents, especially aggregates and hydrated cement paste (ii) Quality of the pore structures, (iii) Quality of interfacial transition zone, (iv) Degree of compaction, (v) Adequate curing of concrete in green stage, (vi) structural or non-structural cracks in concrete.

Degree of impermeability in a certain concrete depends on its functional use. Coefficients of permeability has been determined by researchers experimentally with increasing pore sizes. IS 3085 gives a detailed procedure to determine permeability of concrete and cement mortar.

## UNIT SUMMARY

This unit introduced different grades of concrete and provisions of IS 456. Duff Abram water cement (w/c) ratio law, significance of w/c ratio, selection of w/c ratio for different grades, maximum w/c ratio for different grades of concrete for different exposure conditions as per IS 456 have been discussed in detail. Properties of fresh concrete such as workability and factors affecting workability of concrete have been described. Determination of workability of concrete by slump cone, compaction factor, Vee-Bee Consistometer and prescribed workability requirement for different types of concrete works have been outlined. Also, properties of hardened concrete such as strength, durability, impermeability have been depicted in detail.

# EXERCISES

## Multiple Choice Questions

1. Two statements associated with concrete are given. Select the correct option with regard to these statements.
 1: As the compaction factor increases, slump decreases.
 2: Slump test helps in qualitative understanding of the setting time of concrete.
 (a) Statement 1 is false and statement 2 is true
 (b) Statement 1 is true and statement 2 is false
 (c) Statement 1 and statement 2 are true
 (d) Statement 1 and statement 2 are false
2. As per IS 456:2000, the permissible limit for sulphates in water to be used for making concrete is
 (a) 100 mg/lit (b) 200 mg/lit
 (c) 400 mg/lit (d) 500 mg/lit
3. What is the permissible limit of organic matter present in water for mixing concrete as per IS 456-2000?
 (a) 400 mg/l (b) 2000 mg/l
 (c) 3000 mg/l (d) 200 mg/l
4. Concrete mix design for RCC is carried out using IS ________ code.
 (a) 10262 (b) 456
 (c) 383 (d) 800
5. The slump recommended for mass concrete is about
 (a) 25 mm to 75 mm (b) 50 mm to 100 mm
 (c) 100 mm to 150 mm (d) 125 mm to 150 mm
6. Select the correct statements
 1: Rounded aggregates produce concrete with high workability and low strength.
 2: Angular aggregates produce concrete with high workability and low strength.
 3: Rounded aggregates produce concrete with low workability and high strength.
 4: Angular aggregates produce concrete with low workability and high strength.
 (a) 1 and 2 (b) 1 and 4
 (c) 2 and 3 (d) 3 and 4
7. The concrete slump recommended for beams and slabs with medium workability
 (a) 25 to 50 mm (b) 25 to 75 mm
 (c) 30 to 125 mm (d) 50 to 100 mm
8. If 375 ml or g of water is required to have 1875 g cement paste of normal consistency, the percentage of water is
 (a) 20% (b) 25%
 (c) 30% (d) 40%

9. According to IS: 456-2000, the minimum grade recommended for reinforced concrete is
   (a) M15 (b) M25
   (c) M20 (d) M30
10. According to IS:456-2000, the smallest grades of High Strength Concrete is
   (a) M55 (b) M60
   (c) M65 (d) M70
11. As per IS 269, a maximum of ____ % by mass can be added as performance improvers in plain Portland cement:
   (a) 10 (b) 5
   (c) 2.5 (d) 0
12. Which of the following materials are not added to the kiln in the manufacturing of Ordinary Portland Cement?
   (a) Coal (b) Clay
   (c) Gypsum (d) Limestone
13. In Optical microscopy, the white (bright) spots in the image represents the _____ phase
   (a) $C_2S$ (b) $C_3S$
   (c) $C_3A$ (d) $C_4AF$
14. The formation of Bogue's compounds for Ordinary Portland Cement from the raw materials are completed
   (a) At the mid length of kiln (b) In the preheater
   (c) Only after leaving the kiln (d) At the end of kiln
15. As per IS 269, a maximum of 5% of performance enhancer can be added, it is called performance enhancer because
   (a) It increases the strength of the concrete
   (b) It increases efficiency (reduces net energy emission and cost) of cement production mill
   (c) It decreases the pollution caused by cement mill
   (d) None of them
16. A quick-setting cement has an initial setting time of about
   (a) 50 minutes (b) 40 minutes
   (c) 15 minutes (d) 5 minutes
17. Fineness of cement is measured in the units of
   (a) volume/mass (b) mass/volume
   (c) area/mass (d) mass/area
18. The initial setting time of cement depends most on
   (a) tri-calcium aluminate (b) tri-calcium silicate
   (c) tri-calcium alumino-ferrite (d) di-calcium silicate
19. Which compound of cement is responsible for strength of cement?
   (a) Magnesium oxide (b) Silica
   (c) Alumina (d) Calcium sulphate

20. Which type of cement is recommended in large mass concrete works such as a dam?
    (a) Ordinary Portland (b) High Alumina
    (c) Low-heat Portland (d) Portland Pozzollona

## Answers for Multiple Choice Questions

1. (d), 2. (c), 3. (d), 4. (a), 5. (a), 6. (b), 7. (d), 8. (b), 9. (c), 10. (c), 11. (b), 12. (a), 13. (d), 14. (c), 15. (b), 16. (d), 17. (c), 18. (a), 19. (b), 20. (c)

## Short and Long Answer Type Questions

1. What are the reasons for the use of concrete as a building material?
2. Define Workability of concrete and elaborate the factors affecting it.
3. Explain Slump cone test for workability of concrete.
4. Compare the results of Slump test and Compaction factor test of workability of concrete.
5. A batch of 5 m$^3$ of concrete was made with the following:
   Cement used = 32 bags
   Water used = 490 L
   Find the water-cement ratio adopted and the cement content of the mix.
6. Compare the relative merits and demerits of slump cone test and compaction factor test.
7. What parameter affect the Permeability of concrete?
8. What do you understand by the carbonation of concrete and how does it affect the durability of concrete structures?
9. Define and explain durability of concrete.
10. Explain physical and chemical durability.
11. Define the maturity of concrete factor affecting it.
12. Find the maturity of concrete, (a) 7 days curing at an average temperature of 18°C, (b) for 28 days curing at constant temperature of 18°C.
13. A concrete structure is cured at an average temperature of 20°C during day and 10°C during night. Find the maturity of concrete for a curing period of 7 days and 28 days. Assume datum temperature as −11°C.

## PRACTICAL

To be given as Unit VI

## KNOW MORE

**Q.** Do you know difference between Durability and Serviceability?

Durability can be stated as the ability of a structure to continue to remain functional, without the requirement of excessive maintenance or repair, when subjected to normal conditions over its design/service life of structure. It can be simply understood as the long lastingness of the structure.

Serviceability is the acceptable performance at service load during design life of structure under normal conditions. A good serviceable structure means it controls deflection, durability, excessive vibration, fire resistance within its design life under normal circumstances.

**Q.** Provide minimum values of nominal cover required to meet durability of Concrete as per IS: 456-2000.

| Exposure | Minimum Nominal Concrete Cover in mm |
|---|---|
| Mild | 20 |
| Moderate | 30 |
| Severe | 45 |
| Very severe | 50 |
| Extreme | 75 |

## REFERENCES AND SUGGESTED READINGS


1. Gambhir, M.L., *Concrete Technology*, Tata McGraw Hill Publishing Co. Ltd., Delhi.
2. Shetty, M.S., *Concrete Technology*, S. Chand and Co. Pvt. Ltd., Ram Nagar, Delhi.
3. Santhakumar, A. R., *Concrete Technology*, Oxford University Press, New Delhi.
4. Neville, A. M. and Brooks, J.J., *Concrete Technology*, Pearson Education Pvt. Ltd., New Delhi.
5. Neville, A. M., *Concrete Technology*, Pearson Education Pvt. Ltd., New Delhi.
6. Sood, H., Kulkarni P. D., Mittal L. N., *Laboratory Manual in Concrete Technology*, CBS Publishers, New Delhi.
7. Kumar, V., Kumar, R., Mandal, S. and Sinha, A.N. (2005). "*Admixtures for Underwater Concreting for Repair of Cracks in the Structure.*" Proceedings of the International conference on "*Our World in Concrete & Structures*", Singapore.
8. Diamond, S. (1999). "*Unique response of LiNO3 as an alkali silica reaction-preventive admixture.*" Cement and concrete research, Vol. 29(8), 1271-1275.
9. Amhudo, R. L., Tavio and Raka, I. G. P. (2018). "*Comparison of Compressive and Tensile Strengths of Dry-Cast Concrete with Ordinary Portland and Portland Pozzolana Cements.*" Civil Engineering Journal, 4(8), 1760-1771.
10. Gonnerman, H. F. and Shuman, E. C. (1928). "*Flexure and Tension Tests of Plain Concrete,*" Major Series 171, 209, and 210, Report of the Director of Research, Portland Cement Association, November, 149-163.
11. Shetty, M. S. and Jain, A. K. (2019), *Concrete Technology: Theory and Practice*, S. Chand and Co. Ltd., New Delhi.

# 3 Concrete Mix Design and Testing of Concrete

## UNIT SPECIFICS

Through this unit we have discussed the following aspects:

- The different methods of mix design and steps towards an economic and durable mix design using the provisions of IS 10262 have been explained in detail. The steps of a typical mix design without admixtures has been detailed.
- The existing methods to test the compressive strength of concrete cubes at different ages have been discussed. Also the interpretation and co-relation of test results have been explained.
- The two major Non- destructive testing of concrete such as Rebound hammer test and Ultrasonic pulse velocity have been described in terms of their working principle.
- The factors affecting the test results of rebound hammer test have been described as per IS 13311 (Part 2) & IS 516 (Part 5). Similarly, the provisions of IS 13311 (Part I) & IS 516 (Part 4) have been discussed on the factors affecting the pulse velocity test results.

At present the construction industry is using self-compacting concrete and pumped concrete in large scale. So, the mix-design aspects of such special concretes have been introduced. The non-destructive testing procedures of hardened concrete have been discussed in detail as per relevant Indian Standards. Comparative analysis of such test data to reach a conclusive decision on the quality and acceptability of the concrete has been further explained.

A large number of multiple-choice questions as well as questions of short and long answer types marked in two categories following lower and higher order of Bloom's taxonomy, a list of references and suggested readings are given in the unit so that one can go through them for practice. It is important to note that for getting more information on various topics of interest some QR codes have been provided in different sections which can be scanned for relevant supportive knowledge.

## RATIONALE

The fundamental concepts introduced in this Unit will help students to determine the proportions of ingredients of concrete to produce a durable and economic concrete mix. The aspects of non-destructive testing of hardened concrete have also been discussed. These tests are often conducted to assess the quality of reinforced as well as plain concrete structures. These topics are relevant to understand whether the quality of concrete produced are acceptable in terms of their uniformity and strength.

## PRE-REQUISITES

Statistical concepts: mean and standard deviation, basic physics of ultrasonic wave propagation.

## UNIT OUTCOMES

List of outcomes of this unit is as follows:

**U3-O1:** To understand the procedure to design concrete mixes of different grades based on appropriate selection of water cement ratio and ingredients of concrete.

**U3-O2:** To learn the inter relationships of strength of hardened concrete measured by different methods.

**U3-O3:** To learn the procedure to conduct non-destructive testing of hardened concrete and factors influencing the test results using rebound hammer test and ultrasonic pulse velocity test.

| Unit-3 Outcome | EXPECTED MAPPING WITH COURSE OUTCOMES (1 - Weak Correlation; 2 - Medium Correlation; 3 - Strong Correlation) | | | | |
|---|---|---|---|---|---|
| | CO-1 | CO-2 | CO-3 | CO-4 | CO-5 |
| U3-O1 | 2 | 3 | 3 | 2 | 1 |
| U3-O2 | 1 | 3 | 2 | 1 | 1 |
| U3-O3 | 1 | 2 | 2 | 3 | 1 |

## 3.1 CONCRETE MIX DESIGN

**Introduction**

Concrete comprises of different ingredients such as cement, water, sand, coarse aggregates and admixtures. Among these, admixtures are optional ingredients added to get desired properties in fresh state. All these ingredients have to be mixed in certain proportions to obtain concrete of desired quality. Considering variability in properties of these constituent materials, obtaining proportions of these ingredients usually requires both competence and experience. This process of selecting suitable ingredients in right proportions with an intent to produce concrete of desired quality is called concrete mix design.

### 3.1.1 Objectives

The final aim of concrete mix design is to produce a concrete mix with desired properties. This aim can be achieved if desired properties of concrete in fresh and hardened states are met. Apart from exhibiting desired properties, the obtained concrete mix should be economical. Therefore, the process of concrete mix design aims to achieve following major objectives:

- **Workability**: In fresh state, the concrete mix should be easy to transport, place, compact and finish. This is summarized as concrete mix having adequate workability. In mix design practice, this is implemented by considering a target range for slump value. Table 2.2 reports desired slump value for some typical construction practices.
- **Strength**: In hardened state, the concrete should achieve strength required to satisfactorily perform intended functions. This is usually expressed as grade of concrete, i.e., MXX, where M stands for mix and XX denotes characteristic compressive strength in N/mm$^2$. Characteristic compressive strength is the strength below which compressive strength of not more than 5% of concrete cube samples are expected to fall.
- **Durability**: The hardened concrete should also exhibit high durability. In order to achieve durability, concrete should have minimal porosity. The aggregates used should also be inert so that alkali-aggregate reaction is restricted. Shrinkage should also be kept under check to avoid cracking and spalling of concrete, which may lead to corrosion of steel reinforcement.

- **Economy**: The concrete mix should be as economical as possible. For instance, in case of pumpable concrete, high value of target slump can be achieved with increasing use of superplasticizers. However, since superplasticizers are quite expensive, an experienced concrete mix designer is likely to optimally select proportions of fine and coarse (CA10 and CA20) aggregates.

Apart from these objectives, projects requiring large volumes of concrete also tend to use **green concrete.** Green concrete refers to a concrete mix which utilizes waste materials including industrial by-products, such as fly ash, silica fume and slag, while meeting above mentioned objectives.

### 3.1.2 Methods of Mix Design

Several methods of mix design have been developed over time, for proportioning ingredients of concrete with an aim to achieve satisfactory properties in fresh and hardened states. Some of them are: (i) Volumetric method (ii) Arbitrary proportion (iii) Fineness modulus method (iv) Maximum density method (v) Surface area method (vi) Indian Road Congress (IRC 44) method (vii) High strength concrete mix design (viii) Mix design based on flexural strength (ix) Grading curve method (x) ACI Committee 211 method (xi) British Department of Environment (DoE) method and (xii) Indian Standard (IS 10262:2019) method

Some of these methods have become obsolete because of their limitations and drawbacks. For example, volumetric method of mix design could not result in similar concrete mix in situations with different temperature and relative humidity as volumes of different ingredients of concrete vary with environmental conditions. Most modern concrete mix designs follow ACI Committee 211 method, DoE method and Indian Standard IS 10262 method. In India, mix design is conducted using specifications of IS 10262. It prescribes the procedural steps involved in obtaining proportions of different ingredients of concrete.

Considering variability in properties of ingredients, the obtained concrete is also likely to have a variability in its properties. Therefore, in order to ascertain that the concrete mix possesses desired properties in fresh and hardened states, it is important to understand aspects of statistical quality control.

**Statistical Quality Control**

As observed in Section 2.4.1 of this book, a number of factors, including properties and proportions of ingredients, influence compressive strength of concrete which is the most important indicator of concrete quality. Considering possible variations in these factors, it is impossible to accurately assess strength and quality of concrete by testing just one specimen. Since one of the tested specimens may have unusually poor strength, testing very few samples may lead to a very rigid criteria for declaring the specimen fit for construction. On the other hand, owing to huge costs, testing a very large number of concrete specimens for compressive strength using compression testing machine (CTM) is not possible. Though non-destructive tests can be used on a very large number of specimens without incurring additional costs, these tests are mere indicative of quality of concrete and cannot reliably predict the compressive strength. Therefore, it is prudent to conduct limited number of destructive tests using CTM and apply statistical quality control to ascertain whether the designed mix would result in concrete with desired properties.

Statistical quality control is a scientific approach to understand the realistic variabilities in properties of materials so that specifications for tolerance limits can be laid properly. If properties of most (certain percentage) of the tested specimens fall within these tolerance limits, it is practical to assume that a random specimen would exhibit desired quality with a high probability. Therefore, statistical quality control is a trade-off between economy and risk. If higher limit is imposed on percentage of tested specimen falling within tolerance limits, the risk is lowered but the mix may become uneconomical. On the other hand, if the tolerance limits are set too lenient, the mix is highly economical but the risk is greatly increased. We need to establish a rational balance between economy and risk.

Compressive strength of concrete is measured by testing concrete cubes (with sides 100 mm or 150 mm) in compression testing machine (CTM). Though these cubes are sampled and cast from the same concrete mix, they exhibit variation in compressive strength due to variation in properties and proportions of mix ingredients. If a large number of cubes are tested and the results are plotted as a histogram, the results are observed to follow normal distribution curve as shown in Fig. 3.1. Normal distribution is characterised using two parameters, viz. mean and standard deviation.

Mean strength is the average of strength values obtained upon testing different concrete cubes. For instance, if $N$ cubes are tested and $i^{\text{th}}$ cube has a compressive strength of $x_i$, the mean compressive strength $\overline{x}$ is given by the following expression.

$$\overline{x} = \frac{\sum_{i=1}^{N} x_i}{N}$$

Variation of compressive strength of a certain specimen from the mean compressive strength is represented by standard deviation. Standard deviation is defined as root mean square of variance, where variance is defined as the difference between sample strength and mean strength $\left(x_i - \overline{x}\right)$. Therefore, standard deviation is computed as shown below. It is to be noted that mean of squared variance values are calculated by dividing the sum by $\left(N-1\right)$.

$$\sigma = \sqrt{\frac{\sum_{i=1}^{N}\left(x_i - \overline{x}\right)^2}{N-1}}$$

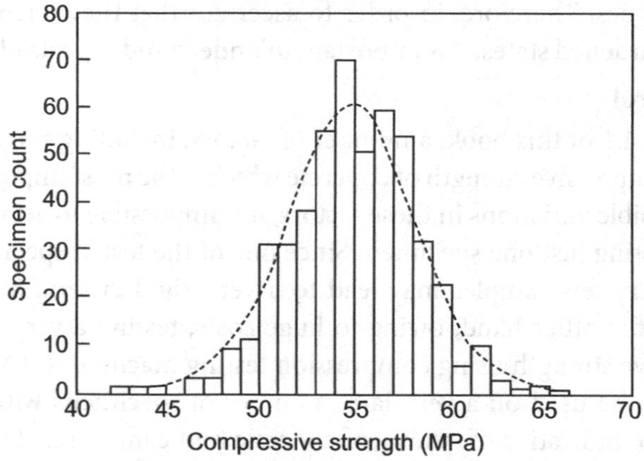


**Fig. 3.1:** Distribution of compressive strength of concrete

Standard deviation expressed as percentage of mean value is further termed as coefficient of variation. Therefore, to define normal distribution of the test results, the second parameter can be either standard deviation or coefficient of variation. A typical example calculation of mean and standard deviation for testing done on a set of 30 concrete cube samples is presented in Table 3.1. IS 456 prescribes testing of a minimum of 30 concrete cubes for reliable estimation of standard deviation.

**Table 3.1:** Calculation of mean and standard deviation for compressive strength of cube samples

| Sample No. (*i*) | Compressive Strength $(x_i)$ in MPa | Variance $(x_i - \bar{x})$ in MPa | Squared Variance $(x_i - \bar{x})^2$ |
|---|---|---|---|
| 1 | 29.4 | -1.9 | 3.73 |
| 2 | 31.7 | 0.4 | 0.14 |
| 3 | 39.3 | 8.0 | 64.46 |
| 4 | 32.9 | 1.6 | 2.69 |
| 5 | 34.2 | 2.9 | 8.64 |
| 6 | 36.8 | 5.5 | 29.80 |
| 7 | 33.9 | 2.6 | 6.65 |
| 8 | 27.1 | -4.2 | 17.82 |
| 9 | 28.7 | -2.6 | 6.51 |
| 10 | 29.6 | -1.7 | 2.93 |
| 11 | 23.9 | -7.4 | 54.33 |
| 12 | 24.4 | -6.9 | 47.49 |
| 13 | 30.0 | -1.3 | 1.69 |
| 14 | 34.0 | 2.7 | 7.18 |
| 15 | 26.7 | -4.6 | 20.80 |
| 16 | 33.7 | 2.4 | 5.56 |
| 17 | 37.5 | 6.2 | 37.93 |
| 18 | 30.1 | -1.2 | 1.49 |
| 19 | 31.9 | 0.6 | 0.34 |
| 20 | 37.2 | 5.9 | 35.27 |
| 21 | 38.1 | 6.8 | 46.91 |
| 22 | 22.5 | -8.8 | 76.76 |
| 23 | 27.0 | -4.3 | 18.58 |
| 24 | 30.6 | -0.7 | 0.46 |
| 25 | 33.8 | 2.5 | 6.40 |
| 26 | 21.8 | -9.5 | 90.27 |
| 27 | 28.0 | -3.3 | 10.83 |
| 28 | 33.1 | 1.8 | 3.24 |
| 29 | 33.8 | 2.5 | 6.15 |
| 30 | 37.2 | 5.9 | 35.03 |
| *N* = 30 | Sum = 938.7 | | Sum = 650.1 |
| | Mean Strength: | | Standard Deviation: $\sigma = \sqrt{\dfrac{\sum_{i=1}^{N}(x_i - \bar{x})^2}{N-1}} = 4.7$ |

The value of compressive strength below which not more than 5% specimens are expected to fall is usually called characteristic compressive strength ($f_{ck}$) of concrete. In other words, 95% of samples are expected to have compressive strength equal to or more than $f_{ck}$. For the test results shown in Table 3.1, $f_{ck}$ is observed to be 22.5. This is obtained by arranging observed compressive strength in descending order and choosing the 29th value (equal to or more than 95 percentiles in this case).

To obtain a concrete mix exhibiting satisfactory properties for most specimens the same is designed for a strength larger than $f_{ck}$. This is termed as target mean strength or design mean strength ( $f_{ck}^{'}$ ) and is determined using following expression.

$$f_{ck}^{'} = f_{ck} + K\sigma$$

Here, $K$ is Himsworth constant and $\sigma$ is the standard deviation. Himsworth constant represents the probability with which compressive strength of an untested sample is likely to pass or fail. Higher $K$ value indicates higher design strength which would imply high probability that specimens have compressive strength exceeding $f_{ck}$. With $f_{ck}$ defined as compressive strength with 95% confidence (95% samples to have strength higher than $f_{ck}$), $K$ is assigned a value of 1.65.

Standard deviation represents the spread of compressive strengths of tested specimens, and is expected to be higher for higher grades of concrete. IS 456 specifies standard deviation values for different grades of concrete which can be assumed while obtaining the target mean strength $f_{ck}^{'}$. These values are listed in Table 3.2. However, standard deviation values prescribed by IS 10262 are used in concrete mix design. The values prescribed by IS 10262 are the same as that by IS 456 for concrete up to M50. For higher grade concrete, only IS 10262 prescribes values for standard deviation.

**Table 3.2:** Standard deviation values for different grades of concrete

| Grades of concrete | Assumed standard deviation (MPa) |
|---|---|
| M10, M15 | 3.5 |
| M20, M25 | 4.0 |
| M30, M35, M40, M45, M50 | 5.0 |

### 3.1.3 Procedural Steps of Mix Design as per IS 10262

In India, mix design is conducted as per guidelines prescribed in IS 10262. In this context, following data need to be specified for designing a concrete mix:

(i) **28-days Characteristic compressive strength ($f_{ck}$)**: Typically, not more than 5% of the samples are expected to have 28-days compressive strength less than $f_{ck}$. This is usually expressed as grade of concrete MXX, where XX denotes $f_{ck}$ in MPa.

(ii) **Type of cement and grade of cement**: Different types of cements exhibit different properties such as specific gravity. It will be evident from the IS 10262 procedural steps that the quantity of coarse and fine aggregates to be used per unit volume of concrete depends on specific gravity of cement.

(iii) **Standard deviation of the compressive strength**: As described in Section 3.1.2, standard deviation of compressive strength helps us obtain target mean strength. This target mean strength acts as design strength for the concrete mix.

(iv) **Desired degree of workability**: It is usually expressed as target slump value in mm or as a compaction factor. Different concreting applications require different slump and some of these values are listed in Table 2.2. Target slump value often dictates whether superplasticizers are to be used.

(v) **Maximum water-cement ratio and minimum cement content**: Limits on water-cement ratio and cement content are specified depending on exposure conditions, with an intent of achieving desired durability. For instance, a lower value for maximum water-cement ratio and a higher value for cement content is prescribed for concrete structures exposed to harsh environmental conditions. For concrete with normal weight aggregates of maximum size 20 mm, these values are prescribed in Table 5 of IS 456, and are as presented in Table 3.3.

(vi) **Type and maximum size of aggregates to be used**: Shape and size of aggregates are primarily responsible for workability of the mix. Therefore, these factors influence water demand in the concrete mix.

(vii) **Water absorption capacity and moisture content in aggregates**: As discussed in Sections 1.5.5 and 1.6.5 of this book, water absorption capacity and moisture content in fine and coarse aggregates affect water-cement ratio required for adequate strength and workability.

(viii) **Use of admixtures**: Use of mineral and/or chemical admixtures affect properties of fresh concrete. If admixtures are to be used, type and dosage of admixtures are to be decided based on desired properties of fresh concrete.

Some other data such as transportation time, method of placing and compacting the fresh concrete and degree of site control are also desirable. Other specific requirements such as early strength development and resistance against chemical attacks should also be specified.

**Table 3.3:** Maximum water-cement ratio and minimum cement content for concrete with different exposure conditions

| Exposure Conditions | Plain Concrete | | Reinforced Concrete | |
|---|---|---|---|---|
| | Maximum water-cement ratio | Minimum cement content (kg/m$^3$) | Maximum water-cement ratio | Minimum cement content (kg/m$^3$) |
| Mild | 0.60 | 220 | 0.55 | 300 |
| Moderate | 0.60 | 240 | 0.50 | 300 |
| Severe | 0.50 | 250 | 0.45 | 320 |
| Very Severe | 0.45 | 260 | 0.45 | 340 |
| Extreme | 0.40 | 280 | 0.40 | 360 |

The steps involved in obtaining proportions of different ingredients of concrete are outlined below. An illustrative example for concrete mix design is presented after the procedural steps.

**Step 1: Target Strength for Mix Proportioning**

As discussed earlier, in order to achieve desired strength in most cases, the concrete mix is designed for a higher strength as compared to characteristic compressive strength ($f_{ck}$). The target strength ( $f'_{ck}$ ) is calculated using following two relations and the higher of the two values is considered.

$$f'_{ck} = f_{ck} + 1.65\sigma$$

$$f'_{ck} = f_{ck} + X$$

Here σ denotes standard deviation and $X$ is another factor based on grade of concrete, and are prescribed by IS 10262:2019 in Tables 1 and 2 respectively. These values are listed in MPa in Table 3.4. These values of σ and $X$ should be used only in case of good site control. Good site control is characterized by proper storage of cement, weigh batching of all materials, controlled addition of water, regular checking of all materials, aggregate grading and moisture content, and regular checking of workability and strength. If there are deviations and site control can be designated as fair, the values for σ are increased by 1 MPa. For concrete mixes with grades M65 and above, the standard deviation may be obtaining as shown in Table 3.1, upon testing a minimum of 30 cube samples.

**Table 3.4:** Values of σ and *X* for different grades of concrete

| Grade of concrete | Value of σ | Value of *X* |
|---|---|---|
| M10, M15 | 3.5 | 5.0 |
| M20, M25 | 4.0 | 5.5 |
| M30, M35, M40, M45, M50, M55, M60 | 5.0 | 6.5 |
| M65, M70, M75, M80 | 6.0 | 8.0 |

**Step 2: Selection of water-cement ratio**

While change in water-cement ratio leads to significant change in compressive strength of concrete, use of ingredients with different properties may produce concrete with different compressive strength for the same water-cement ratio. Therefore, relationship between water-cement ratio and strength of concrete should be established for the material actually being used. In case of absence of data about properties of ingredients, water-cement ratio should be adopted from Fig. 3.2. The adopted water-cement ratio should be limited to maximum water-cement ratio for durability requirements depending on the desired grade of concrete and the exposure conditions, obtained from Table 3.3.

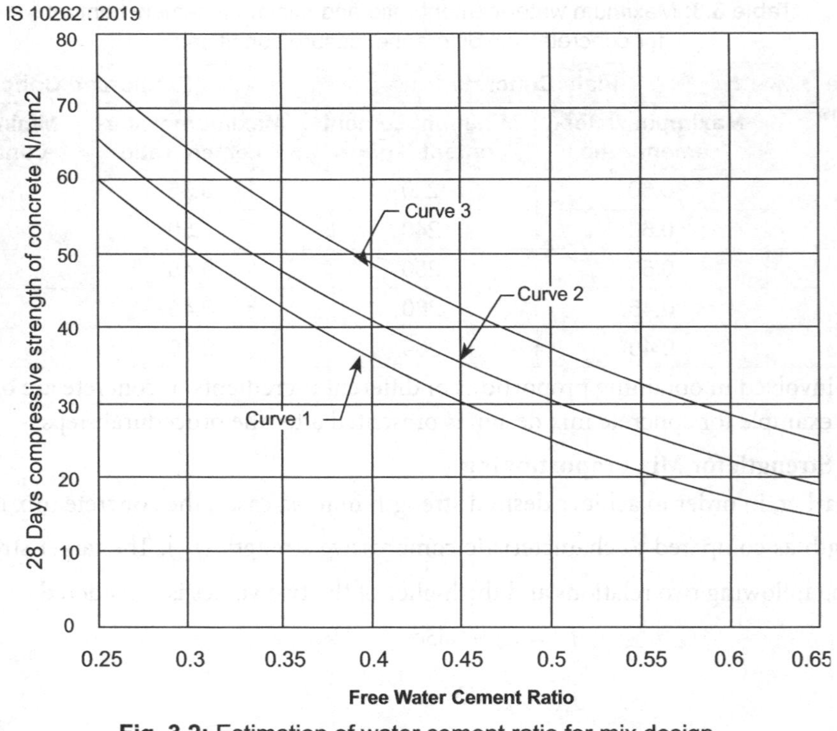


**Fig. 3.2:** Estimation of water cement ratio for mix design

Curve 1: for expected 28 days compressive strength of 33 and < 43 N/mm$^2$.

Curve 2: for expected 28 days compressive strength of 43 and < 53 N/mm$^2$.

Curve 3: for expected 28 days compressive strength of 53 N/mm² and above.

**Notes:**

1. In the absence of data on actual 28 days compressive strength of cement, the curves 1, 2 and 3 may be used for OPC 33, OPC 43 and OPC 53, respectively.
2. While using PPC/PSC, the appropriate curve as per the actual strength may be utilized. In the absence of the actual 28 days compressive strength data, curve 2 may be utilized.

**Step 3: Estimation of air content**

In case of concrete without use of air entraining admixtures, amount of entrapped air is assumed as given in Table 3.5. These values are adopted from Table 3 of IS 10262:2019. If air content is estimated for at least 5 samples, actual value of air content can also be adopted.

**Table 3.5:** Approximate air content in non-air-entrained concrete

| Nominal Maximum Size of Aggregates (mm) | Entrapped Air (% of Volume of Concrete) |
|---|---|
| 10 | 1.5 |
| 20 | 1.0 |
| 40 | 0.8 |

**Step 4: Selection of water content and use of admixtures**

A number of factors such as shape, size, texture of aggregate, workability, water-cement ratio, type and content of cement, use of chemical admixtures (especially water reducing admixtures) and environmental conditions, influence water demand in concrete. For instance, an increase in aggregate size, a reduction in water-cement ratio and slump, and use of rounded aggregates and water reducing admixtures reduce the water demand. On the other hand, increased temperature, cement content, slump, water-cement ratio, aggregate angularity and a decrease in the proportion of coarse to fine aggregates leads to increased water demand.

The amount of water to be mixed per unit volume of concrete is determined using Table 4 of IS 10262:2019 which is reproduced here as Table 3.6. This water content is for concrete with a target slump value of 50 mm and prepared using angular coarse aggregates in saturated surface dry conditions.

**Table 3.6:** Water content per cubic metre of concrete

| Nominal Maximum Size of Aggregate (mm) | Water Content (kg per m³ of concrete) |
|---|---|
| 10 | 208 |
| 20 | 186 |
| 40 | 165 |

Use of rounded aggregates lowers the water demand for achieving same degree of workability. Therefore, to achieve concrete mix with target slump value of 50 mm, water content obtained from Table 3.6 should be reduced by approximately 10 kg, 15 kg and 20 kg if sub-angular aggregates, gravels with some crushed particles and rounded gravels are respectively used.

If the target slump value is higher, water content needs to be increased. Therefore, water content should be increased or decreased by about 3 percent for each increase or decrease of 25 mm in target slump value. If necessary for site control, the modifications in water content due to change in aggregate type and target slump value should be established by trial.

If water reducing admixtures (plasticizers) or high range water reducing admixtures (super-plasticizers) are used, target slump can be achieved with use of lesser water. With use of plasticizers and super-plasticizers, the water content should be decreased by 5-10 % and 20-30 % respectively. The actual reduction depends on the actual quantity of admixtures used in the concrete mix. While typical dosage range for plasticizer is 0.3-0.5% leading to water reduction of 8-12%, typical dosage range for superplasticizers is 0.5-1.5% leading to water reduction of 15-30% (Annexure G of IS 10262). It should be noted that in concrete mix design, the term "admixtures" usually refers to either water reducing admixtures (plasticizers) or high range water reducing admixtures (superplasticizers).

These modifications in water content due to change in aggregate type, desired slump and use of plasticizers or superplasticizers are implemented in the same order as described above.

**Step 5: Calculation of cement content or cementitious material content**

While Ordinary Portland Cement (OPC) comprises of cement particles, blended cements such as Portland Pozzolana Cement (PPC) and Portland Slag Cement (PSC) contain pozzolanic materials which lead to formation of secondary cementitious products. Therefore, in case of blended cements, cement content is described by cementitious material content which comprises of cement and pozzolans. The cement content or cementitious material content per unit volume of concrete is calculated using water content per unit volume of concrete and water-cement ratio, as shown below.

$$\textit{Cement or cementitious material content} = \frac{\textit{Water content}}{\textit{Water cement ratio}}$$

If blended cement comprises of large portions of mineral admixtures (such as fly ash, slag or silica fume), cementitious material content may have to be increased. For instance, if fly ash replacement level is 20% or more, cementitious material content is increased by 10% and water-cementitious materials ratio is recalculated.

The calculated cement content or cementitious material content should be more than the minimum cement content for durability requirements depending on the desired grade of concrete and the exposure conditions, obtained from Table 3.3. Further, to avoid shrinkage cracks, cement content should be limited to 450 kg/m$^3$.

**Step 6: Proportioning of coarse and fine aggregates in the total aggregate content**

To produce concrete of satisfactory workability, aggregates should comprise of coarse and fine aggregates in suitable proportions. Table 3.7, adopted from IS 10262, provides volume of coarse aggregates per unit volume of total aggregates for water-cement ratio (or water-cementitious materials ratio) of 0.50. These values should be suitably modified for variations in water-cement ratio. For every increase/decrease of 0.05 in water-cement ratio, the proportion of volume of coarse aggregates to that of total aggregates should be decreased/increased by 0.01. Volume of fine aggregates to that of total aggregates is obtained by subtracting this value from 1.

**Table 3.7:** Volume of coarse aggregate per unit volume of total aggregate for water-cement ratio (or water-cementitious materials ratio) of 0.50

| Nominal Maximum Size of Aggregates (mm) | Volume of coarse aggregate per unit volume of total aggregate for different grading zones of fine aggregate | | | |
|---|---|---|---|---|
| | Zone I | Zone II | Zone III | Zone IV |
| 10 | 0.54 | 0.52 | 0.50 | 0.48 |
| 20 | 0.66 | 0.64 | 0.62 | 0.60 |
| 40 | 0.73 | 0.72 | 0.71 | 0.69 |

It can be observed that this volumetric proportion of coarse aggregates depends on nominal maximum size of coarse aggregates and grading zone of fine aggregates. Larger coarse aggregate particles owing to lower specific surface area require lesser mortar and therefore lower fine aggregate content. Therefore, higher the nominal maximum size of aggregates, higher is the coarse aggregate proportion. On the other hand, coarser sand (Zone I) suggest lower proportion of coarse aggregates.

It should be understood that these values are for angular coarse aggregates and fine aggregates obtained from natural sources, both in saturated surface dry conditions. Appropriate adjustments may be made in case of variations in aggregate types, sources and moisture content.

As mentioned in Section 1.6, coarse aggregates used in concrete mix usually comprise of two components, CA10 and CA20, mixed together. These have nominal maximum size of 10 mm and 20 mm respectively. These two components should be combined in suitable proportions to result in an overall grading conforming to Table 7 of IS 383. However, this proportioning of CA10 and CA20 requires some experience. Commonly used fractions for CA10 and CA20 are 1:2 and 2:3. The ratio of CA10 and CA20 should be chosen depending upon the slump requirements as described below.

As per Table 2 of IS 383, for well graded aggregate of 20 mm nominal size, percentage passing through IS sieve designation of 10 mm sieve size is 25-55%. It can be divided into three ranges: (i) 25-35% (for this range, the specific surface area (SSA) of aggregates is minimum, so for the same amount of cement and water, it gives maximum slump), (ii) 35-45% (as SSA is medium, it is adopted for medium slump) and (iii) 45-55% (SSA is maximum, so it gives minimum slump).

An illustrative example explains the procedure briefly. Consider the grading of CA10 and CA20 aggregates given in Table 3.8, obtained by the sieve analysis. Let, the mix needs to yield minimum slump, i.e., lower range of slump. So the percentage passing range should vary between 45-55%, the mean value being 50%.

Let us take x% of CA20 and (100-x) % of CA10 aggregates. From the sieve analysis data given in Table 3.8, the percentage passing through 10 mm sieve for CA20 is 0.05% and that for CA10 is 94.65%. So, for minimum slump, equating the percentage passing to 50%, the value of x can be determined as follows.

$$\frac{x}{100} * 0.05 + \frac{100-x}{100} * 94.65 = 50$$

After solving, the value of x is obtained as 47.20. Therefore the proportion CA20 : CA10 will be 47.20 : 52.80, which can be approximated to 45:55 or 50:50. Similarly the ratio for the other cases of medium and low slump could be determined depending up on the prescribed slump requirements.

**Table 3.8:** Sieve analysis data for CA20 and CA10 used to obtain their proportions in concrete mix

| Sl. No. | Test<br>Sieve analysis IS Sieve No. | CA 20 mm (% passing) | CA 10 mm (% passing) |
|---|---|---|---|
| 1. | 20 mm | 92.4 | 100.0 |
| | 10 mm | 0.05 | 94.65 |
| | 4.75 mm | - | 41.5 |
| | 2.36 mm | - | 5.25 |
| | 1.18 mm | - | - |
| | 600 micron | - | - |
| | 300 micron | - | - |

| Sl. No. | Test<br>Sieve analysis IS Sieve No. | CA 20 mm (% passing) | CA 10 mm (% passing) |
|---|---|---|---|
| | 150 micron | - | - |
| 2. | Fineness modulus | 7.076 | 5.58 |
| 3. | Bulk Density (Kg/Litre) | 1.68 | 1.59 |
| 4. | Specific Gravity | 2.84 | 2.83 |

**Step 7: Estimation of coarse and fine aggregate contents**

Quantities of cement, water and admixtures per unit volume of concrete are obtained in steps 4 and 5. Total volume of aggregate is first estimated by volumetric proportioning as shown below. The underlying principle is summing volume of all ingredients in one cubic metre of concrete to one cubic metre. Volume of air content is obtained using Table 3.5. Since most regular constructions use coarse aggregates with MSA of 20 mm, air is usually assumed to occupy 1% of concrete volume, i.e., 0.01 m³.

$$1m^3 = Volume\,of\,air\,content + \frac{Cement\,content}{Specific\,gravity\,of\,cement * 1000} + \frac{Water\,content}{Specific\,gravity\,of\,water * 1000} + Volume\,of\,aggregate$$

Once the total volume of aggregates is obtained, volume of coarse aggregates and volume of fine aggregates are calculated using their proportions obtained in Step 6. Weights of coarse and fine aggregates are then computed based on their specific gravity.

**Step 8: Moisture correction**

Estimation of different ingredients of concrete has been performed in above steps assuming that coarse and fine aggregates are in saturated surface dry (SSD) conditions. However, the recycled aggregates may tend to absorb water or may be carrying free moisture. In such cases, quantities of water, coarse and fine aggregates are modified.

This completes the concrete mix design as quantities of every ingredient has been determined. The concrete mix proportions are then checked by performing trial mixes.

**Step 9: Trial mixes**

Different ingredients, viz., cement, water, sand, aggregates and admixture, are mixed as per designed proportions, to get Trial Mix No. 1. It should be ensured that mixing is done by weight batching, i.e., it involves weighing required quantities of every ingredient.

Workability of Trial Mix No. 1 is measured. If the measured workability satisfies the desired workability and the mix does not undergo segregation and/or bleeding, the ingredients are further mixed in the designed proportions to cast cubes for testing 7-days and 28-days compressive strength.

If workability of Trial Mix No. 1 is not satisfactory, water content and/or admixture content are modified. For instance, if obtained slump value for Trial Mix No. 1 is lower than the desired slump, water and/or admixture content are increased. Keeping the water-cement ratio (or water-cementitious materials ratio) same as in original design mix, quantities of other ingredients, viz. cement, sand and aggregates, are re-calculated. Concrete mix obtained using this new proportioning gives us Trial Mix No. 2. Water-cement ratio is then varied by +/- 10% to obtain two additional trial mixes, called Trial Mix No. 3 and Trial Mix No. 4. Workability test is performed on these three trial mixes (No. 2, 3 and 4). The trial mix providing desired workability and not showing signs of segregation and/or bleeding is selected, to cast cubes for 7-days and 28-days compressive strength tests.

An illustrative example showing concrete mix proportioning is presented in following section.

### 3.1.4 Illustrative Example for Concrete Mix Design as per IS 10262:2019

A reinforced concrete structure is to be constructed in a region with extreme exposure conditions. While the desired slump value of the fresh concrete mix is 80 mm, the hardened concrete is expected to be of M40 grade. Ordinary Portland Cement (OPC) of 53 Grade with specific gravity of 3.14 is available for use. The coarse aggregate comprises of 10 mm MSA (CA10) and 20 mm MSA (CA20). Both CA10 and CA20 are of rounded gravel type and have specific gravity of 2.70 at saturated surface dry (SSD) conditions. However, the provided batch of coarse aggregates is drier than SSD conditions and is expected to absorb water up to 0.5% by its weight. The fine aggregate conforms to Zone II and has a specific gravity of 2.66 at SSD conditions. However, the provided batch of fine aggregates has got wet due to rains and has free surface moisture of 1% by its weight.

Obtain the concrete mix design using Indian Standard Method. Ignore any air entrapped in the concrete.

*Given Data:*

- Grade of concrete: M40
- Exposure conditions: Extreme
- Desired/Target slump = 80 mm
- Cement:
  - OPC (53 Grade)
  - Specific gravity = 3.14
- Coarse aggregates:
  - Type: Rounded gravel
  - Nominal Maximum Size: 20 mm
  - Specific gravity = 2.70 (SSD conditions)
  - Water absorption = 0.5%
- Fine aggregates:
  - Gradation Zone: II
  - Specific gravity = 2.66 (SSD conditions)
  - Free moisture content = 1%

**Step 1: Target strength for concrete mix**

Target mean strength, $f_{ck}' = max\begin{Bmatrix} f_{ck} + 1.65\sigma \\ f_{ck} + X \end{Bmatrix} = max\begin{Bmatrix} 40 + 1.65 * 5 \\ 40 + 6.5 \end{Bmatrix} = 48.25\, MPa$

**Step 2: Selection of water-cement ratio**

From Fig. 3.2, where curve 3 corresponds to use of OPC 53, 28-days target strength of 48.25 MPa gives free water-cement ratio of 0.40. From Table 3.3, maximum water-cement ratio for reinforced concrete exposed to extreme conditions is 0.40. Hence, the assumed water-cement ratio of 0.40 is appropriate.

**Step 3: Estimation of air content**

Since the coarse aggregates have a nominal maximum size of 20 mm, air content is assumed as 1% of the volume of concrete.

**Step 4: Selection of water content and use of admixtures**

Since 20 mm MSA coarse aggregates are used, water content is taken as 186 kg/m³ from Table 3.6.

Use of rounded gravel warrants water content to be reduced by 20 kg. Therefore, the water content is modified to 166 kg/m³.

Since the target slump is 80 mm which exceeds 50 mm by 30 mm, the water content is further modified as $\left(166+166*\frac{3}{100}*\frac{30}{25}\right)=172$ kg/m³.

Since information on use of plasticizers or super-plasticizers is not provided and the slump is also not very high, these admixtures may not be required.

**Step 5: Calculation of cement content or cementitious material content**

Cement content is obtained by dividing water content by water-cement ratio, i.e. $\frac{172\,kg/m^3}{0.40}=430\,kg/m^3$.

This value is adequate considering minimum cement content of 360 kg/m³ for extreme exposure conditions and maximum cement content of 450 kg/m³.

**Step 6: Proportioning of coarse and fine aggregates**

As per Table 3.7, since fine aggregates of Zone II are used and coarse aggregates have a nominal maximum size of 20 mm, volume of coarse aggregates per unit total volume of aggregates is taken as 0.64. However, this value is for water-cement ratio of 0.50. In this example, water-cement ratio is 0.40. Therefore, the volume of coarse aggregates per unit total volume of aggregates is modified to 0.66. Further, it should be noted that using only CA20 may result into excess voids. Therefore, CA20 and CA10 aggregates should be mixed in suitable proportions following slump requirements as discussed using Table 3.8.

At the same time, volume of fine aggregates to the total volume of aggregates is obtained as 1-0.66, i.e. 0.34.

**Step 7: Estimation of coarse and fine aggregate contents**

Using volumetric proportion, we calculate volume of aggregates as shown below.

$$1m^3=\left(\begin{array}{l} Volume\,of\,air\,content+\dfrac{Cement\,content}{Specific\,gravity\,of\,cement*1000} \\ +\dfrac{Water\,content}{Specific\,gravity\,of\,water*1000}+Volume\,of\,aggregates \end{array}\right)$$

$$1m^3=0.01m^3+\frac{430}{3.14*1000}m^3+\frac{172}{1.00*1000}m^3+Volume\,of\,aggregates$$

$$Volume\,of\,aggregates=0.681m^3$$

Therefore, volumes of coarse and fine aggregates are respectively (0.66*0.681) m³ and (0.34*0.681) m³, i.e. 0.45 m³ and 0.23 m³ respectively.

Coarse and fine aggregate contents are then estimated by multiplying their volumes with 1000 times of their respective specific gravities.

Coarse aggregate content = (0.45*2.70*1000) = 1215 kg per m³ of concrete

As rounded gravels are used, the ratio of CA10 and CA20 can be adopted as 35:65. Therefore, quantity of CA10 and CA20 aggregates per m³ of concrete are respectively (0.35*1215) and (0.65*1215), i.e., 425 kg and 790 kg.

Fine aggregate content = (0.23*2.66*1000) = 612 kg per m³ of concrete

**Step 8: Moisture correction**

It is given that provided coarse aggregates tend to absorb water (0.5% by their weight) and provided fine aggregates contain excess water (1% by their weight). Therefore, excess water present in aggregates is calculated as free moisture from fine aggregates minus water to be absorbed by coarse aggregates. This is calculated as ((0.01*612) – (0.005*1215)), i.e. 0.045 kg/m$^3$ which is negligible in this case (compared to used water content of 172 kg/m$^3$).

If this value comes out to be significant, water content in mix design should be decreased. On the other hand, if this value is negative and is significant, we need to increase the water content in mix design. Sometimes, if this value is quite large, corresponding weight of fine and coarse aggregates are also adjusted so that the total volume of concrete mix remains at 1 m$^3$.

**Step 9: Mix design result**

The obtained concrete mix design is usually shown in terms of quantities (per cubic metre of concrete) and ratio (per unit weight of cement) as shown in Table 3.9.

**Table 3.9:** Mix Design for M30 grade of concrete with target slump of 80 mm and given properties of ingredients

| Ingredients | Cement | Water | CA20 | CA10 | Sand | Admixture |
|---|---|---|---|---|---|---|
| Quantity (kg/m$^3$) | 430 | 172 | 790 | 425 | 612 | - |
| Ratio (Per unit weight of cement) | 1 | 0.40 | 1.84 | 0.99 | 1.42 | - |

Cube samples are cast and tested as outlined earlier in Step 9 in Section 3.1.3.

## 3.2 TESTING OF CONCRETE

**Introduction**

As part of quality control of concrete, the hardened concrete is sampled and tested frequently to assess whether the hardened concrete mass complies the requirement of strength. Concrete takes long time to attain strength. Therefore, certain accelerated strength tests are available to assess the probable strength the concrete may achieve. However, standard procedure is to cast a set of cubes and/ or cylinders while casting the concrete structural elements. Generally, these specimens are tested at 7 days and 28 days. Usually 7 days strength is about 60-75% of 28-days strength. So, based on the 7-days strength, if required, the necessary adjustment in concrete ingredients may be done. Thus, frequent testing of concrete is important. IS 456 specifies the testing frequency depending upon the mass of concrete produced. For example, for every 1 to 5 m$^3$ of concrete, at least one set of samples (three cubes) should be tested for quality compliance.

### 3.2.1 Determination of Compressive Strength of Concrete Cubes at Different Ages

As stated above, compression tests on 150 mm size cubes is the most frequently used method of assessing the strength compliance of concrete. Also, at times, cylindrical specimens of size 150 mm diameter and 300 mm height are used. Metal moulds of cast iron are used to cast these samples.

The cube moulds should satisfy the specified tolerance level of 150.2 mm to 149.8 mm. The angle between two internal faces and top and bottom planes should be between 90.5° and 89.5°. Concrete is cast into these moulds and compacted properly by hand compaction, or by machine vibrations. The cubes are then covered by jute bags or similar membranes so that temperature of 25 to 29°C and relative humidity of at least 90% are maintained. After 24 hours of casting, the cubes are put in a curing chamber of potable water with temperature range maintained at 24 to 30°C. After 7 days and 28 days from the time of casting, the cubes are tested in compression testing machine. A set of three cubes are tested and the average stress is calculated for representative strength of the concrete.

After testing, in case a strength value differs from the mean value by more than ±15%, the corresponding reading is known as outlier. The outlier is rejected and the average of the two remaining values are accepted as the representative value of strength.

### 3.2.2 Interpretation and Co-relation of Test Results

The strength of concrete from compression test may be validated by non-destructive testing methods as described in section 3.3. In general, the test results from different methods correlate well, if the tests are conducted in a standard manner.

Ultrasonic Pulse Velocity (UPV) and Rebound Hammer (RH) are continually used to estimate the compressive strength of the concrete. Concrete matrix being very complex, the strength of concrete can be influenced due to even minor change in any of the factors. The factors influencing the strength of concrete are type and size of aggregates, cement content, physical and mechanical factors. To evaluate the compressive strength considering these factors with higher precision, UPV and RH methods are combined henceforth called SonReb. This SonReb method could be used to evaluate the reliability of concrete (Chandok and Kumavat, 2020).

## 3.3 NON-DESTRUCTIVE TESTING OF CONCRETE

**Introduction**

Testing of concrete cubes in the compression testing machines is a destructive test method. The cubes fail after cracking on all four faces and test specimens are completely destroyed. However, several non-destructive testing methods have been devised.

These methods assess the strength of the in-situ structural concrete members, in a manner such that the members are not suffering any permanent damage. Two major NDT methods are (i) Ultrasonic Pulse velocity method and (ii) Rebound hammer method. These methods are widely used for assessing concrete strength and uniformity. While the rebound hammer test provides surface hardness of the concrete, in particular, the pulse velocity method test gives uniformity of the concrete mass of the structure.

### 3.3.1 Rebound Hammer Test

Rebound hammer test, also known as surface hardness test, is a non-destructive testing method of concrete. It provides an easy-to-use and rapid indication of the compressive strength of the concrete. The rebound hammer is also called Schmidt hammer, as it was devised by a Swiss Engineer Ernst Schmidt. The traditionally used hammer consists of a spring-controlled mass that slides on a plunger within a tubular housing. The steps of applying a rebound hammer is detailed in Fig. 3.3. When the plunger of rebound hammer is pressed against the surface of concrete, a spring-controlled constant mass with a specified energy hits concrete surface and it rebounds back. The extent of rebound, which is a measure of surface hardness, is measured on a graduated scale attached to the rebound hammer casing. This measured value is designated as Rebound Number (also, known as rebound index). Concrete with low strength and low stiffness will absorb more energy to yield a lower rebound value. Similarly, hard surface of a concrete of high grade will absorb less energy to give a high value of rebound number.

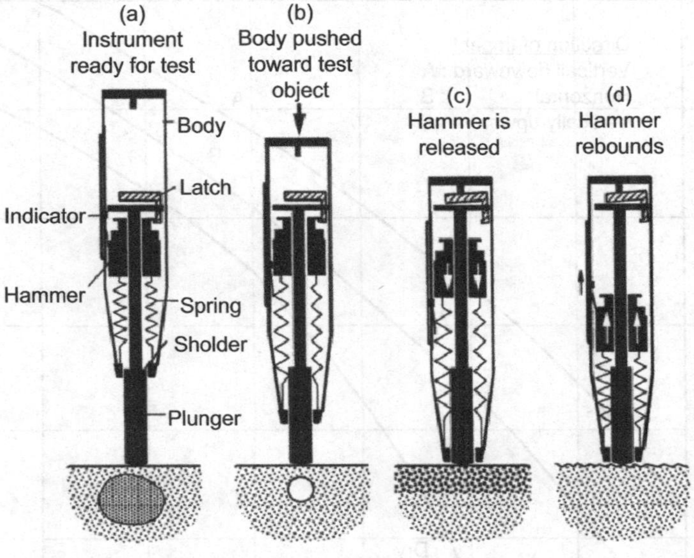


**Fig. 3.3:** Operation of Rebound Hammer (Alyamac et al. 2017)

### 3.3.2 Working Principle of Rebound Hammer Test (IS 13311 Parts 1 and 2 and IS 516 Part 5)

Rebound hammer test method is based on the principle that the rebound of an elastic mass depends on the hardness of the surface against which the mass strikes. The hardness of concrete and rebound hammer reading can be correlated with compressive strength of concrete. Some hammers have the compressive strength graph provided on the body of the hammer and can be read directly from it as per obtained rebound number. The graph provides three curves based on the direction of the hammer, viz., vertically downward, horizontal and vertically upward, as shown in Fig. 3.4. However, since rebound number is a measure of surface hardness of concrete, these correlations provide only estimates of concrete compressive strength. The actual compressive strength obtained using destructive tests (such as concrete cube testing in compression testing machine) may differ from the value obtained using correlations in Fig. 3.4. Rebound number is a good indicator of quality of concrete indicating its homogeneity, uniformity and compaction. Table 3.10 reports how average of observed rebound number values can be used to assess quality of concrete.

The commonly used Schmidt test hammer has a weight of 2 kg and specified impact energy of 2.25 N-m. However, the impact energy varies with the type of concrete to be tested. For example, to test a lightweight concrete or small and impact sensitive part of concrete, the hammer corresponding to impact energy of 0.75 N-m is used. On the contrary, for testing mass concrete, for roads, air-field pavements and hydraulic structures, a larger hammer with impact energy of 30 N-m is used.

The set of apparatus also consists of an abrasive stone and a testing anvil. The abrasive stone is usually made up of silicon carbide or equivalent material. The surface of concrete to be tested is smoothened by rubbing the abrasive stone. The testing anvil is used to calibrate the rebound hammer. It is of cylindrically shape with 150 mm diameter and 150 mm height. The manufacturer of the rebound hammer has to specify the range of readings on the anvil, suitable for a typical rebound hammer.

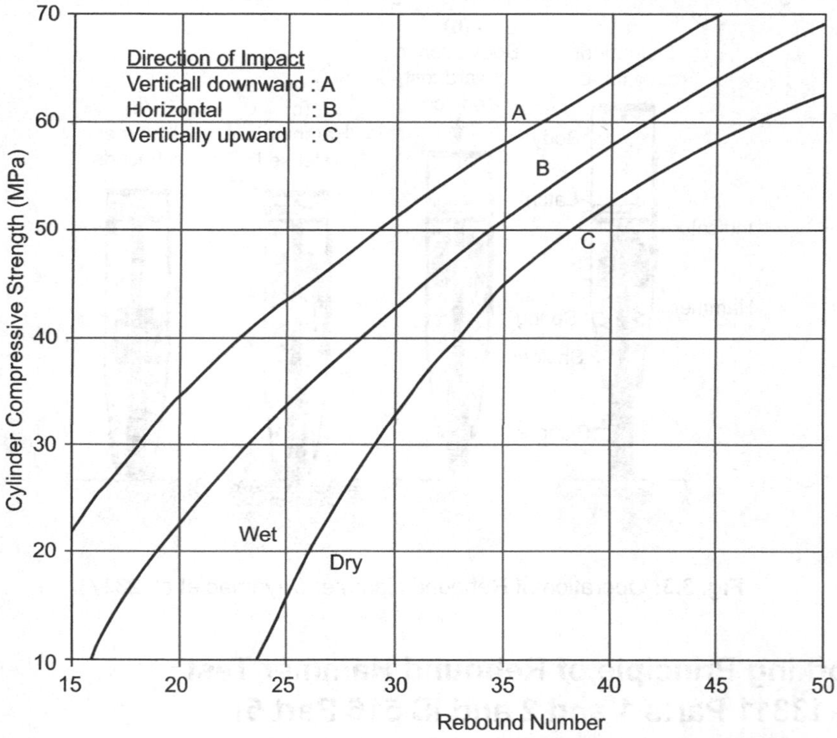


**Fig. 3.4:** Correlation between rebound number and compressive strength of concrete

**Table 3.10:** Qualitative description of concrete based on average value of rebound number

| Average Rebound | Quality of Concrete |
|---|---|
| >40 | Very Good |
| 30-40 | Good |
| 20-30 | Fair |
| <20 | Poor and/or delaminated |
| 0 | Very poor and/or delaminated |

Procedural details of the test

**Rebound Hammer:**

*Procedure:*

1. Calibration of Rebound hammer is to be obtained before performing the test in the field from the testing of existing concrete cubes. Then a correlation between compressive strength of concrete and its rebound number is established.
2. The rebound hammer is checked against the testing anvil before commencement of a test to ensure reliable results. (IS 516 (Part 5/Sec 4):2020).

3. Six readings of rebound indices are taken and average of these reading after deleting outliers as per IS 516 (Part 5/Sec 4):2020 becomes the rebound index for the point of observation.
4. For testing concrete, a smooth, clean and dry surface of concrete is selected. The surface should be smoothened and cleaned of any loosely adhering scale present by rubbing off with a grinding wheel or an abrasive stone. This is to be done because rough surfaces, resulting from incomplete compaction, loss of grout, spalled or tooled surfaces, do not give reliable results.
5. The point of impact should be at least 25 mm away from any edge or shape discontinuity.
6. For taking a measurement, the rebound hammer should be held at right angles to the surface of the concrete member. The test can thus be conducted horizontally on vertical surfaces (preferably) or vertically upwards or downwards on horizontal surfaces. In certain situations, the rebound hammer might have to be held at intermediate angles also. In such cases, the rebound number will be different for the same concrete.

Currently digital angle gauges are available that can be attached to the body of the instrument to allow quick measurement of the angle with respect to concrete surface. However, correlation considering the direction effect can also be developed between equivalent cube compressive strength of concrete cores (minimum 6 samples) with rebound number in vertically upward or downward direction for specific projects.

## 3.3.3 Factors Affecting the Rebound Index

Rebound index is influenced by a number of factors like types of cement and aggregate, surface condition and moisture content, age of concrete and extent of carbonation of concrete.

- **Effect of Type of Cement**

  Compared to concrete made up of Ordinary Portland Cement (OPC), concrete made with high alumina cement can give higher strength (as high as 100 percent). However, super-sulphated cement concrete gives 50 percent lower strength than that using OPC.
- **Effect of Type of Aggregate**

  The aggregate type used in concrete influences the rebound hammer test results. Rebound hammer test results of concrete with normal aggregates (gravels) and crushed rock aggregates have similar correlations. However, concrete made using lightweight aggregates need additional special calibration.
- **Effect of Surface Condition and Moisture Content of Concrete**

  The test is appropriately applicable for concrete with smooth surface. The test is not suitable for rough surfaces such as masonry blocks, honeycombed concrete, no-fines concrete. Also, it is applicable for fully compacted concrete only. Trowelled and floated surfaces are harder than moulded surfaces, and hence, the trowelled surfaces tend to overestimate the strength of concrete.
- **Effect of moisture content**

  A concrete of specified strength with wet surface will give lower rebound number than that calibrated under dry conditions. In structural concrete, this can be about 20 percent lower than that in an equivalent dry concrete. The effect of moisture content on rebound number is presented in Fig. 3.5.

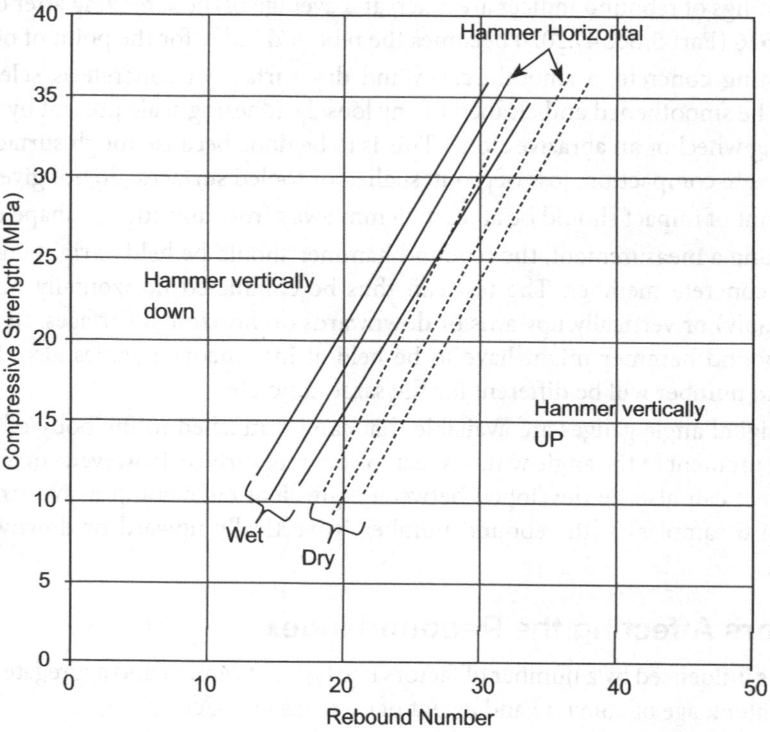


**Fig. 3.5:** Effect of moisture content on rebound number

- **Effect of Curing and Age of Concrete**
  Hardness of concrete increases with time and depends on factors such as initial rate of hardening, subsequent continuity in curing, and conditions of exposure. A properly cured concrete becomes harder with age, leading to increase in rebound number.
- **Effect of Carbonation**
  Carbonation of concrete surface increases the rebound number. Carbonated concrete thus provides an over-estimated strength (as high as up to 50 percent). Experimentally, it is feasible to establish a correction factor between a concrete before and after its carbonation.

### 3.3.4 Ultrasonic Pulse Velocity Test

This test is conducted as per the provisions of IS13311 (part 1) and IS516 (part 5). Ultrasonic pulse velocity test is performed on concrete to assess the internal quality of concrete by passing ultrasonic pulse velocity through it. Quality of concrete can be estimated based on ultrasonic pulse velocity using Table 3.11.

### 3.3.5 Working Principle of UPV Test

When concrete quality is good in terms of density, homogeneity, and uniformity, it exhibits comparatively higher ultrasonic pulse velocity in concrete. On the other hand, if the concrete quality is poor, and cracks exist in the concrete mass, time taken to travel will be higher, resulting into lower velocity.

In case, if the concrete has cracks and voids inside, the strength of pulse velocity is reduced and it passes around discontinuity (as shown in Fig. 3.6), thereby following the longer path for travel consequently, lower velocities are obtained.

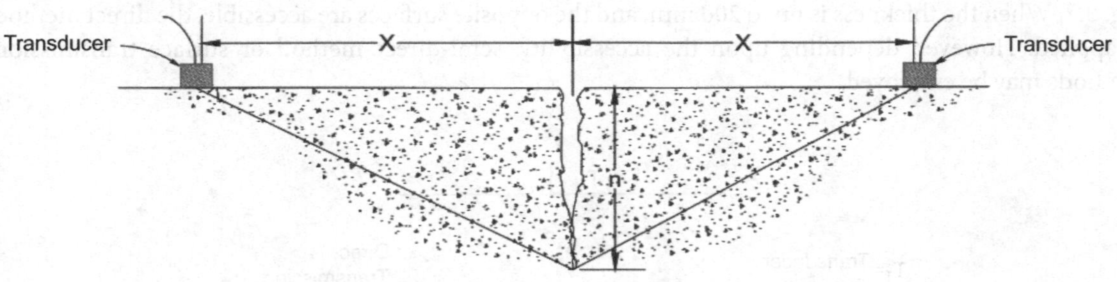


**Fig. 3.6:** The increase in path length due to presence of cracks

**Ultrasonic Pulse Velocity Test Procedure**

During the test, the transducer held in contact with one surface of concrete emits an ultrasonic pulse which traverses a known path length L in the concrete to reach second transducer, also known as receiver, held in contact with the other surface of the concrete member, and the transit time (T) of the pulse to be measured.

The pulse velocity (V) is given by: $V = L/T$

Once the path is discovered by the transducer the pulse velocity is transmitted at a right angle to the surface of the concrete to get the best result.

It is essential that pulse velocity propagated or transmission by the transducer is detected by receiving transducer. To ensure that, sufficient couplant is necessarily applied between the concrete and the face of each transducer. Generally used couplants are petroleum jelly, grease, liquid soap, and kaolin glycerol paste. If the concrete surface is very rough, it is essential to smoothen it before placing the transducer.

Testing shall also be similarly done by INDIRECT method wherever required by placing the probes at adequate distance from each other and noting the UPV values. The distance between the probes should be fed into the UPV meter during the test. Typical distance between probes lies in the range of 150 mm to 400 mm. Table 3.11 adopted from IS: 516 (Part:5/Sec1): 2020 presents the qualitative description of concrete based on UPV test.

**Table 3.11:** Qualitative description of concrete based on ultrasonic pulse velocity

| Pulse Velocity (km/s) | Concrete Quality |
|---|---|
| Above 4.4 km/s | Excellent |
| 3.75 to 4.4 km/s | Good |
| 3.0 to 3.75 km/s | Doubtful |
| Below 3.0 km/s | Poor |

**Test Limitations**

1. When testing is done by indirect method, as per clause 2.4.3.2.5 (IS: 516 (Part:5/Sec1): 2020), the pulse velocity may be increased by 0.5 km/sec for values above 3.0 km/sec.
2. Measurements of UPV values may be affected by other factors like moisture content of concrete, surface texture, temperature of concrete and percentage reinforcement.

**Methods of UPV tests through concrete:**

Depending upon the accessibility of the surfaces and the thickness of the concrete mass, the UPV measurements can be classified as direct, semi-direct and indirect (surface) transmissions as shown in Fig. 3.7. When the thickness is up to 200 mm, and the opposite surfaces are accessible, the direct method is applied. However, depending upon the accessibility, semi-direct method or surface transmission methods may be employed.

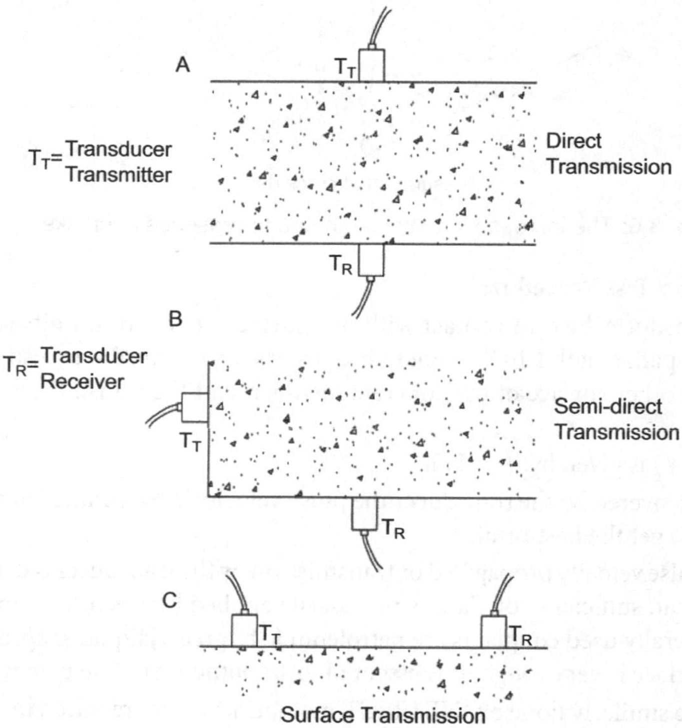


**Fig. 3.7:** Methods of measuring pulse velocity through concrete

## 3.3.6 Factors Affecting UPV Test Results

- **Influence of Surface Conditions and Moisture Content of Concrete**

  The smoothness of the concrete surface under test influences the results of ultrasonic pulse velocity. Therefore, before testing, the surface should be sufficiently smoothened for good acoustical contact by the use of a coupling medium.

- **Influence of moisture condition**

  In general, as per the physics of pulse velocity, it passes faster through a solid or a liquid medium than a vacuum. Therefore, the voids being filled with water, the pulse velocity passes through wet-concrete faster than a dry concrete. So, wet concrete gives increased pulse velocity and thereby, over estimates the strength of concrete.

  The increase is higher for low-strength concrete compared to high-strength concrete. As per IS 13311 (Part1), the pulse velocity of saturated concrete may be up to 2 percent higher than that of similar dry concrete.

- **Influence of Path Length, Shape and Size of the Concrete Member**

  In general, concrete is a heterogeneous material. Hence, during testing concrete, a sufficient path length should be ensured to minimize the error introduced in results due to its heterogeneity. In field work, this does not pose any difficulty, as thickness of structural concrete members are sufficiently higher than the minimum thickness specified by the code. However, small specimens are used in the laboratory, and it can adversely influence the pulse velocity readings. The least lateral dimension of a specimen is a function of natural frequency of the transducer. For example, it is about 80 mm for a transducer of natural frequency of 50 kHz.

- **Influence of Temperature of Concrete**

  When temperature of the tested concrete lies in the range of 5 to 30°C, the results of the pulse velocity measurements are without any significant error. However, between 30 to 60°C, a reduction in pulse velocity up to 5% is likely to occur. Also, below 0°C, the free water freezes within concrete mass, and it gives an increased pulse velocity up to 7.5%.

- **Influence of Stress**

  If concrete is subjected to a stress significantly higher than its capacity, there is a probability of reduction in pulse velocity, as there may be presence of micro-cracks within the concrete mass. This influence is observed to be insignificant, when the stress is lower than about 60 percent of the ultimate strength of the concrete.

- **Limitations of UPV test**

  1. A high degree of operator skill and integrity is required. Hence, there is a need for trained and certified NDT personnel.
  2. In most examinations, there is no permanent record of the inspection as there is in radiography. However, more recent equipment does offer this facility.
  3. In certain materials, like austenitic steel, the large grain size found in welds can cause attenuation and this may mask defects.
  4. Spurious indications and misreading of signals can result in unnecessary repairs.
  5. A standard procedure should be followed when carrying out any ultrasonic examination.

### 3.3.7 Importance of NDT Tests

NDT is a comprehensive way to locate surface and subsurface flaws and defects that could have an adverse impact on safety, reliability, and the environment. It can also be employed to estimate the size of these flaws and defects. The advantages of non-destructive testing are that they are safe, affordable, and quick in evaluating the quality of hardened concrete.

## UNIT SUMMARY

This unit discussed steps towards an economic and durable mix design using the provisions of IS 10262 and IS 456. An example illustrating these steps for a M40 grade concrete without admixtures has been provided. The existing methods to test the compressive strength of concrete cubes, their interpretation and co-relation have been explained. Popularly used non- destructive testing (NDT) methods, viz., rebound hammer test and ultrasonic pulse velocity test, have been described with their working principles. Factors affecting NDT test results have also been described.

# EXERCISES

## Multiple Choice Questions

1. Match the following List I and List II

| List I (Test name) | List II (IS code ) |
|---|---|
| (a) Ultrasonic Pulse Velocity | (i) IS 10262 |
| (b) Rebound Hammer | (ii) IS 516 |
| (c) Concrete Mix Design | (iii) IS 13311(Part1) |
| (d) Compressive, flexural and split tensile strength of Hardened Concrete | (iv) IS 13311 (Part2) |

2. Match the modular ratio of concrete for given grade

| List I (value of modular ratio) | List II (Grade of concrete) |
|---|---|
| (a) M20 | (i) 10.98 |
| (b) M25 | (ii) 13.33 |
| (c) M30 | (iii) 7.18 |
| (d) M40 | (iv) 9.33 |

3. The ratio of modulus of steel to that of concrete is called
   (a) Modular value (b) Modular ratio
   (c) Young modulus (d) none of them
4. Calculate the target mean compressive strength at 28 days curing, for M20 grade concrete, as per IS 10262-2009 .
   (a) 26.6 N/mm$^2$ (b) 20.0 N/mm$^2$
   (c) 22.4 N/mm$^2$ (d) 28.7 N/mm$^2$
5. Schmidt's Rebound Hammer technique is used to measure:
   (a) Tensile Strength (b) Compressive Strength
   (c) Thickness of member (d) Surface hardness
6. As per IS : 10262: 2019, the standard deviation for M25 concrete is:
   (a) 4.0 (b) 3.5
   (c) 4.5 (d) 5.0
7. Approximate value of shrinkage strain in concrete is
   (a) 0.03 (b) 0.003
   (c) 0.0003 (d) 0.00003
8. Strength of concrete increases with
   (a) Increase in w/c ratio (b) Decrease in w/c ratio
   (c) Decrease in size of aggregates (d) Decrease in curing time
9. Strength of concrete increases with
   (a) Increase with w/c ratio (b) Increase in fineness of cement
   (c) Decrease in size of aggregates (d) Decrease in curing time

**10.** Approximate ratio of flexural compressive strength to characteristic compressive strength of concrete is

(a) 0.25 (b) 0.33
(c) 0.5 (d) 0.05

**11.** The characteristic strength of concrete is

(a) Higher than average cube strength
(b) Lower than average cube strength
(c) Same as average cube strength
(d) Higher than 90% of average cube strength

**12.** The nominal mix corresponding to M20 grade concrete is

(a) 1:1:2 (b) 1:1.5:3
(c) 1:1:3 (d) 1:2:4

**13.** The proper size of mould for testing compressive strength of cement is

(a) 7.05 cm cube (c) 15 cm cube
(b) 10.05 cm cube (d) 12.05 cm cube

**14.** Tensile strength of concrete is measured by

(a) direct tension test in the universal testing machine
(b) applying compressive load along the diameter of the cylinder
(c) applying third point loading on a prism
(d) applying tensile load along the diameter of the cylinder

**15.** The approximate ratio of strength of 150 mm × 300 mm concrete cylinder to that of 150 mm cube of the same concrete is

(a) 1.25 (b) 1.00
(c) 0.85 (d) 0.50

**16.** The optimum number of revolutions over which concrete is required to be mixed in a mixer machine is

(a) 10 (b) 25
(c) 50 (d) 100

**17.** The ratio of direct tensile strength to that of modulus of rupture of concrete is

(a) 0.10-0.25 (b) 0.50-0.75
(c) 0.85-0.95 (d) Above 1.0

**18.** The use of super-plasticizers as admixture is to

(a) increase compressive strength of concrete
(b) lower water cement ratio, thereby strength is increased
(c) reduce the setting time of concrete
(d) lower cement content, thereby strength is increased

**19.** On which one of the following factors, does strength of concrete primarily depend?

(a) Quality of coarse aggregate (b) Quality of fine aggregate
(c) Fineness of cement (d) Water-cement ratio

**20.** Why is super plasticizer added to concrete?

(1) To reduce the quantity of mixing water

(2) To increase the workability

(3) To increase the quantity of cement

(4) To increase the quantity of mixing water

Select the correct answer using the codes given below:

(a) 1 and 2 (b) 1, 3 and 4

(c) 2 and 4 (d) 4 only

**21.** The working principle of rebound hammer test is based on

(a) Rebound deflections (b) Radioactive waves

(c) Ultrasonic pulse (d) Creep-recovery

**22.** Which one of the following is the correct expression for the target mean strength $f_m$ of concrete mix ?

(a) $f_m = k^*f_{ck} + S$ (b) $f_m = f_{ck} + k^*S$

(c) $f_m = f_{ck} + S$ (d) $f_m = f_{ck} + k$

where, fck is characteristic strength, k is Himsworth constant and S is standard deviation.

**23.** What is the ratio of flexural strength (f ) to the characteristic compressive strength of concrete ($f_{ck}$) for M25 grade concrete ?

(a) 0.08 (b) 0.11

(c) 0.14 (d) 0.17

**24.** Which of the following tests estimates the dynamic modulus of elasticity of samples of concrete?

(a) Compression test (b) Ultrasonic pulse velocity test

(c) Split test (d) Tension test

**25.** In a concrete mix, if the maximum size of coarse aggregate is increased, the proportion of fine to coarse aggregate should be

(a) Increased (b) Decreased

(c) Kept the same (d) Not dependent on size of aggregates

## Answers for Multiple Choice Questions

1. a-iii, b-iv, c-i, d-ii

2. a-ii, b-i, c-iv, d-iii

3. (b), 4. (a), 5. (d), 6. (a), 7. (c), 8. (b), 9. (b), 10. (b), 11. (b), 12. (b), 13. (a), 14. (b), 15. (c), 16. (b), 17. (b), 18. (b), 19. (d), 20. (a), 21. (a), 22. (b), 23 (c), 24. (b), 25. (b)

## Short and Long Answer Type Questions

1. How is non-destructive testing different from destructive testing of concrete?
2. Explain the working principle of ultrasonic pulse velocity test.
3. Why is the rebound hammer test also known surface hardness test?
4. What are the merits and demerits of self compacting concrete?

5. What are the material properties of coarse and fine aggregate required for mix design?
6. Describe the method of assessing the ratio of CA10 and CA20 based on the slump requirement and IS 383.
7. What are the factors governing the mix design?
8. Describe the requirements of limiting water cement ratio and cement content for different exposure conditions as per IS 456.
9. A reinforced concrete construction, expected to be exposed to severe environment, requires M30 grade of concrete with desired slump value of 75 mm. Ordinary Portland Cement (OPC) of 43 grade with specific gravity of 3.15 is readily available. The coarse aggregate comprises of CA10 and CA20, having angular texture and specific gravity of 2.65 under saturated surface dry conditions. However, the coarse aggregate samples are available as air dry, and is expected to absorb water up to 1% of its weight. The fine aggregates conform to Zone III and has a specific gravity of 2.60 under saturated surface dry conditions. However, because of recent rains, the fine aggregate has free surface moisture around 1.5% of its weight. Obtain the concrete design mix using Indian Standard Method.
10. Using Indian Standard Method, find out the quantities and mix proportions for a concrete mix to be used in constructing a structure exposed to severe environmental conditions. The concrete mix has a target slump value of 80 mm and a target mean strength of 48 MPa. The nominal cover to the steel reinforcement is 40 mm. Ordinary Portland Cement with specific gravity of 3.15 is to be used. The available coarse aggregate has two components, CA10 and CA20. Each component has specific gravity of 2.65 (measured under SSD conditions) and water absorption capacity of 0.8% of its weight. The fine aggregate conforms to Zone III and has a specific gravity of 2.60 under SSD conditions. However, the available fine aggregates contain free surface moisture of 1.2% of its weight. Both coarse and fine aggregates are crushed type.

## PRACTICAL

To be given as Unit VI

## KNOW MORE

There are evidence of the use of surkhi (powdered brick) and surkhi mortar in India from around 2nd century BC. The key to strength development of lime-surkhi mortar was thorough mixing and sustained ramming. The final product exhibited strength as well as impermeability, at times superior to Roman mortar.

## REFERENCES AND SUGGESTED READINGS


1. Gambhir, M.L., *Concrete Technology*, Tata McGraw Hill Publishing Co. Ltd., Delhi.
2. Shetty, M.S., *Concrete Technology*, S. Chand and Co. Pvt. Ltd., Ram Nagar, Delhi.
3. Santhakumar, A. R., *Concrete Technology*, Oxford University Press, New Delhi.
4. Neville, A. M. and Brooks, J.J., *Concrete Technology*, Pearson Education Pvt. Ltd.

5. Neville, A. M., *Concrete Technology*, Pearson Education Pvt. Ltd., New Delhi.
6. Sood, H., Kulkarni P. D., Mittal L. N., *Laboratory Manual in Concrete Technology*, CBS Publishers, New Delhi.
7. Shetty, M. S. and Jain, A. K. (2019), *Concrete Technology: Theory and Practice*, S. Chand and Co. Ltd., New Delhi.
8. Chandak, N. R. and Kumavat, H. R. (2020). "*SonReb Method for Evaluation of Compressive Strength of Concrete*." IOP Conf. Ser.: Mater. Sci. Eng. 810 012071.
9. Alyamac, K. E., Tas, Y., Ulas, M. A., and Ghafari, E. (2017). "*Feasibility analysis of NDT methods using to estimate the concrete strength as part of urban regeneration*", International Conference on Advances and Innovations in Engineering (ICAIE), Elazığ, Turkey.

# 4 Quality Control of Concrete and Concreting Operations

## UNIT SPECIFICS

Through this unit we have discussed the following aspects:

- The measures to ensure quality production of concrete are discussed. The concreting operations, viz., batching, mixing, transportation, placing, compacting, finishing and curing of concrete have been discussed in detail to adhere to specified workmanship;
- Materials of formwork used for beams, slabs, columns and requirement of good formwork have been outlined. Also, their stripping time for removal of formwork have been described based on IS 456 stipulations;
- The importance of waterproofing, the methods and materials used in construction works are described in detail;
- The types of joints and materials used for filling the joints are discussed including the steps towards proper joint treatment between old concrete and new concrete.

The practical applications of the topics are discussed for generating further curiosity and creativity as well as improving problem solving capacity.

Besides giving a large number of multiple choice questions as well as questions of short and long answer types marked in two categories following lower and higher order of Bloom's taxonomy, assignments through a number of numerical problems, a list of references and suggested readings are given in the unit so that one can go through them for practice. It is important to note that for getting more information on various topics of interest some QR codes have been provided in different sections which can be scanned for relevant supportive knowledge.

Based on the content, there is a "Know More" section. This section has been carefully designed so that the supplementary information provided in this part becomes beneficial for the users of the book.

## RATIONALE

The basics of concreting operations to ensure quality concrete have been introduced in this Unit. The same will enable students to understand the precautions necessary at every stage of concreting works. The types of formwork and their removal time depending upon type of structural members will provide a deep insight into good concreting practice. Nowadays, waterproofing compound are being used on a large scale. So the basics of types of water proofing compounds and materials used for the same will help the students to use the approach scientifically whenever, the same is required in construction. Joints are inevitable in concreting works. The joints used in concrete construction will enhance the basics of providing them properly in concrete structures.

## PRE-REQUISITES

Properties of ingredients of concrete, effect of each ingredient on durability of concrete

## UNIT OUTCOMES

List of outcomes of this unit is as follows:

**U4-O1:** To understand the steps of concreting operations such as batching, mixing, placing, compacting to finishing and curing of concrete to produce a durable and good quality concrete.

**U4-O2:** To learn the formworks used in concreting and the proper time of removal of the same after sufficient strength is achieved by concrete.

**U4-O3:** To know the importance of water proofing, the procedure and the materials used for the same in concreting operations.

**U4-O4:** To learn the types of joints used on site during concreting operations and the suitable filling materials used in the such joints for construction works.

| Unit-4 Outcomes | EXPECTED MAPPING WITH COURSE OUTCOMES (1- Weak Correlation; 2- Medium Correlation; 3- Strong Correlation) | | | | |
|---|---|---|---|---|---|
| | CO-1 | CO-2 | CO-3 | CO-4 | CO-5 |
| U4-O1 | 3 | 2 | 2 | 3 | 2 |
| U4-O2 | 1 | 3 | 2 | 3 | 1 |
| U4-O3 | 1 | 1 | 2 | 3 | 3 |
| U4-O4 | 1 | 1 | 1 | 2 | 2 |

## 4.1 CONCRETING OPERATIONS

**Introduction**

For a concrete structure to adequately carry desired loads throughout its design life, the concrete used should be of good quality. Good quality concrete implies that concrete should possess and exhibit desirable properties both in fresh and hardened states. Production of such concrete requires careful planning and execution of a number of concreting operations. These operations are performed while the concrete is in fresh state, and are listed as follows in the sequence: (i) Batching, (ii) Mixing, (iii) Transporting, (iv) Placing, (v) Compacting, (vi) Finishing, and (vii) Curing. This section explains these concreting operations in detail.

### 4.1.1 Batching

Once the concrete mix is designed as per IS 10262, as illustrated in Unit III, ingredients of the concrete are to be mixed in designed proportions. Batching refers to the process of measurement of materials for preparing concrete. Batching is usually performed either by volume batching or weigh batching. As these names suggest, volume and weigh batching refer to measurement of quantities of ingredients of concrete through volume and weight respectively.

Volume batching is an inferior method to weigh batching for measuring materials for making concrete, where the measurements are performed using gauge boxes of certain volume. Gauge boxes shown in Fig. 4.1(a), often called *farmas*, are made of timber or steel plates. This batching method is inferior because of difficulty and inaccuracy involved in measuring granular materials such as aggregates using gauge boxes. For instance, moist sand in loose condition would contain less sand as compared to the same volume of dry compacted sand. Moreover, the correction due to water absorption capacity and/or free surface moisture in aggregates cannot be applied. It is therefore prudent to avoid use of volume batching in order to produce good quality concrete.

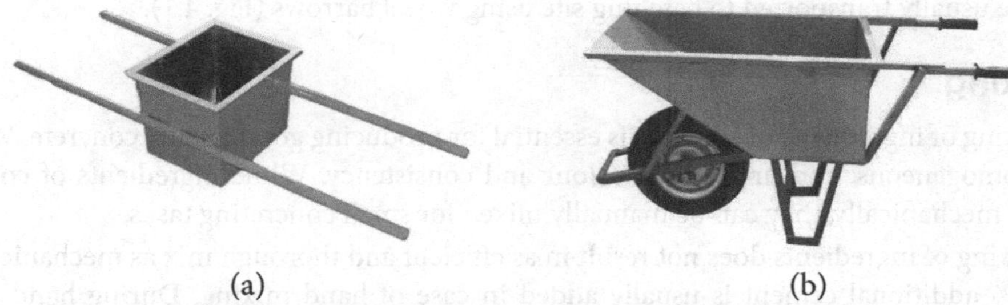

(a) (b)

**Fig. 4.1:** (a) Gauge box (*farma*) and (b) Wheel barrow

On the other hand, weigh batching refers to the proportioning of concrete ingredients where each material is measured to their weight. Weigh batching of concrete ingredients promotes simplicity and accuracy at the same time. Corrections due to water absorption capacity and/or free moisture in coarse and fine aggregates, can be easily applied, provided water absorption capacity and free moisture content are known. These values are obtained by testing small samples of given coarse and fine aggregates.

Depending on nature and scope of the job, different types of weight batchers are available. For small projects, a platform-type weighing balance or a simple spring balance is commonly used. In mid-size projects, the weighing facility usually comprises of two weighing buckets mounted on a central spindle about which they can rotate. Each bucket is connected to spring loaded dials through a system of levers to indicate the load. As the buckets can rotate about the spindle, one of these buckets can discharge material into the mixer while the other is being used to weigh other ingredients. In large projects where, enormous quantities of concrete mix are required, automatic weighing equipment is used. An automatic weighing equipment consists of a hopper in which an ingredient is weighed through a lever-arm system, two interlinked beams and jockey weights. Since these jockey weights are several orders smaller in magnitude than the weight they represent, this arrangement with large hopper can be used to weigh large quantities of concrete ingredients without any difficulty. These hoppers can then further feed the material directly into the mixer through a swivel gate. At times, automatic weigh batching equipment are able to record weight of material delivered in each batch, and the data can be assessed through a computer. In modern batching plants, sensor probes can detect water absorption capacity and free moisture present in aggregates, and then can automatically perform corrections while batching aggregates.

It is a common practice to measure quantity of cement in terms of number of bags consumed in preparing the mix. A standard cement bag contains 50 kg of cement. Water used in mixing concrete can be measured either by mass or volume. This is acceptable considering density of water to be roughly 1000 kg/m$^3$ at usual ambient temperatures.

Further it is important to properly store all the ingredients of concrete. Out of all ingredients, storage of cement is to be done with utmost care, as it starts setting in contact with moisture present in humid air. This leads to gradual deterioration of the efficiency of the cement. Absorption of moisture more than 2% by its mass, leads to reduction in strength. Finer cement such as OPC 53 is more prone to this phenomenon. Therefore, cement should be transported and stored in a damp-proof enclosure. Regular inspection of storage place should be carried out. However, storage period should be minimized as far as possible.

Once the cement bags are stored in a place, they should only be taken out only before making concrete. Relocation of the same is not advisable as it increases the risk of cement absorbing moisture. Aggregates should be preferably stored in an enclosed space away from direct sunlight and rain. This ensures adequate moisture content in aggregates and avoids deterioration in their properties. These ingredients are usually transported to batching site using wheel barrows (Fig. 4.1).

### 4.1.2 Mixing

Thorough mixing of ingredients of concrete is essential for producing good quality concrete. Well mixed concrete is homogeneous, and uniform in colour and consistency. While ingredients of concrete are usually mixed mechanically, they can be manually mixed for small concreting tasks.

Hand mixing of ingredients does not result in as efficient and thorough mix as mechanical mixing. Therefore, 10% additional cement is usually added in case of hand mixing. During hand mixing of concrete, coarse and fine aggregates are spread in alternate layers on a smooth impervious surface. Cement is poured over it and materials are thoroughly mixed in dry condition by turning the mixture over and over again using shovel(s). This mixing is continued till uniform colour of the mix is achieved. The dry mix is then spread out over the mixing surface and measured water is slowly sprinkled over the dry mix. Further mixing is performed while simultaneously sprinkling the water. Addition of water should be slow and gradual to ensure mix exhibits homogeneity and uniformity in colour and consistency.

However, for most concreting applications, mixing is performed using machines. This ensures efficient as well as economical mixing process. Mixers can be broadly categorised as batch mixers and continuous mixers. Ingredients are batched and fed into batch mixers to produce a certain quantity of concrete. On the other hand, materials are continuously fed in designed proportions into a continuous mixer which continuously discharges concrete mix. While most projects use batch mixers, continuous mixers are used in mass concreting applications (such as dams) requiring very large quantities of concrete. Batch mixers can be of pan type or drum type depending on shape of the mixer (Fig. 4.2). Pan type mixers are more efficient. However, the drum type mixers are convenient for feeding the materials and discharging the concrete mix. Drum mixers can be further defined as tilting, non-tilting, reversing or forced action type. Even upon thorough mixing, irrespective of the mixer used, the initially discharged mix contains excess of coarse aggregates and the finally discharged mix contains more of matrix. Therefore, the discharged mix has to be re-mixed a bit to prevent segregation of ingredients of the concrete.

**Fig. 4.2:** Types of concrete mixers: Pan type (left), Drum type (right)

In order to achieve proper mixing of ingredients, adding of ingredients to the mixer has to be done in the right sequence. About half of the coarse aggregate is taken in the skip followed by about half of the fine aggregate. Cement is then completely poured followed by the remaining half of coarse and fine aggregates. Such placement of aggregates and cement prevents cement from spilling and blowing away while feeding the materials into the mixing drum/pan from the skip. About one-fourth of the total water is first added to the rotating drum. This makes the drum wet and does not allow cement sticking to the blades or the bottom of the drum. The dry mix, comprising of cement, sand and coarse aggregates, is then fed into the drum. It is followed by the remaining (three-fourth) water. Water should be fed simultaneously with the dry mix preferably.

Mixing of concrete is defined at the instant water is fed into the mixer drum. Initial setting time and final setting time are measured from this instant. During mixing, the drum is usually rotated for 25 to 30 revolutions, at 15 to 20 revolutions per minute. Therefore, the mixing time is usually in the range of 1.5 to 2.5 minutes. Mixers with larger drum capacities require longer mixing time. Fig. 4.3 shows effect of mixing time on strength of concrete. It should be noted that reducing mixing time with an intent of faster concrete production can significantly impair strength development of concrete. At the same time, prolonged mixing leads to water evaporation, segregation, breaking of some aggregate particles due to abrasion and attrition, and loss of air in air-entrained concrete. Therefore prolonged mixing, at times, leads to poor workability of the concrete mix.

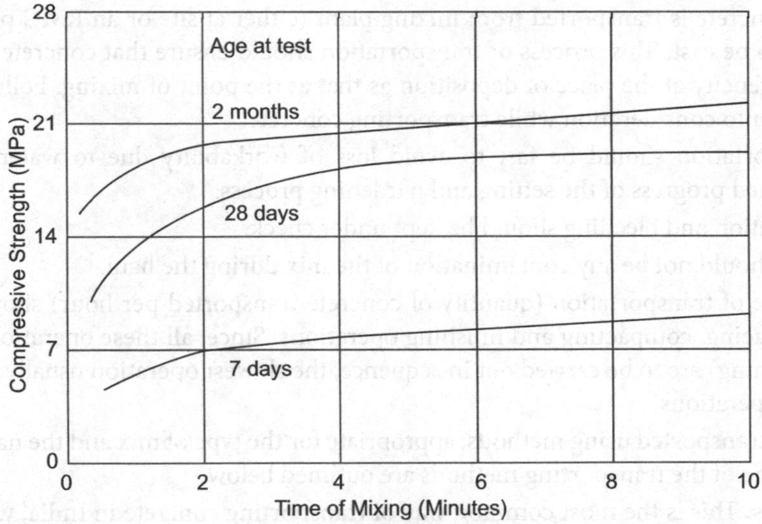


**Fig. 4.3:** Effect of mixing time on compressive strength of concrete

If water reducing admixtures (plasticizers/ super-plasticizers) are to be used, some portion of water is held back. The admixture is then mixed with that remaining water and added to the drum about 1 minute after the mixing. If mineral admixtures like fly ash, silica fume and slag are to be used, they are mixed in the dry ingredient mix before adding to the rotating drum. When any admixture is used, the concrete is mixed for slightly longer time (say, 30 seconds more) so that the required property modification is achieved in fresh concrete.

Concrete mixers are often used continuously for long durations, say several hours. The mixers should therefore be well maintained. Immediately at the end of every use, concrete drum should be thoroughly cleaned so that no concrete sticks to the drum and its blades. If concrete is allowed to stick, it is going to set and it will be difficult to remove at a later stage. The drum should be further tilted or covered to avoid deposition of rain water.

In large projects such as construction of high-rise buildings, dams and tunnels, where large quantities of concrete are required, ready mixed concrete (RMC) are commonly used. RMC is prepared in factory-controlled environment and is transported using special trucks called transit mixers. These trucks are equipped with a drum having rotating ability. In case of long hauls, the concrete is mixed intermittently to avoid setting and undue stiffening of concrete. Continuous mixing is avoided in order to avoid bad effects of prolonged mixing. At times, construction engineers at site find the delivered RMC either undue stiff or even set. Excessively stiff or set mix should be discarded as it can lead to non-uniformity, honeycombing and poor durability in structures. However, if the delivered RMC exhibits slight stiffening, it should be remixed with slight quantity of water. This remixing of concrete with addition of just the required amount of water is called tempering of concrete. A small quantity of cement is also sometimes added while retempering, to ensure constant water-cement ratio. However, addition of extra water during initial mixing to prevent undue stiffening during the haul should not be practiced. Further, retempering should not be performed if the haul time is too long (say, more than 2 hours). In such cases, intermittent mixing of concrete during the haul should be carefully performed.

### 4.1.3 Transportation

After mixing, concrete is transported from mixing plant (either at site or an RMC plant) to formwork where it needs to be cast. This process of transportation should ensure that concrete exhibits the same degree of homogeneity at the place of deposition as that at the point of mixing. Following precautions should be taken into consideration while transporting concrete:

- Transportation should be fast to avoid loss of workability due to water evaporation and continued progress of the setting and hardening process.
- Segregation and bleeding should be kept under check.
- There should not be any contamination of the mix during the haul.
- The rate of transportation (quantity of concrete transported per hour) should be compatible with placing, compacting and finishing operations. Since, all these operations (from batching to finishing) are to be carried out in sequence, the slowest operation usually guides the pace of other operations.

Concrete is transported using methods, appropriate for the type of mix and the nature of concreting applications. Some of the transporting methods are outlined below.

**Mortar pans:** This is the most common way of transporting concrete in India, where people carry concrete in mortar pans to the point of deposition. It can be conveniently used for concreting applications at, above or below the ground level. It is labour intensive and should only be used for small projects. Though it prevents segregation of ingredients, larger surfaces of concrete are exposed leading to rapid water evaporation in hot and arid conditions. This can lead to a loss of workability. Mortar pans should be washed to make it clean and wet, before it is used to transport concrete.

**Wheel barrows:** Wheel barrows are suitable if the point of deposition is at the ground level. They are also commonly used when concrete is to be transported for longer distance, as compared to mortar pans. However, the concrete is prone to segregation due to vibrations coming from rough ground surface. In order to minimize segregation, wheel barrows can be equipped with pneumatic wheels and wooden plank can be placed on the ground. These measures can significantly reduce vibrations and thereby prevent segregation and bleeding.

**Cranes, hoists and ropeways:** If concreting is to be performed at greater heights such as construction of high-rise buildings, cranes are the most suitable means to transport concrete from the point of mixing to the point of deposition. Cranes can carry concrete both horizontally and vertically using its boom. Concrete is carried either in skips or buckets. While a skip can deliver concrete through discharge door at bottom, buckets need to be tilted while depositing concrete. In case of locations inaccessible by cranes, hoist assembly with skips/buckets may be used to transport concrete from ground level to higher elevations. If concreting is to be performed at locations difficult to access such as valleys or rivers, ropeways are used to carry concrete. Skips or buckets can be conveniently used with ropeways. Ropeways are most suitable means to transport concrete in case of dams and piers of river bridges. The size of skips and buckets in case of cranes and ropeways can vary depending on scale of concreting. Medium size skips and buckets carry 0.5 $m^3$ of concrete in a single haul. The transported concrete should be deposited from the least possible height, as deposition from large height can lead to segregation.

**Trucks, dumpers, jubilee wagons and transit mixers:** For large concreting tasks located at ground level, trucks, dumpers and jubilee wagons can be used to transport and deposit concrete. Since jubilee wagons require rails for their movement, trucks and dumpers are more commonly used. Dumpers and trucks can easily transport 2 to 5 $m^3$ of concrete at one time. The internal surface of dumpers and trucks must be wetted before loading concrete. The exposed surface of concrete should be covered with tarpaulin sheets to avoid evaporation of free water. If the hauling distance is long as commonly found in case of RMC, concrete should be transported in transit mixers. Even in these cases, the haul time (from mixing to deposition) should be restricted to 2 hours and the drum should not be rotated for more than a total of 300 revolutions.

**Belt conveyors:** Belt conveyors are rarely used to transport concrete because of two major problems. Firstly, concrete is prone to segregation at locations with steep belt slopes, change of belt direction and belt passing over rollers due to vibrations. Secondly, belt conveyors expose concrete over large stretches which may lead to evaporation induced poor workability in case of hot and arid weather conditions. Due to these inherent disadvantages, belt conveyors are used to transport concrete only in mass concrete applications such as gravity dams where large quantities of concrete of lower grades are used.

**Chutes and tremie pipes:** Chutes are used to transport concrete from ground level to a lower level. This method of transporting concrete is therefore suitable for foundations. The slope of the chute should be selected based on consistency of the concrete mix, and should not be flatter than 1 vertical to 2.5 horizontal. If the chute is very steep, it may result in concrete mix falling under gravity leading to segregation. If the chute is very flat, transporting concrete may not be feasible. For concreting cast in-situ piles, steel casing is first inserted. Steel reinforcement cage is then inserted into the steel casing, followed by insertion of tremie pipes. Tremie pipes transport concrete to the point of concreting which can be tens of metres below ground level. Further, concrete should be deposited from the least possible height to prevent segregation.

**Pumps and pipelines:** In order to achieve good quality homogeneous concreting in inaccessible regions with dense reinforcement such as pile foundations or to carry concrete over large horizontal and vertical distances, concrete needs to be transported using pumps and pipelines. Hydraulic piston pumps are the most commonly used pumps, and comprise of three parts, viz., concrete receiving hopper, valve system and power transmission system. System of pumps and pipelines have made construction of skyscrapers possible. Concrete which can be transported through pumps and pipelines is called pumpable concrete. Pump pressure rating must exceed the calculated flow resistance. Therefore, pumpable concrete usually has a higher water-cement ratio.

As outlined in Unit III, IS 10262 recommends water content to be increased by 10% in case of pumpable concrete. The target slump for pumpable concrete usually exceeds 100 mm. The diameter of the pipeline is usually taken as 3 to 4 times the maximum size of aggregates for an efficient transportation of concrete. The pumping pressure falls with length of pipeline and bends in pipeline network, and therefore pipeline geometry should be adequately designed before transporting the concrete mix.

### 4.1.4 Placing

Placing of concrete refers to the process of depositing concrete in the desired location. Timber or steel formworks are often used to mould concrete in desired shapes. However, for raft foundations, the concrete may be directly placed in an earth mould. Good placing of concrete leads to uniform and homogeneous concrete without honeycombing, resulting in durable structures.

While placing concrete on earth as in case of foundations and rigid pavements, the earth bed should be scrapped off for any loose soil, vegetation matter and other wastes. Any tree root passing through or close to the foundation dimensions must be chopped, charred and tarred in order to prevent its further outgrowth into the foundation. If the earth surface is dry, it should be made wet so that earth does not tend to absorb water from the concrete. In case of thin rigid pavements, polyethylene film should be used in between concrete and ground surface to prevent earth from absorbing water from concrete. If the earth surface is too wet, the slush needs to be removed to expose a firm earth surface. In case of seepage through the foundation region, the flow of water should be diverted before placing the concrete.

When concrete is to be placed in formworks as in the case of beams, slabs and columns, a number of good practices need to be followed. Firstly, the reinforcement cage is checked for correct placement (such as provision of appropriate cover and spacing between tie bars). The joints between planks and sheets (in case of timber and steel formworks respectively) should be plugged effectively to prevent cement matrix from escaping the formwork while placing concrete. Mould releasing agents should be applied to the inner surfaces of formworks, for easy stripping of formwork. However, this application should be done carefully so that reinforcement bars remain free of any such agent. If reinforcement cage is very dense as in the case of columns, placing of concrete should be slow enough to prevent congestion and blocking. Further, it is common to witness deposition of concrete from a height in case of columns, which can result in segregation. To avoid segregation, tremie pipes and chutes are commonly used to place concrete from the least possible height. In case of thin sections with dense steel reinforcement and cables such as in case of box sections of a prestressed bridge girder, it is nearly impossible to place concrete from the top to reach every portion at the bottom of the box. In such cases, small openings on sides are made and concrete is pumped through these openings. The spacing between these openings depends on thickness, density of steel bars and span of sections, and often requires expert judgement.

For underwater applications, concrete is usually placed using bottom dump buckets or tremie pipes. Bottom dump buckets do not allow ingress of water once closed. These buckets are filled with concrete, closed and taken to the required point of concrete deposition. They are then electro-mechanically opened to slowly pour out the concrete. However, this method does not give satisfactory results as certain amount of concrete surely get washed away. Sometimes, dry or semi-dry mixes of cement, fine and coarse aggregates are filled in cement bags, and these bags are then deposited on the underwater bed. However, this method usually leads to formation of large undesirable voids. Tremie pipes are the best suited means to place underwater concrete. Tremie pipes, usually 200 mm in diameter, have a funnel attached at the top end and a plug attached at the bottom end. These pipes are lowered such that bottom end reaches the point where concrete is to be placed. The bottom plug prevents water from entering the tremie pipe. Concrete with good consistency and cohesion is then filled into the tremie pipe using the top funnel. The tremie pipe is then slightly raised and given a jerk, which tends to open the bottom plug and the concrete gets deposited at the desired location. The operation is continued till the concrete level reaches above the water level. Self-compacting concrete (SCC) is commonly used in underwater concrete applications. SCC is characterised by very high workability, which is often measured using slump flow test rather than slump cone test.

When thick concrete sections are to be laid as in case of raft foundations, piers, abutments and dams, concrete is usually placed in layers. Thickness of each layer depends on mode of compaction used. Methods of compaction are outlined in Section 4.1.5. Typical layer thickness varies from 150 mm to 300 mm and 350 mm to 450 mm respectively, in case of reinforced concrete structures and mass concrete structures. These layers should be placed in quick succession to avoid formation of cold joints. In this regard, the exposed surface should be cleaned off with water jet. In case of dams, sand blasting is also adopted to clean the surface. The idea is to leave the surface rough to enable good bond between the two layers. In case of mass concreting structures such as dams, dowel bars and/or bond stones may be used to achieve good bond between two layers.

### 4.1.5 Compaction

Good quality concrete has two important characteristics, strength and durability. Both these properties require high density of concrete which implies lesser entrapped air voids. Compaction is a necessary process for expelling these entrapped air voids in order to obtain concrete with desired strength and durability. A concrete mix with good workability is likely to have low entrapped air. On the other hand, stiff concrete mixes with poor workability are likely to have high amount of entrapped air. Therefore, good workable mixes require lesser compaction efforts as compared to poor workable mixes.

Fig. 4.4 shows that concrete considerably loses its strength if entrapped air is not removed. For instance, if concrete has 5% of voids, it tends to lose almost 30% of its strength. Further, concrete with 10% of voids has less than half of its desired strength. This explains significance of compaction in good concreting practice. Depending on concreting application, different methods of compaction are adopted. Some of them are outlined below.

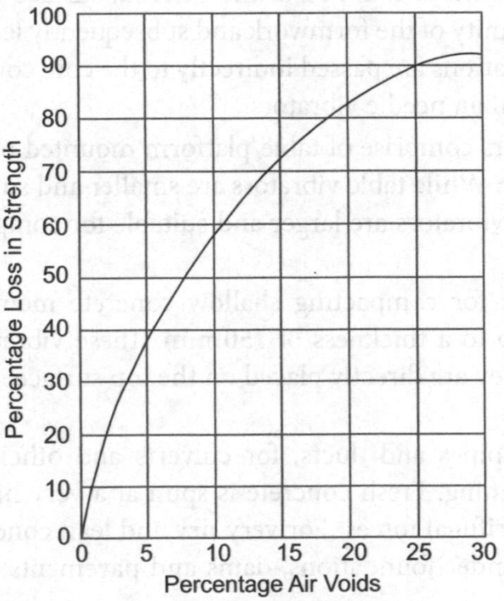


**Fig. 4.4:** Loss in compressive strength due to air voids

**Hand Compaction:** Hand compaction is adopted in small projects or in case of concrete members with large amount of reinforcement where mechanical compaction is usually not recommended. Hand compaction is achieved either by rodding, ramming or tamping. Rodding comprises of poking concrete using a steel rod which is 2 metres long and 16 mm in diameter with a bulleted end. Ramming is usually performed on unreinforced foundation concrete, and is not permitted for concrete placed in formwork supported on struts (such as slabs in upper storeys). Tamping is suitable for compacting slabs and rigid pavements with lesser thickness of concrete. Tamping comprises of beating the top surface of concrete by 10 cm X 10 cm wooden cross beam. When concrete is to be compacted by hand, concrete mix should exhibit good workability with slump value exceeding 75 mm. In case of thick concrete elements, concrete is compacted in layers with thickness ranging from 150 mm to 200 mm.

**Mechanical Compaction:** Mechanical vibrations are the most effective and efficient method of compacting concrete. Even stiff mixes (exhibiting slump as low as 40 mm) can be compacted using this means. Therefore, mechanical compaction is also suitable for compacting high strength concrete with low water-cement ratio. The idea is to apply vibrations to set the fresh concrete particles in motion, leading to reduced friction between them and setting up a temporary liquefaction. This enables easy settlement of concrete with minimum air voids. Mechanical compaction is suitable in cases where congestion of reinforcement and/or inaccessibility of concrete in formwork makes hand compaction infeasible. It is also the preferred means for concrete made using angular and rough aggregates as such concrete is likely to have very poor workability. Further, in large projects, mechanical compaction is faster and economical as compared to hand compaction.

Mechanical compaction of concrete is achieved using vibrators. Needle vibrator, also called as immersion vibrator, is the most commonly used vibrator (Fig. 4.5). This comprises of a power unit, a flexible shaft and a needle. The needle has a length of 250 mm to 900 mm and a diameter of 20 mm to 75 mm. Compacting concrete in mass concrete structures such as dams, where concrete is to be compacted in thick layers, requires bigger needles. Needle vibrators impart vibrations at around 12000 rpm.

In case of precast construction, structural members are cast in factory environments. In such cases, especially for columns and walls with congested reinforcement, form vibrators are used. The arrangement comprises of a vibrating unit which is clamped to the external surface of the formwork. This imparts vibrations to the concrete in vicinity of the formwork and subsequently leads to good compaction across the section. However, since vibrations are passed indirectly to the core concrete from the cover concrete, form vibrators are less efficient than needle vibrators.

Table and platform vibrators comprise of table/platform mounted on a spring assembly which are vibrated using an electric motor. While table vibrators are smaller and suitable for compacting concrete cubes in laboratories, platform vibrators are larger and suitable for compacting prefabricated elements such as railway sleepers.

Surface vibrators are used for compacting shallow concrete members such as slabs and rigid pavements, and are effective up to a thickness of 150 mm. These vibrators should never be used for concrete over 250 mm thick. They are directly placed on the top surface, and vibrations are imparted at around 4000 rpm (Fig. 4.5).

Construction of concrete pipes and ducts, for culverts and other special applications, involve compaction of concrete by spinning. Fresh concrete is spun at a very high speed which leads to very efficient compaction using centrifugal forces. For very dry and lean concrete mixes spread over a very large area such as those used under foundations, dams and pavements, vibratory rollers are used for compaction.

(a) (b)

**Fig. 4.5:** (a) Needle vibrator and (b) Surface vibrator

As discussed above, compaction using mechanical vibrators is more efficient than hand compaction. However, use of mechanical vibrators should be practiced with certain precautions outlined below.

(i) The formworks should be strong, stiff and well-sealed to avoid any loss of cement paste.
(ii) Compaction of concrete should progress in layers of small thickness, say not more than 400 mm. While using needle vibrator, it should be immersed to full depth of the concrete layer.
(iii) Needle vibrator should be inserted as vertical as possible, at a typical interval of 400 to 450 mm. This interval should not exceed 8 times the needle diameter.
(iv) The needle vibrator should be inserted quickly to allow air to escape easily, and should be removed slowly to ensure closing up of concrete surface.
(v) Vibrations should not be excessive at any location. Prolonged vibration can lead to segregation and laitance, making concrete prone to freezing and thawing under wet conditions. While using needle vibrators, 10 to 15 seconds of vibrations are usually sufficient.

Once the concrete is compacted, concrete surface needs to be finished as per requirements.

## 4.1.6 Finishing

Finishing is the process to achieve a good, uniform and smooth surface of concrete members. For beams and columns, most of the surfaces are moulded (i.e., most surfaces are cast with formwork). But, finishing is important for slabs in buildings and rigid pavements for roads and airstrips as top surface is exposed. The degree of smoothness varies based on applications. For instance, building slabs need to have a very smooth surface, while concrete pavements such as roads and airstrips should have some degree of roughness to offer skid resistance. Surface finishes on concrete are usually classified as formwork finishes, surface treatments and applied finishes.

In formwork finishes, concrete surface is finished using specially designed formwork. For instance, columns with chamfered edges can be obtained by adequately preparing the formwork.

A smooth concrete surface is obtained by surface treatment using floats and trowels. Floats are usually made of wood or steel. Use of wooden floats should be followed by steel floats for a smooth surface finish. If a slightly rough surface is desirable as in the case of pavements, surface is raked lightly or broomed.

Applied finishes refer to desired finish on exterior surface of concrete structures. The surface is cleaned, roughened and then kept wet for sufficient time. A mortar of proportion 1:3 (cement:sand) is then usually applied. Further application of white or pigmented cement (wall putty) is also warranted in residential construction to obtain a smooth wall surface to form a good base for paints.

Typical finishing of concrete structures comprises of following steps:

(i) Screeding: Excess concrete is struck off using a straight edge, to remove bumps and hallows and to obtain uniform levelled surface.

(ii) Floating: It removes the irregularities left after screeding and firmly embeds the large aggregate particles.

(iii) Trowelling: Floating is followed by trowelling to obtain a smooth and wear resistant surface. It is performed using a steel trowel.

Once concrete surface is finished, concreting operations are said to be completed. However, in order to obtain durable concrete structures, we need to provide conducive environment for concrete to develop strength and impermeability. This is achieved by adequate curing of concrete.

### 4.1.7 Curing

In Unit III, it is mentioned that water used in making concrete serves two purposes, viz., hydration of cement and filling of voids in gel pores. Water absorption tendency and free moisture present in aggregates are taken into consideration while obtaining the quantity of water to be used in making concrete. However, when a concrete member is cast, it is exposed to environmental conditions. Some portion of water from concrete is likely to get evaporated rendering insufficient water availability for hydration of cement. This can be prominent near the exposed surface of the concrete, especially in hot and arid climates. This can hamper the strength development in concrete. Incomplete hydration of cement can further lead to shrinkage cracks leading to poor durability of the structure. Therefore, loss of water from concrete due to evaporation should be checked. This is possible by ensuring desirable conditions of ambient temperature and sufficient moisture. This process of maintaining ambient temperature and ample moisture in concrete, so as to enable unhindered hydration of cement and eliminate shrinkage, is called curing.

Efficient curing in the early period of hydration leads to good strength development and durability of concrete. On the other hand, ignoring curing in the early stages can lead to poor quality concrete with irreparable loss. It is therefore important to adopt efficient and continuous curing practices for concrete during the early stages. Fig. 2.8 shows effect of curing on the development of compressive strength of concrete. It is observed that continuously cured concrete exhibits much desirable properties as compared to concrete cured for short period.

A number of factors, such as cement type and weather conditions, influence curing requirements. Blended cements contain mineral admixtures such as fly ash, slag and silica fume, and therefore react slowly than Ordinary Portland Cement (OPC). Therefore, concrete made using blended cement needs to be cured for longer period of time as compared to concrete made with OPC. In hot weather conditions, hydration rate is significantly increased along with rate of evaporation. Therefore, concreting in hot weather requires efficient curing during the initial stages. At the same time, concreting in cold weather would require curing for a prolonged time.

Different methods for curing are used depending on the concrete member and the scale of project. These can be broadly categorised as water curing, membrane curing and steam curing. However, there are several modern methods of curing suited for specific applications.

**Water curing:** It is the most economical curing method, and is suitable for most applications. It is done in different ways, viz. ponding, and immersion, spraying and wet covering. In case of slabs in buildings and rigid pavements, small ponds are made using sand/saw dust barriers and these ponds are filled with water. This process of curing is called ponding. Precast concrete members and pretensioned elements (such as railway sleepers) are immersed in curing tanks filled with water. Concrete cubes and cylinders to be tested in laboratory for compressive strength are also kept under water in curing tanks. This method is usually referred as immersion. Vertical members such as columns and walls are cured by spraying water, typically in morning and evening. If the weather conditions are hot and dry, vertical surfaces are also covered with wet gunny bags, jute mats and hessian clothes. These wet coverings ensure ample moisture content and ambient temperature throughout the day. Water can be periodically sprayed to keep these coverings wet.

**Membrane curing:** Water curing requires large quantities of water, making it not feasible in regions with acute water scarcity. In such cases, curing compounds are sprayed on the concrete surface. These liquid substances form a surface coating/membrane which do not allow water to evaporate and thereby ensure conditions conducive for hydration of cement. These compounds are usually sprayed after brief spell of water curing, say for a day or two. Since application of curing compounds is not followed by water curing, multiple coats may be required for effective sealing of surface to prevent evaporation of water. Apart from bituminous and rubber compounds, impermeable membranes such as polyethylene and polyester films can also be used. Concreting in inaccessible places and in projects with possibility of poor-quality control should adopt membrane curing rather than water curing.

**Steam curing:** It comprises of exposing concrete members to steam. This provides high temperature leading to rapid hydration and therefore quick strength development. At the same time, steam also ensures ample moisture content in the concrete. It should be understood that application of dry heat will accelerate hydration as well as evaporation, which will hinder hydration and promote shrinkage. Steam curing is most suitable for precast and prefabricated concrete members as it usually involves placing the concrete member in a steam chamber.

**High pressure steam curing:** Steam curing may adversely affect the compressive strength of concrete. High pressure (typically eight times the ambient atmospheric pressure) steam curing is applied to overcome this problem. This is done in cylindrical steel chambers, called as autoclaves.

**Electrical Curing:** Concrete is cured by passing alternating current of low voltage (30 – 60 V) and high ampere through electrodes in the form of plates. These plates are fixed on the two opposite faces of the concrete members, covering entire concrete surfaces. An impermeable rubber membrane is used to prevent water evaporation from the concrete during the electrical curing process.

**Infra-Red Curing:** It has been used in Russia mainly, although, it is rarely practised in India. The rapid increase in temperature does not affect the final strength of the concrete. This method is particularly used in curing of hollow concrete sections.

## 4.2 FORMWORK FOR CONCRETING

### Introduction

Formwork are moulds that enable concrete to take desired shape and size. The dimensional accuracy of concrete member depends on fabrication and finish of formwork. For in-situ concreting, formwork accounts for roughly 30% to 50% of the concreting cost. Moreover, the speed of construction depends on fabrication and erection speed of formwork. Therefore, formwork is an important component of concrete construction.

### 4.2.1 Types of Formwork for Beams, Slabs and Columns

While formwork for columns includes shutters all around its cross-section along its height, formwork for beams and slabs comprise of shutters for soffit and sides while leaving the top exposed. Formwork for beams and slabs are also supported by a number of vertical members, called props. Steel props are easy to install compared to bamboo props, and can be easily operated using jacks while removing the formwork.

### 4.2.2 Materials used for Form Work

- **Timber:** Timber formwork is the most conventionally used formwork in construction because they can be easily cut and joined to obtain desired shape and size. Timber used for formwork should be light-weight, seasoned and free from termites.
- **Steel:** Steel formwork provides smoother surface than timber formwork. It is suitable for curved surfaces in circular columns, water tanks, silos, chimneys, tunnels, culverts and retaining walls. It can also be assembled and removed at a faster pace. Steel formwork is strong and durable, and can be reused several times, hence economical also.

Other materials such as aluminium, plywood, fabric and plastic are also used for making formwork required for specific applications.

### 4.2.3 Requirements of a Good Formwork

Formwork is an important component of plain and reinforced concrete construction. A good formwork should satisfy following requirements:

(i) The formwork should have properly sealed edges to avoid leakage of cement paste.

(ii) The formwork should be rigid and strong. In case of columns and walls, it should be able to withstand hydrostatic pressure of fresh concrete. Formwork for slabs should be able to carry dead and live loads.

(iii) The formwork should have dimensional accuracy so that members are cast with desired dimensions. This is ensured in IS 456, by allowing tolerance limits for formwork suitable for different purposes, as outlined in Table 4.1.

(iv) The internal surfaces of formwork should be smooth and clean, and it should not leave stains and undesirable texture on surfaces of concrete members.

(v) The formwork should be durable and reusable.

**Table 4.1:** Allowable tolerance in formwork for structural members

| S. No. | Member description | Allowable tolerances |
|---|---|---|
| 1. | Cross-sectional dimensions of beams and columns | +12 mm and -6 mm |
| 2. | Dimensions of foundations<br>(i) Plan dimensions<br>(ii) Eccentricity<br><br>(iii) Thickness | <br>+50 mm and -12 mm<br>0.02 times the footing width; limited to 50 mm<br>±0.05 times thickness |

### 4.2.4 Stripping Time for Removal of Formwork as per IS 456

The process of removing formwork from the hardened concrete members is called stripping. Formwork is typically removed when concrete exhibits strength at least twice the expected stress at removal of formwork. Stripping time depends on a number of factors such as:

(i) Concrete member, viz., beam, slab, column etc.: Stripping time for columns is much smaller compared to beams and slabs, as shown in Table 4.2.

(ii) Type of cement and admixture used in concrete: Concrete made of blended cement and with mineral admixtures (such as fly ash, silica fume and slag) exhibit slower strength development. Therefore, stripping time can be longer than that in case of concrete made of OPC.

(iii) Curing conditions: Adequately cured concrete tends to develop strength at a good pace, which may permit early stripping of formwork.

(iv) Environmental conditions: Hot weather conditions lead to rapid hydration and thereby rapid strength development. Concreting in hot and humid conditions usually allow slightly early stripping of formwork.

It is emphasized that, if PPC is used in construction, curing as well as stripping time should be suitably increased by 3 to 5 days.

**Table 4.2:** Stripping time for formwork as per IS 456

| S. No. | Type of formwork | Minimum stripping time |
|---|---|---|
| 1. | Vertical formwork to column walls and beams | 16 to 24 hours |
| 2. | Soffit formwork to slabs<br>(Props to be re-fixed immediately after removal of formwork) | 3 days |
| 3. | Soffit formwork to beams<br>(Props to be re-fixed immediately after removal of formwork) | 7 days |
| 4. | Props to slabs<br>(i) Span up to 4.5 m<br>(ii) Span over 4.5 m | <br>7 days<br>14 days |
| 5. | Props to beams<br>(i) Span up to 4.5 m<br>(ii) Span over 4.5 m | <br>14 days<br>21 days |

## 4.3 WATERPROOFING

**Introduction**

Waterproofing of concrete is an important aspect to produce a durable concrete. This section details the importance of waterproofing, the methods practised in general construction works and materials used for this purpose.

### 4.3.1 Importance and Need of Waterproofing

Due to this surface tension in capillary pores of hydrated cement paste, concrete inherently tend to absorb water by capillary suction or pulling in potential. Water proofing admixtures prevent the 'pulling in' of water by capillary suction. If water enters the concrete body by this suction, there is a probability of increased corrosion of reinforcement embedded in concrete. The perfection achieved in water proofing depends on the workmanship to a large extent and the environmental factors, as well as the type of the structure.

Waterproofing is a method which prevents water from penetrating into the concrete mass. Waterproofing is essentially important as it ensures concrete to remain dry. Waterproofing prevents humidity from building up inside the house and thereby protects things inside the house from humidity induced damages. The permeability of concrete is reduced significantly due to use of plasticizers, super-plasticizers, and pozzolanic materials. IS 2645 describes the requirements of these water proofing compounds. They make the concrete hydrophobic, and at times reduce permeability to some extent. Water is repelled from the surface of concrete, due to presence of water-repellent chemicals on the surface of the concrete. Calcium or aluminium stearate or oleate, butyl stearate, stearic acid, several vegetable and animal fats are commonly used as water-proofing chemicals.

### 4.3.2 Methods and Materials of Waterproofing

The commonly used methods of waterproofing can be broadly classified as integral water proofing and externally applied water proofing measures. Integral water proofing uses compounds integrally mixed with the ingredients of concrete. Cementitious waterproofing is the most common integral waterproofing practice.

The externally applied measures of water proofing are liquid waterproofing membrane, bituminous membrane, bituminous coating, and polyurethane liquid membrane. In each of these approaches, the surface is coated by a layer of corresponding material. This layer forms a continuous membrane, also called coating. This coating permanently adheres to the concrete surface, after forming a thin impermeable membrane.

**Cementitious water proofing materials**

Cementitious waterproofing materials are the easiest and most commonly used method of waterproofing in construction. The materials for cementitious waterproofing are readily available in solid, liquid or powder form. These products are ready-mixed rapid setting compounds. They consist of pore filling compounds such as sodium silicate, aluminium and zinc sulphate, aluminium and calcium chlorides.

Some of these compounds, usually in powdered form, are mixed with cement, or in liquid form mixed with mixing water before preparing the green concrete. Such compounds are also called as integral water proofing compounds. These compounds accelerate the setting time and make concrete more impervious.

These compounds will be effective in providing desired results, in case the concrete is constantly under wet or damp conditions. Following the manufacturer's instructions, a thorough mix is prepared and applied on the wet concrete surface, such as railways/ road subways, bridges, toilet floors.

**Mineral based polymer modified coatings**

These are slurry coating specially modified by processed hydraulically setting powder and a liquid polymer component. The final slurry is applied with brushes in two coats to form a durable waterproofing coat. Further, in certain applications, mortar screeding or tiles are provided on top of these coatings. It is suitable in sunken slabs of bathrooms.

**Chemical damp proof course (DPC)**

This course is provided at the plinth level to stop capillary rise of ground water through walls. In old structures, to get rid of dampness, such DPC is injected at the plinth level by drilling holes with an aim to seal the capillaries.

**Water proofing adhesive for tiles, marble and granite stones**

These are polymer based hydraulically setting adhesives used to fix glazed tiles. These adhesives provide water proofing quality to the walls. For example, swimming pool floors and side walls tiles are fixed this way. The bonding quality and long-term durability of the adhesives are making such applications more popular.

**Liquid waterproofing membrane**

The liquid membrane consists of three coats, viz., a primer coat and two top coats. The application of the coatings is either by spraying, rolling, or trowelling. The liquid layer forms a thin membrane and offers comparatively higher flexibility than the cementitious types of waterproofing. The membrane should be water resistant, solar reflective, elastic and durable. These are suitable to apply on roof slabs to repair the micro-cracks due to variation in temperature or long-term shrinkage.

The liquid, over a short period of time, cures into a rubbery coating on the concrete surface. The elongation properties of the coat can reach as high as 280%. The durability of the waterproofing coating depends on the type of polymer used for making of the liquid waterproofing chemical.

Liquid waterproofing membrane can be of a spray-applied liquid layer composed of polymer-modified asphalt. Polyurethane liquid membranes in separate grades for trowel, roller, or spray are also available from manufacturers.

**Bituminous Membrane Waterproofing**

Bituminous membrane waterproofing is another widely used method. They are applied more often to water proof low-sloped roofs. The bituminous waterproofing membrane formed on the concrete surface is self-adhesive in nature. Self-adhesive compounds mainly comprise of asphalt, polymers, and fillers. Moreover, certain resins and oils are added to improve adhesion characteristics. Since the bonding properties of the membrane reduce faster with time, the self-adhesive type of bituminous membrane has a low shelf life.

Such membranes are of two types, viz., exposed and covered types. The exposed type layer often has granular mineral aggregate to withstand the wear and tear of the weathering. For certain types of membrane, it may often be provided with protective screed to prevent the puncture of the membrane.

**Bituminous Coating Waterproofing**

Bituminous coatings (asphalt coating) are based on bitumen-based materials. They are highly flexible protective coats depending on their specific formulation and characteristic polymerization grade. The flexibility and protection against water can be influenced by the polymer grade and reinforcement of fiber.

These applications ensure an excellent protective coating and waterproofing, particularly on surfaces such as concrete foundations. They are not suitable for concrete surfaces exposed to sunlight. In case of exposure to direct sunlight, they are suitably modified with a more flexible material such as polyurethane or acrylic-based polymers. Emulsion-based bitumen coatings are also capable of providing a water proofing layer. These coatings produce a tough but elastic film (elasticity is relatively lower than bituminous membranes) on the concrete surface.

It is to be noted that the fillers used in concreting, viz., hydrated lime or the dust of normal weight aggregates, are different from joint fillers. Also, silicone resins are different from water proofing chemicals, despite being water repellents. Silicon based water repellents are used to stop moisture migration through external masonry walls.

**Polyurethane Liquid Membrane Waterproofing**

Polyurethane liquid membrane method of waterproofing is used for flat roof area and surfaces exposed to weathering. This waterproofing method is expensive. Such membranes provide higher flexibility. Polyurethane is highly sensitive to the presence of moisture. Therefore, it is necessary to ensure dry surface before its application. It is also suggested to evaluate the moisture content of the concrete slab properly.

Some waterproofing innovations are (i) use of nano-technology in waterproofing (ii) crystalline waterproofing (iii) self-healing, water-repellent, spray-on coating (iv) ultra-water-resistant surfaces and (v) torch on membrane waterproofing.

## 4.4 JOINTS IN CONCRETE STRUCTURES

**Introduction**

At times, the length of a structure exceeds the possible length of concreting at one go using the available resources. Therefore, it becomes necessary to provide joints between two successive concreting sessions. The locations of such joints avoid maximum bending moments and shear forces. This section describes types of joints and their treatment for concreting over an existing old concrete surface, and the materials suitable for filling such joints.

### 4.4.1 Types of Joints

**Movement Joints**

Such a joint is designed to allow for slight movement between adjacent sections of a structure. Thus, movement joints eliminate external restraints on a structure. The joint should be constructed with specific requirements to keep the joint watertight. The design should provide for exclusion of grit, debris and other unwanted material which would prevent the closing of the joint. The material for construction of movement joints should not undergo permanent distortion or extrusion during its intended life. These materials should not be affected by temperature variations, exposure to light and evaporation of plasticizer solvent. Movement joints are further classified as (i) contraction joint (ii) expansion joint and (iii) sliding joints.

**Contraction Joints**

A movement joint designed to support concrete contraction, that has a planned discontinuity but no initial gap between the concrete on either side of the joint, is called as contraction joint. The well-spaced contraction joints help in controlling shrinkage cracking. The spacing of contraction joint increases with the increasing slab thickness due to the higher resistance to shrinkage offered by thicker slabs. Table 4.3 provides an estimated spacing based on slab thickness (Shetty & Jain, 2019).

**Table 4.3:** Spacing between successive contraction joints

| Thickness of Slab (mm) | Joint Spacing (m) |
|---|---|
| 10 | 7.5 |
| 15 | 13.0 |
| 20 | 14.0 |
| ≥ 25 | 17.0 |

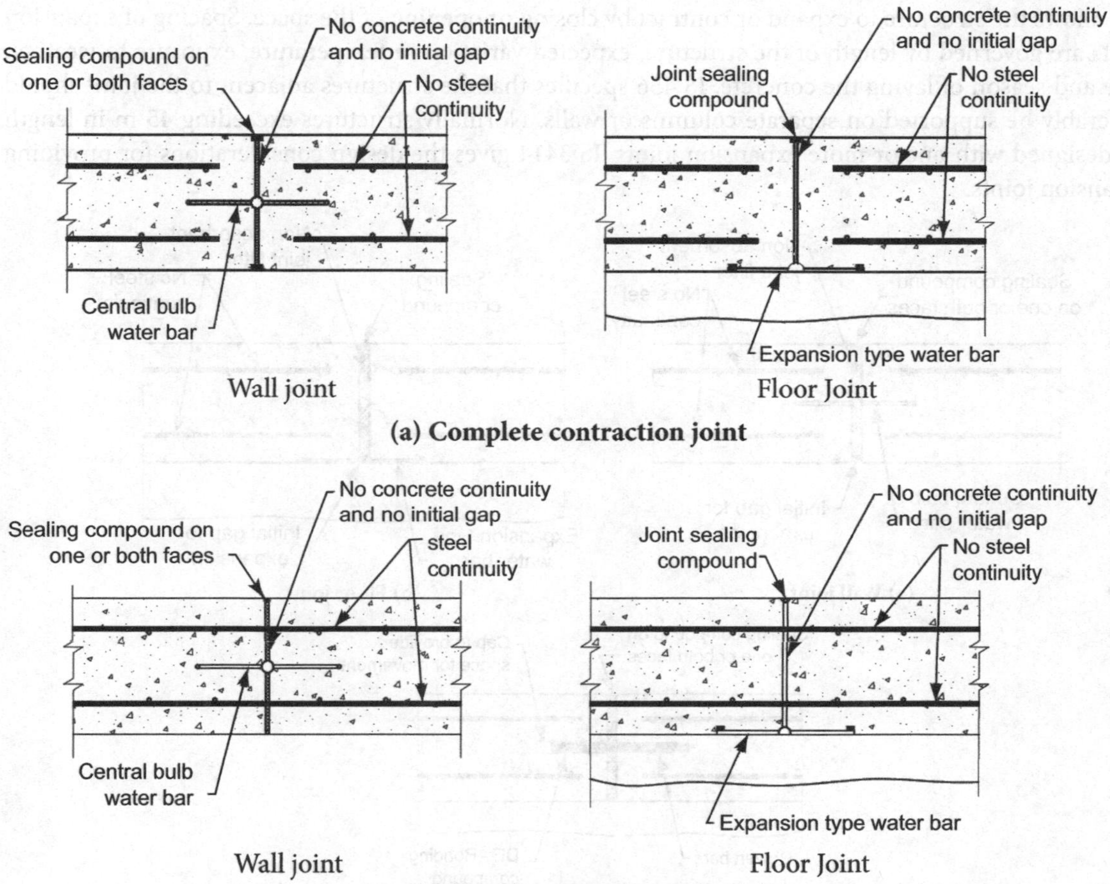

**(b) Partial contraction joint**

**Fig. 4.6:** Schematic diagram of contraction joints (IS 3370 Part I)

The contraction joints may be complete (Fig. 4.6a) or partial (Fig. 4.6b). The partial contraction joints give some restraint but are meant to accommodate a predetermined contraction of concrete. Towards this, concrete industrial floors and pavements are cast in alternate bays and the remaining set of alternate bays are cast after sufficient time to allow maximum possible shrinkage.

Both the concrete and the reinforcing steel are discontinued in complete contraction joints, but in partial contraction joints, only the concrete is not continuous while the reinforcing steel continues on either side of the joint. A water bar must be present, either in the middle of a wall (Fig. 4.6) or on the floor's soffit. IS 3370 Part 1 recommends to provide water bars for walls with thickness more than or equal to 300 mm. Sometimes, a shear key can be provided to account for shear across the face. A water bar may be included in a partial contraction joint, if necessary, in the middle of a wall or on the soffit of a floor.

**Expansion Joint**

This type of joint is designed to tolerate thermal expansion as experienced in large dimension concrete roof slabs. The joint is completely discontinuous in both the concrete and the reinforcement (Fig. 4.7). A water bar of the expansion type is necessarily installed, either in the middle of a wall (Fig. 4.7a) or on the soffit of a floor. Expansion joint needs an initial space between the adjacent components of a structure that allows the structure to expand or contract by closing or opening of the space. Spacing of expansion joints are governed by length of the structure, expected variation in temperature, exposure to weather, time and season of laying the concrete. IS 456 specifies that the structures adjacent to the joint should preferably be supported on separate columns or walls. Normally structures exceeding 45 m in length are designed with one or more expansion joints. IS 3414 gives the design considerations for providing expansion joints.

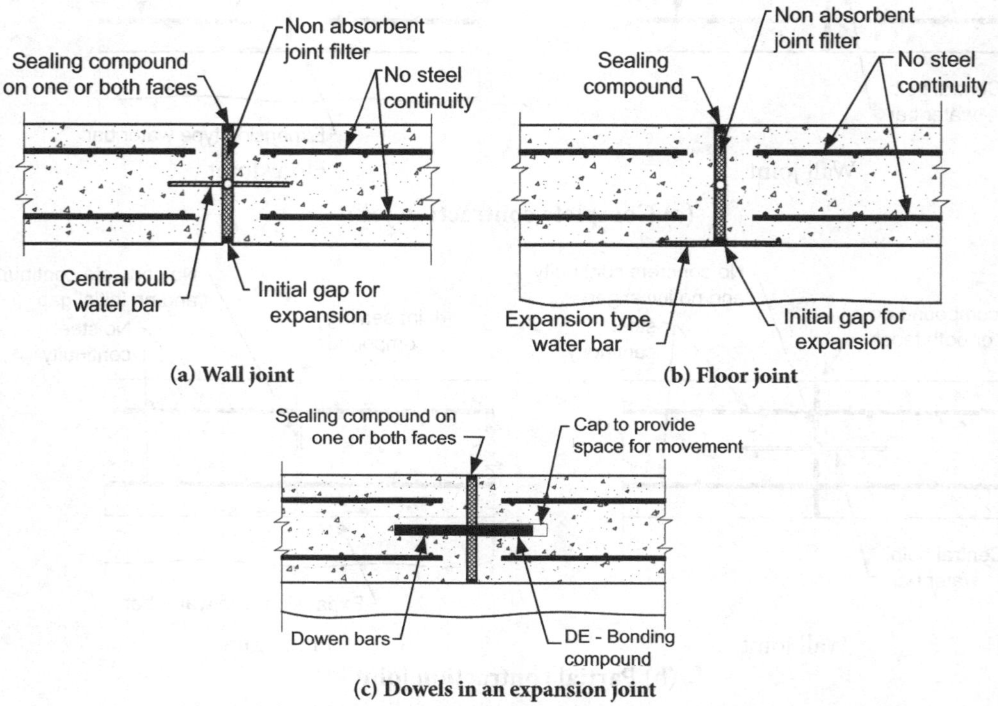


**Fig. 4.7:** Schematic diagram of expansion joints (IS 3370 Part I)

## Sliding Joint

A sliding joint is a movement joint that enables sliding motion between two structural elements. This has a complete discontinuity in both the reinforcement and the concrete, and a unique arrangement is developed to allow for relative movement at the joint location. A typical application between wall and floor in some cylindrical tank designs is detailed below in Fig. 4.8.

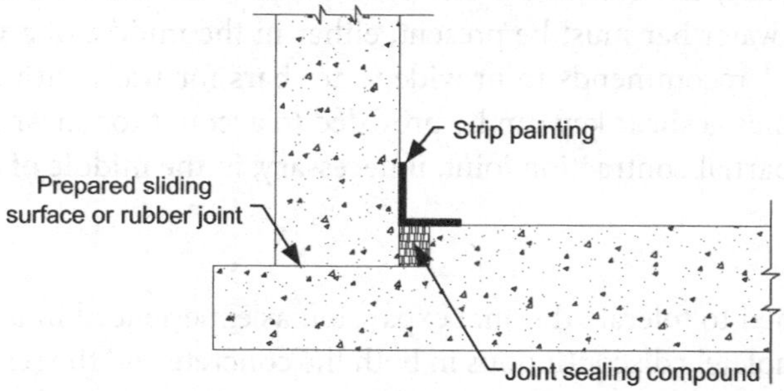


**Fig. 4.8:** Schematic diagram of a sliding joint (IS 3370 Part I)

### Construction Joints

A construction joint in a structural component, is made to achieve monolithic structural element without allowing for further relative displacement (Fig. 4.9). Before starting of construction, the designer should specify the location, where the joints should be placed at the design stage. Construction joints should be grouted, if necessary. To pour a new concrete on an old concrete surface, the precautions and steps to be taken are illustrated in section 4.4.2. At the junction of column and beam, columns are cast few centimeters below the bottom level of beams.

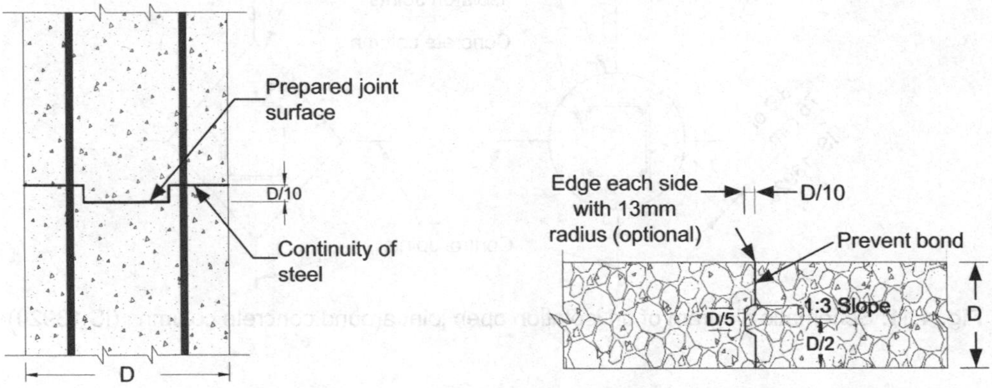


**Fig. 4.9:** Schematic diagram of a construction joint (IS 3370 Part I)

### Temporary Open Joints

A temporary open joint is a space that is momentarily created between the concrete of two adjacent structural components. After a sufficient amount of time has passed after construction, and before the structure is used, the space is duly filled with concrete, either entirely or with the addition of suitable jointing materials (Fig. 4.10). Precautions are taken to achieve water tightness after the addition of proper jointing materials. The water-tightness of the concrete must be maintained after the joints have been filled. This type of joints is generally capable of achieving a partial or full degree of contraction.

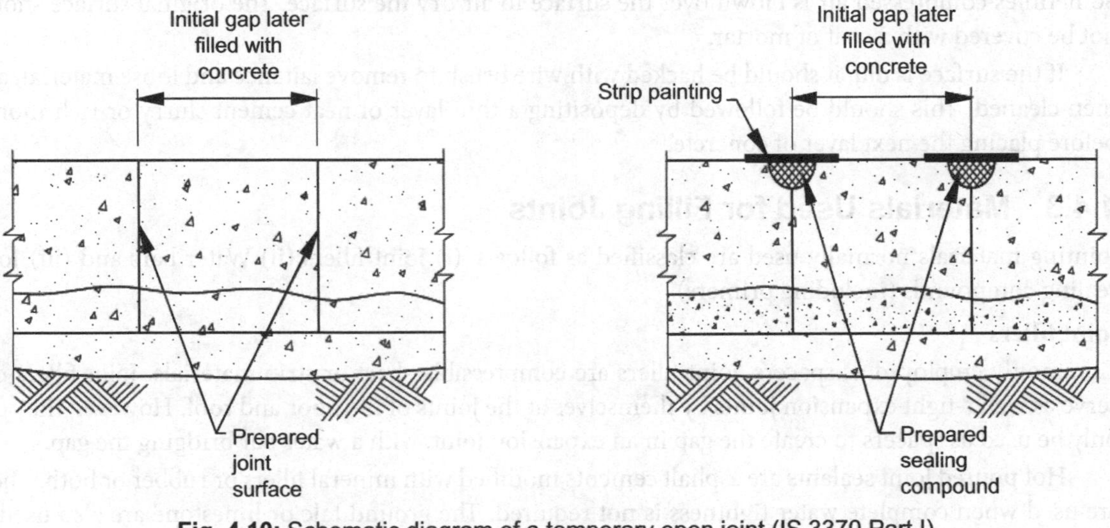


**Fig. 4.10:** Schematic diagram of a temporary open joint (IS 3370 Part I)

**Isolation Joints**

When a concrete floor meets structural elements, such as columns, walls and foundations, the movements of the concrete floor is different from those of the structural elements. Isolation joints (Fig. 4.11) are provided at these locations to ensure compatibility at these structural discontinuities. The width of the joint is usually 12-15 mm. These joints are filled with suitable joint fillers to avoid ingress of moisture or debris.

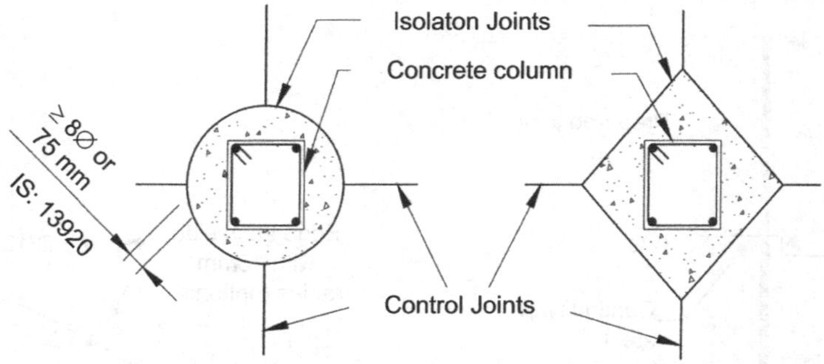


**Fig. 4.11:** Schematic diagram of an isolation open joint around concrete columns (IS 13920)

## 4.4.2 Methods for Joining Old and New Concrete

It is important to correctly connect the old concrete with the new concrete at construction joints. To strengthen the bonding and create sufficient aggregate interlock, the surface of the earlier pour needs to be adequately roughened. Applying a surface retarder right away after concreting the previous pour would be another way to ensure bonding between successive layers of concrete. The surface retarder should be applied to the form work for vertical surfaces.

If the joint surface is not roughened before the concrete is hardened, the laitance is removed by applying a jet of water. In some cases, the laitance should be removed by sand blasting or by a scrabbler. Prior to pouring fresh concrete, the joint surface needs to be cleaned and dampened for at least six hours. Sometimes compressed air is blown over the surface to air dry the surface. The original surface should not be covered with a coat of mortar.

If the surface is old, it should be hacked with wire brush to remove laitance and loose material, and then cleaned. This should be followed by depositing a thin layer of neat cement slurry or rich mortar before placing the next layer of concrete.

## 4.4.3 Materials Used for Filling Joints

Jointing materials normally used are classified as follows: (i) Joint fillers (ii) Water bars and (iii) Joint sealing compounds (including primers).

**Joint fillers**

Commonly employed as spacers, joint fillers are compressible sheet or strip materials. Joint fillers can serve as water-tight expansion joints by themselves at the joints of the floor and roof. However, they can only be used as spacers to create the gap in an expansion joint, with a water bar bridging the gap.

Hot poured joint sealants are asphalt cements modified with mineral fillers or rubber or both. These are used when complete water tightness is not required. The ground talc or limestone are also used as fillers.

**Water bars**

Water bars are prefabricated strips of impermeable material that are fully or partially implanted in the concrete during construction to span across the joint and produce a long-lasting water-tight seal throughout the entire range of joint movement. For instance, water bars can be centrally corrugated Z-shaped strips or a central longitudinal hollow tube.

Metal sheets, natural or synthetic rubbers, and plastics like polyvinyl chloride are the materials utilized to make the water bars (PVC). If the liquids kept or the environment around the liquid holding structure is not solely corrosive, then galvanized iron sheets may also be utilized with the engineer's judgement.

**Joint sealing compounds (including primers)**

Joint sealing compounds are impermeable ductile materials which are required to provide a water- tight seal by adhesion with the concrete throughout the range of joint movements. These materials are based on asphalt, bitumen or coal tar pitch with or without fillers such as limestone, slate dust, asbestos fibre, chopped hemp, rubber or other suitable material. These are usually applied after construction or just before the structure is put into service, by pouring in hot or cold state.

## UNIT SUMMARY

This unit explains concreting operations, viz., batching, mixing, transportation, casting, finishing and curing, to ensure proper quality of construction. Materials and requirements of good formwork have been briefly outlined along with their stripping time for different types of structural members based on IS 456 stipulations. Waterproofing materials and methods practised in general construction works are described in detail. Types of joints and materials used for filling the joints are discussed along with steps to ensure proper joint treatment between old concrete and new concrete.

## EXERCISES

### Multiple Choice Questions

1. The maximum content (kg/m$^3$) of ordinary Portland cement in a design mix of concrete (1 m$^3$) is
   (a) 350 (b) 400
   (c) 450 (d) 500
2. For walls, columns and vertical faces of all structural members, the form work is generally removed after __________
   (a) 16 to 24 hours (b) 3 days
   (c) 7 days (d) 14 days
3. Quality control helps to __________ the risks of overdesign that __________ the overall cost.
   (a) Maximize, Increase (b) Minimize, Increase
   (c) Maximize, Decrease (d) Minimize, Decrease

4. A construction joint is provided where
   (a) Bending moment is small
   (b) Shear force is small
   (c) A member is supported by another member
   (d) All options are correct
5. Which of the following defines concrete?
   (a) Homogenous materials mixed together
   (b) Mixture of cement, water and aggregates
   (c) Both (a) and (b)
   (d) Neither (a) nor (b)
6. Which of the following types of joints are known as movement joints?
   (a) Contraction joint
   (b) Expansion joint
   (c) Sliding joint
   (d) All of the above
7. Increasing the paste content in concrete causes an
   (a) Increase in the viscosity
   (b) Decrease in the viscosity
   (c) Increase in the static yield stress
   (d) Both (b) and (c)
8. The optimum dosage of superplasticizer with a given binder depends upon
   (a) Water/binder ratio
   (b) Type of superplasticizer used
   (c) Binder composition
   (d) All of the above
9. With regard to pumping of concrete, identify the incorrect statement
   (a) Pipe diameter should be at least 3 times maximum aggregate size
   (b) Higher water cement ratio is beneficial for pumping
   (c) A slump of 100-150 mm is recommended
   (d) Aluminium pipes can be used
10. As per the Indian standards, the maximum limit to use recycled aggregate as a replacement is ______ percentage for plain concrete.
    (a) 20
    (b) 25
    (c) 30
    (d) 35
11. The type of aggregate suggested for use in regions susceptible to acid attack is:
    (a) Calcite
    (b) Illite
    (c) Hematite
    (d) Orthoclase
12. Three identical concrete cubes (A, B and C), made with the same concrete mix, are loaded in compression to failure. The rate of loading is different for each cube, with the rate for A being lower than that for B, and that for B being lower than that for C.

    Now, which of the following statements is true in the context of strength recorded for the three cubes?
    (a) Strength of A = Strength of B = Strength of C
    (b) Strength of A < Strength of B < Strength of C
    (c) Strength of A > Strength of B > Strength of C
    (d) Information provided is not sufficient to draw any conclusion

13. Two batches (A & B) of concrete mix are designed, with the characteristic strength ($f_{ck}$) of A and B being 60 MPa and 30 MPa, respectively. If the modulus of elasticity (MOE) of batches A and B (given as $E_A$ and $E_B$, respectively) is calculated using the provisions in IS 456:2000, which of the following best represents the ratio of $E_A/E_B$?
(a) $\sqrt{2}$ (b) $1/\sqrt{2}$
(c) 2 (d) ½

14. Which of the following is not recommended for mass concreting?
(a) Use of higher coarse aggregate size
(b) Increasing the coarse aggregate content
(c) Replacing a part of cement by fly ash
(d) Use of accelerating admixtures

15. Which of the following cannot be used for underwater concrete placement?
(a) Use of concrete pumps (b) Use of Tremie Pipe
(c) Use of bottom discharge buckets (d) Shotcreting

16. *In the context of shotcreting, consider the following statements:*
Statement – 1: Shear strength of concrete has a critical role to play when shotcreting is carried out in layers.
Statement – 2: Workmanship plays a critical role in quality control of shotcreting process.
Choose the best alternative among the following:
(a) Both the statements are TRUE
(b) Statement-1 is TRUE and Statement-2 is FALSE
(c) Statement-1 is FALSE and Statement-2 is TRUE
(d) Both the statements are FALSE

17. The following figure shows the cross section of a concrete cylinder loaded along the diameter. The nature of stress at points 'A' and 'B' will be__

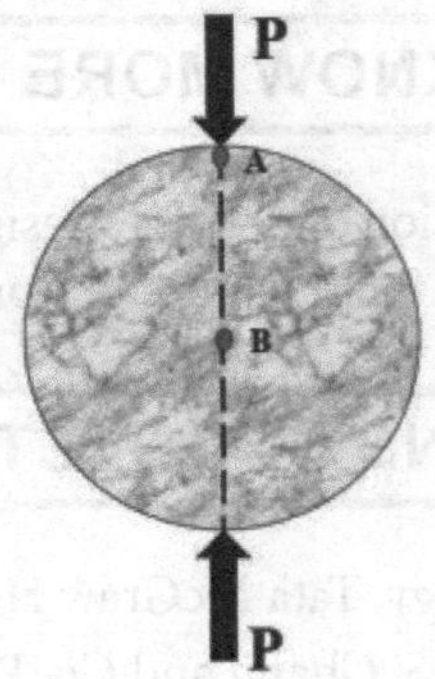


(a) Compressive at both points (b) Tensile at both points
(c) Tensile at 'B' and compressive at 'A' (d) Compressive at 'B' and tensile at 'A'

18. The optimum number of revolutions over which concrete is required to be mixed in a mixer machine is
(a) 10 (b) 25
(c) 50 (d) 100

**19.** Batching refers to
(a) Controlling the total quantity at each batch
(b) Weighing approximately, the quantity of each material for a job before mixing
(c) Controlling the quantity of each material into each batch
(d) Adjusting the water to be added in each batch according to the moisture content of the materials being mixed in the batch

**20.** What is the correct sequence of operations involved in concrete production?
(a) Batching-mixing-transportation-placing
(b) Mixing-batching-placing-transportation
(c) Transportation-placing-mixing-batching
(d) Placing-transportation-mixing-batching

**21.** Transportation of concrete mix by pumps is very convenient, particularly, in case of
(a) Tunnel-lining (b) Cement concrete pavement
(c) High-rise buildings (d) All of the above

**22.** The mix design for pavement concrete is based on the
(a) Flexural strength (b) Characteristic compressive strength
(c) Shear strength (d) Bond strength

## Answers for Multiple Choice Questions

1. (c), 2. (a), 3. (d), 4. (d), 5. (b), 6. (d), 7. (a), 8. (d), 9. (d), 10. (b), 11. (a), 12. (b)
13. (a), 14. (d), 15. (d), 16. (a), 17. (c), 18. (b), 19. (c), 20. (a), 21. (d), 22. (a)

## PRACTICAL

To be given as Unit VI

## KNOW MORE

Good concreting practice is based on provision of properly designed joints. Such joints are able to release moments at specific locations, thus making the structure less prone to damages.

## REFERENCES AND SUGGESTED READINGS

1. Gambhir, M.L., *Concrete Technology*, Tata McGraw Hill Publishing Co. Ltd., Delhi.
2. Shetty, M.S., *Concrete Technology*, S. Chand and Co. Pvt. Ltd., Ram Nagar, Delhi.
3. Santhakumar, A. R., *Concrete Technology*, Oxford University Press, New Delhi.
4. Neville, A. M. and Brooks, J.J., *Concrete Technology*, Pearson Education Pvt. Ltd.
5. Neville, A. M., *Concrete Technology*, Pearson Education Pvt. Ltd., New Delhi.
6. Sood, H., Kulkarni P. D., Mittal L. N., Laboratory Manual in *Concrete Technology*, CBS Publishers, New Delhi.
7. IS 3370 (Part 1) – 2019

# 5 Admixtures and Types of Special Concrete

## UNIT SPECIFICS

Through this unit we have discussed the following aspects:

- The description of properties and objectives of using five types of popularly used admixtures, viz., accelerating admixtures, retarding admixtures, water reducing admixtures, air entraining admixtures and super plasticizers.
- Special types of concretes, such as ready mix concrete, fibre reinforced concrete, high performance concrete, self-compacting concrete and light weight concrete, have been discussed along with their properties, advantages and limitations.
- Effect of cold and hot weather on concrete, and precautions to be taken while concreting in these weather conditions have been elaborated.

The practical applications of the topics are discussed for generating further curiosity and creativity as well as improving problem solving capacity.

Besides giving a large number of multiple choice questions as well as questions of short and long answer types marked in two categories following lower and higher order of Bloom's taxonomy, assignments through a number of numerical problems, a list of references and suggested readings are given in the unit so that one can go through them for practice. It is important to note that for getting more information on various topics of interest some QR codes have been provided in different sections which can be scanned for relevant supportive knowledge.

Based on the content, there is a "Know More" section. This section has been carefully designed so that the supplementary information provided in this part becomes beneficial for the users of the book.

## RATIONALE

The current concreting practice mostly uses admixtures to modify the properties of concrete in fresh as well as hardened state. Therefore, this unit describes five types of admixtures, viz., accelerating admixtures, retarding admixtures, water reducing admixtures, air entraining admixtures and super plasticizers. Nowadays special concretes are frequently used for specific requirements. This unit explains properties, advantages and limitations of certain special concretes, viz. ready mix concrete, fibre reinforced concrete, high performance concrete, self-compacting concrete and light weight concrete. Considering wide variability in the climatic conditions of India, it is important to understand effects of cold and hot weather on concrete. Concreting in these weather conditions requires specific precautions, which have also been elaborated in this unit

## PRE-REQUISITES

Properties of ingredients of concrete

## UNIT OUTCOMES

List of outcomes of this unit is as follows:

**U5-O1:** To understand purpose of using accelerating admixtures, retarding admixtures, water reducing admixtures, super plasticizers (high range water reducing admixtures) and air entraining admixtures.

**U5-O2:** To learn about special concretes such as ready mix concrete, fibre reinforced concrete, high performance concrete, self-compacting concrete and light weight concrete.

**U5-O3:** To understand effect of cold weather on concrete and precautions to be taken while concreting in cold weather conditions.

**U5-O4:** To understand effect of hot weather on concrete and precautions to be taken while concreting in hot weather conditions.

| Unit-5 Outcomes | EXPECTED MAPPING WITH COURSE OUTCOMES (1- Weak Correlation; 2- Medium Correlation; 3- Strong Correlation) | | | | |
|---|---|---|---|---|---|
| | CO-1 | CO-2 | CO-3 | CO-4 | CO-5 |
| U5-O1 | 1 | 1 | 3 | 2 | 3 |
| U5-O2 | 3 | 3 | 3 | 3 | 2 |
| U5-O3 | 1 | 1 | 2 | 3 | 2 |
| U5-O4 | 1 | 1 | 2 | 3 | 2 |

## 5.1 ADMIXTURES IN CONCRETE

**Introduction**

Admixtures are materials that are added to concrete to improve properties of concrete in fresh stage. These are optional ingredients which are added during mixing of basic ingredients such as cement, water and aggregates. Till a century ago, admixtures were rarely used in making concrete. However, concrete is being used in ever-evolving applications requiring it to be suitable for diverse conditions. For instance, high-rise buildings require high strength concrete to be pumped to great heights. As observed in Unit III, high strength concrete is typically marked by low water-cement ratio making it difficult to pump. Over the last century, different types of admixtures have been developed so that concrete exhibits desired properties. It is important to assess the compatibility of the admixture with cement, for which Marsh cone test is used. This also helps to determine the optimum dosage of admixture.

Depending on their composition, admixtures are broadly classified into two classes, viz. mineral admixtures and chemical admixtures. Commonly used mineral admixtures are fly ash, silica fume, slag and rice husk ash. While fly ash, silica fume and slag are industrial by-products, rice husk ash is obtained upon burning of rice husk which comes from de-husking of paddy grains. Mineral admixtures are often confused with cement additives. When the same materials are added to cement clinkers at the time of grinding, they are called cement additives. The main objective of using mineral admixture in concrete or additives in cement is to impart pozzolanic properties which lead to formation of additional cementitious gel improving durability of concrete.

On the other hand, chemical admixtures are chemical compounds added to impart desired properties to fresh concrete. Commonly used chemical admixtures are water reducing admixtures, accelerating admixtures, set retarding admixtures and air entraining admixtures. In field practice, mineral admixtures are often used as cement additives in form of blended cement such as Portland Pozzolana Cement (PPC) and Portland Slag Cement (PSC). Further, Water Reducing Admixtures (WRA) and High Range Water Reducing Admixtures (HRWRA), also known as plasticizers and superplasticizers, are the most commonly used chemical admixtures. Therefore, the term *admixtures* in practice usually implies plasticizers and/or superplasticizers. The upcoming subsections explain purpose, properties and applications of different types of chemical admixtures. This is followed by a brief outline of some commonly used mineral admixtures.

### 5.1.1 Water Reducing Admixtures

Concrete requires different degree of workability for different applications. For instance, deep beams, box girders, walls of overhead water tanks, cast in-situ piles, and sections with dense steel reinforcement such as beam-column junctions require concrete with high workability. In case of high-rise buildings and most of above cases, concrete is usually pumped and transported using pipes. At the same time, most of these constructions involve high strength concrete. From Unit III, it is clear that high strength concrete is prepared with low water-cement ratio. Therefore, in such situations, excess water cannot be added to achieve required workability. In fact, increasing workability of concrete by use of excess water should never be acceptable, as it makes concrete highly prone to segregation and bleeding.

Some of the conventional methods to obtain highly workable concrete mix are: (i) using well-graded coarse and fine aggregates, (ii) increasing size of coarse aggregates, (iii) increasing proportion of CA10 in coarse aggregates, (iv) increasing proportion of fine aggregates relative to coarse aggregates, and (v) increasing the cement content. However, each of these methods can marginally improve the workability, making highly workable concrete (with target slump over 150 mm) difficult to prepare. This problem is resolved with use of water reducing admixtures.

Water Reducing Admixtures (WRAs), also known as plasticizers, comprises of charged polymer compounds. They get adsorbed on the cement particles in the concrete mix, leading to repulsive forces between cement particles, due to zeta potential. The dispersion of cement particles makes free water available in the concrete mix, increasing its workability. The working principle of WRAs is also explained in terms of steric hindrance.

The name *water reducing admixtures* comes from the fact concrete with same desired slump (workability) requires lower water content if these admixtures are used. This reduction in water demand is usually of the order of 5% to 15% at recommended dosage of plasticizer. There are admixtures which can reduce water demand up to 30%. They are called High Range Water Reducing Admixtures (HRWRAs) or super-plasticizers. Typical recommended dosage for plasticizers and super-plasticizers is 0.5% to 2% by mass of cement or binder. Reduction in water demand upon usage of these admixtures depends on admixture make, admixture dosage and properties of cement (chemical composition, fineness and consistency). Recommendations from the manufacturer and specialist literature should be referred while designing concrete mix with these admixtures.

If WRA/HRWRA is used along with same water content, green concrete exhibits increased workability. As shown in Table 5.1, these admixtures can be used with intent of improved workability, increased strength or economical concrete mix. Values in Table 5.1 are mere indicative for example purpose, and need not get completely reflected in an actual test.

**Table 5.1:** Different purposes of water reducing admixtures

| | Cement content (kg/m3) | Water cement ratio | Water content (kg/m3) | Obtained Slump (mm) | 7-days compressive strength (MPa) | 28-days compressive strength (MPa) |
|---|---|---|---|---|---|---|
| Control mix | 300 | 0.62 | 186 | 50 | 25 | 37 |
| Mix with improved workability | 300 | 0.62 | 186 | 100 | 26 | 38 |
| Mix with increased strength | 300 | 0.56 | 168 | 50 | 34 | 46 |
| Economical mix | 270 | 0.62 | 168 | 50 | 25.5 | 37.5 |

Some of the common constituents of WRAs/plasticizers are:

(i) Anionic surfactants, such as lignosulphonates and their derivatives, and salts of sulphonates hydrocarbons.

(ii) Non-ionic surfactants, such as polyglycol esters, and acid of hydroxylated carboxylic acids.

(iii) Other products such as carbohydrates.

Super-plasticizers use different polymers as their base. Two most commonly used polymers are Sulphonated Melamine Formaldehyde Condensate and Sulphonated Naphthalene Formaldehyde Condensate.

In a later section on air-entraining admixtures, it will be evident that use of air-entraining admixtures also tends to enhance fluidity and thereby workability of the concrete mix. However, air entrainment also lowers compressive strength of concrete. Therefore, a good plasticizer/super-plasticizer should not promote air entrainment in concrete.

We have learnt that charged polymer compounds in plasticizers/super-plasticizers get adsorbed on the surface of cement particles. This hinders the hydration process. Therefore, use of plasticizers/super-plasticizers may slightly retard setting process and strength development.

## 5.1.2 Accelerating Admixtures

Accelerating admixtures accelerate the setting process and the rate of strength development in concrete during early stages. These admixtures are usually used when early strength gain is desirable. Some of the applications of accelerating admixtures are listed as follows:

(i) They are used in rapid construction of high-rise structures as lower storeys need to develop strength to expedite the construction process. This is highly relevant in urban centres where there is an urge to put a structure to service at the earliest (time is money).

(ii) They are used to lower the curing time of the concrete. This is relevant in sites where prolonged curing cannot be achieved due to scarcity of water for curing or expected poor quality control.

(iii) They are used to permit early removal of formwork, which can be reused to expedite concrete casting operations.

(iv) They are often used in cold weather concreting applications to partially compensate for slow hydration due to low temperature.

(v) These admixtures are also used in emergency repair and retrofit of structures. For instance, repair of a damaged overpass needs to be done swiftly without hindering the traffic for a long time. This would imply early stripping of formwork.

Since accelerating admixtures accelerate the hydration process, it increases the heat of hydration resulting in cracks. Therefore, these admixtures should not be used in case of hot weather and mass concreting (e.g., dams) applications.

Calcium chloride and calcium nitrite are commonly used as accelerating admixtures. However, calcium chloride has been found to be detrimental to reinforced concrete and prestressed concrete structures, as it promotes corrosion of steel reinforcement and cables. Therefore, use of calcium chloride should be restricted to plain concrete construction. On the other hand, calcium nitrite is a corrosion inhibitor. Maximum dosage of accelerating admixtures is 2% by mass of cement or binder. Some modern accelerating admixtures can even lead to setting of cement in less than 5 minutes. Such formulations are usually used in making self-compacting concrete for underwater applications.

At times, water reducing admixtures and accelerating admixtures are used together in a concrete mix. This improves the workability without retarding the strength development process. If accelerating materials such as triethanolamine chlorides, calcium nitrite and nitrates are already added to plasticizers/super-plasticizers, such admixtures are called accelerating plasticizers.

### 5.1.3 Retarding Admixtures

Retarding admixtures retard the setting process and thereby delays hardening of the concrete. Though this reduces the early strength, long-term strength is not affected. Some of the common applications of retarding admixtures are listed below.

(i) They are used in ready mix concreting applications with long haul time, to retain workability of the concrete mix.

(ii) These admixtures are usually used in hot weather applications where the hydration is already accelerated by high temperature. This is done to prevent cracking of concrete.

(iii) They are also added to concrete mix for mass structures such as dams and foundation rafts, to reduce heat of hydration and thereby prevent cracking of concrete.

(iv) These admixtures are also used to prevent formation of cold joints between two concreting sessions.

(v) They are used in applications like deep piles and tunnels where concrete is to be carried through long pipelines.

An interesting application of retarding admixture is to obtain concrete surfaces with exposed aggregate look. This is done by spraying retarding admixtures on surfaces of formwork before putting it in place, which delays hardening of surface concrete without affecting the rest of the concrete. When the formwork is removed, the unhardened matrix is washed off using water jet to achieve a surface with exposed aggregates.

Calcium sulphate is the most commonly used retarding admixture. In fact, gypsum is added to cement clinkers while grinding for the same reason, i.e., to avoid flash set of cement. Other set retarding admixtures include cellulose products, starch, sugar, soluble zinc salts and soluble borates. Retarding admixtures should be administered in required dosage carefully. For instance, adding sugar 0.05% by mass of cement delays setting time by 4 hours. However, adding sugar 2% by mass of cement completely prevents the setting.

If an admixture serves as both water reducing admixture and retarding admixture, it is called retarding plasticizer. This product is widely used in ready mix concrete industry to avoid slump loss during long haul transportation.

### 5.1.4 Air Entraining Admixtures

When air entraining admixtures is added to concrete mix, millions of air bubbles are formed in the concrete. These bubbles are non-coalescing which means they do not form groups and are uniformly distributed throughout the concrete mass. These bubbles are typically 5 microns to 80 microns in size. These bubbles act as ball-bearings and enhance workability of the concrete mix. They also make concrete less prone to segregation and bleeding. Also, concrete becomes permeable increasing its resistance to frost action and chemical attacks. However, this can affect durability of concrete exposed to harsh environmental conditions. Another less desirable effect is slight reduction in compressive strength of concrete. However, air entrained concrete can be used for non-load bearing applications such as infill walls in moment resisting framed structures. Autoclaved Aerated Concrete (AAC) blocks are commonly used for such applications.

Foaming agents such as synthetic detergents, petroleum acids, animal and vegetable fats, and natural wood resins are the most commonly used air entraining admixtures. Entrained air should not be confused with entrapped air. While entrained air bubbles are formed intentionally by use of air entraining admixtures, entrapped air bubbles get formed due to poor workmanship in concreting operations such as placing and compaction. Entrapped air bubbles are much larger in size, typically ranging between 10 microns and 1000 microns.

### 5.1.5 Mineral Admixtures

Fly ash, silica fume and slag are the most commonly used mineral admixtures in concrete. They are obtained as by-products from different industries, as reported in Table 5.2. They impart pozzolanic properties, and therefore using these mineral admixtures lead to slow early strength gain and slightly higher long-term strength due to formation of secondary cementitious products. These secondary cementitious products lead to reduced permeability and thereby impart durability to concrete against chemical attack. Rice husk ash, obtained by controlled burning of rice husk, is also sometimes used as pozzolanic material. It has specific gravity of 2 to 2.6, particle size of 1 to 10 microns and silica ($SiO_2$) content of 75% to 80%.

**Table 5.2:** Properties of commonly used mineral admixtures

| Properties | Fly ash | Silica fume | Slag |
|---|---|---|---|
| Source | Thermal power plants using pulverised coal as fuel | Ferrosilicon alloy industries | Cast iron (pig iron) industries |
| Particle size | Less than 10 microns | Around 0.1 microns | Around 10 microns (slightly larger than fly ash) |
| Specific gravity | 2.0 to 2.5 | 2.1 to 2.5 | 2.8 to 2.9 |
| Silica ($SiO_2$) content | 45% to 60% | 85% to 95% | 35% to 40% |
| Percentage replacement level by mass of cement/binder (if used as cement additive) | 20% to 25% | Less than 10% | 25% to 60% |

## 5.2 TYPES OF SPECIAL CONCRETE

**Introduction**

Due to advent of new construction chemicals, improved supplementary cementitious materials and advanced cement production technology, the construction industry nowadays use a variety of special concretes. This section introduces some of the popular special concretes and describes their properties, advantages and limitations.

Cement Concrete has to perform its intended functions for more than 75 years. It has to withstand chemical attack natural process like carbonation, abrasion of vehicles in case of pavement concrete and high differential temperature during summer and winter therefore there is a need to modify the microstructure of it to improve mechanical properties(Compressive and tensile strength), reduce permeability, increase thermal insulation. Therefore, this section describes the following special concrete such as ready-mix concrete (RMC), fibre reinforced concrete (FRC), high-performance concrete (HPC), self-compacting concrete (SCC), and lightweight concrete (LWC).

### 5.2.1 Ready-Mix Concrete

Ready-mix concrete (RMC) is produced in a batch plant, according to each specific job requirement stipulated by the user. This concrete is transported to the site in a ready-to-use form. IS 4926 describes it as the concrete mixed in a stationary mixer in a central batching and mixing plant or in a truck mixer and supplied in a fresh condition to the purchaser either at a site or into the purchaser's vehicle. The code specifies that the concrete from the truck mixer should be discharged within a maximum of 2 hours from the time of loading.

RMC was first patented in Germany in 1903. In India, it started in the 1950s and flourishing on a large scale in 1980s. Uniformity requirements of RMC includes parameters, viz., unit weight, air content, slump, coarse aggregate content, and average compressive strength. The IS 4926 stipulates one sample per 50 m$^3$ of concrete or every 50 batches, whichever has a larger frequency.

**Types of Ready-Mix Concrete**

Based on the mixing of the different ingredients, there are three types of ready mix concrete (RMC).

**Transit mix concrete**

All the basic ingredients of the concrete including water are fed directly into the truck mixer. During the loading of the material, the mixer drum is made to revolve faster than the normal charging speed. Also, transit mix concrete can be of three types as

(i) **Concrete mixed at site:** In this case, during transportation towards the site, the drum is revolved at a slow speed of about 2 rpm. As soon as it arrives the site, prior to discharging the mix, a maximum speed of 12 to 15 rpm for nearly 70 to 100 revolution is attained to ensure homogeneous mixing.

(ii) **Concrete mixed in transit:** The drum speed is kept medium during the transit time (about 8 rpm for about 70 revolutions). After about 70 revolutions, the revolution speed is slowed down to a speed of 2 rpm only till discharging the concrete.

(iii) **Concrete mixed in the yard:** The drum is revolved at high-speed of 12 to 15 rpm, with all the ingredients, for about 50 revolutions in the RMC plant yard. The concrete is then transported with slow revolution throughout the transit time.

**Shrink mix concrete**

Such concrete is partially mixed in the mixer located at the RMC plant. Thereafter, the remaining mixing is carried out in drum mixer mounted on the truck. The extent of mixing, required in the transit mixer, is dependent on the mixing already done in the central mixing plant. A set of tests are usually carried out to ascertain the requirement of mixing in the drum mixer mounted on the truck.

**Central-mix concrete**

Initially, such concrete is thoroughly mixed in the RMC plant, also called a central batching plant. Then the well-mixed concrete is loaded into the truck mixer. During the transit, the truck mixer performs the task of agitation only. At times, when the green concrete is of low workability, or the site is quite close to the RMC plant, non-agitating units or dump trucks may also be employed.

**Advantages of Ready-Mix Concrete**

1. The concrete produced by RMC plants has a uniform and assured standard quality. Stringent quality control through testing of materials, standardized process parameters and continuous monitoring of key practices ensure production of such a durable concrete.
2. Mechanized operations ensure faster construction practices. The output of a RMC plant is 10 to 12 times greater than that of site mix concrete plant.
3. Proper handling and mixing practices save the cement consumption by about 12%.
4. Air pollution, caused by cement particles and dust from aggregates, decreases as ready mix concrete make use of bulk concrete.
5. More durable structure with longer service life can be constructed using RMC.
6. As human resources used in RMC plants are lesser, the chance of human errors is reduced.
7. As concrete is procured directly from RMC plants, no space is required for storing raw materials at site.
8. In RMC, as materials are stored and used in bulk quantities, wastage of material is reduced.

**Limitations of Ready-Mix Concrete**

1. In case, the job site is far from the RMC plant, transit time being high, significant loss in workability occurs. This will require additional water or admixtures to maintain the target workability. It is important to check the slump value of concrete before pouring it into the formwork.
2. Traffic jams on the way to site may result into early setting of concrete in the transport vehicle only. This will deteriorate the quality of construction. So, addition of admixtures is recommended to delay the setting period, which in turn increases the cost of production.

### 5.2.2 Fibre Reinforced Concrete

Fibre Reinforced Concrete is a composite material impregnated additionally with fibrous material. Discrete uniformly dispersed suitable fibres are added to concrete to increase its structural integrity in terms of its tensile resistance, and toughness. The fibres control cracking due to plastic shrinkage and to drying shrinkage. Thus reduced micro-cracks results in reduction of the permeability of concrete. Also, the fibres get interlocked and entangled around aggregate particles. This reduce the workability but increases resistance to segregation.

There are many types of Fibre-Reinforced Concrete currently practised in India, viz., steel Fibre reinforced concrete, glass fibre reinforced concrete, Slurry Infiltrated Fibre Concrete (SIFCON), and slurry infiltrated (fibre) mat concrete (SIMCON).

### Steel-Fibre Reinforced Concrete

Steel fibre is a metal reinforcement usually round in shape, diameter ranging from 0.25 to 0.75 mm. The rectangular cross section, obtained by slitting the sheets of 0.15 to 0.41 mm thickness and 0.25 to 0.90 mm width, are also used. The aspect ratio of fibres, the ratio of length to diameter, vary from 30 to 250.

A small amount of steel fibre in concrete increases resistance to cracking, impact, fatigue, flexural tensile strength and durability. SFRC is commonly used in construction of flooring, precast applications such as manhole covers, concrete pipes, machine foundations, inner lining of tunneling such as fibre shotcrete, refractory concrete, heavy-duty concrete pavements in highways and airfields, hydraulic structures with resistance to cavitation or erosion damage.

### Polypropylene Fibre Reinforced (PFR) Concrete

Polypropylene fibre is a synthetic fibre used in concrete to control cracking due to plastic and drying shrinkage. It increases the impact strength of concrete. These fibres are claimed to reduce the permeability of concrete.

The other synthetic fibres used in concrete are acrylic, aramid, polyester, polyethylene and polyvinyl alcohol. Synthetic fibres are either from textile or petrochemical industry. Asbestos mixed with Portland cement, called asbestos cement, has high flexural strength

Such fibres belong to the group of poly olefins, are partially crystalline and non-polar, harder, resistant to acids, alkalies, organic solvents and more heat resistant than polyethylene. It is a white rugged material manufactured from propylene gas with a catalyst titanium chloride.

### Glass Fibre Reinforced Concrete

Glass fibre reinforced concrete consists of numerous extremely fine fibres of glass. It has high tensile strength 1020-4080 N/mm$^2$. Glass fibre is not as rigid as carbon fibre, but cheaper and significantly less brittle. Glass fibres are used as a reinforcing element to form a strong and lightweight fibre-reinforced polymer (FRP) composite material. CEM-FIL, trade name of a fibre, is an alkali resistant variety with improved durability.

### Carbon fibres

This type of fibre, composed mainly of carbon atoms, has low density but high tensile strength and Young's modulus. The cement fibre composite also has significantly high modulus of elasticity and flexural tensile strength. Also, it has a low thermal expansion, high chemical resistance, and a high temperature tolerance.

### Factors affecting properties of FRC

The factors affecting FRC are descried briefly in this section.

#### Relative fibre matrix stiffness

Modulus of elasticity and tensile strength of fibres affect the tensile strength of FRC. Certain low modulus fibres, such as polypropylene and nylon, increase the toughness and resistance to impact. High modulus fibres (steel, glass and carbon type) increases strength and stiffness of the FRC.

#### Volume of fibres

Normally with the increase in fibre content the tensile strength and toughness of FRC increases. However, beyond certain percentage, the segregation and harshness of concrete and mortar take place.

#### Aspect ratio of fibres

Research on varying aspect ratio shows that increase of aspect ratio upto 75 helps in increased ultimate strength of concrete. However beyond that, the strength as well as toughness decreases.

| Aspect ratio | Relative strength | Relative toughness |
|---|---|---|
| 0 | 1.00 | 1.0 |
| 25 | 1.50 | 2.0 |
| 50 | 1.60 | 8.0 |
| 75 | 1.70 | 10.5 |
| 100 | 1.50 | 8.5 |

The other factors such as orientation of fibres, workability and compaction of concrete, size of coarse aggregates mixing procedure also affect the properties of the FRC. A steel fibre content higher than 2% by volume and aspect ratio more than 100 may result in balling mechanism, where all the fibres accumulate at one place. This results in low strength and should be carefully avoided.

**Limitations of Fibre-reinforced concrete**

(i) A fibre-reinforced concrete can adversely affect workability, especially in the case of steel fibre-reinforced concrete.

(ii) Uniform distribution of fibres throughout concrete may be affected by the danger of fibres balling during mixing.

(iii) Fibre-reinforced concrete is heavier than non-fibre concrete. Steel fibres may increase the danger of corrosion.

(iv) Fibre-reinforced concrete is more expensive than ordinary concrete.

### 5.2.3 High Performance Concrete

High performance concrete (HPC) is a substantially durable concrete having certain characteristics which will be maintained during its design time.

High-performance concrete characteristics are developed for particular applications and environments. The American Concrete Committee on HPC includes the following six criteria:

(i) Ease of placement and compaction without segregation,

(ii) Long term mechanical properties,

(iii) Early-age strength,

(iv) Toughness,

(v) Long life in severe environments, i.e., durability

(vi) High Performance Concrete for Highway application on the subsequent strength, durability, and w/c ratio criteria.

High strength concrete may not be necessarily a high performance concrete. HPC should possess high modulus of elasticity, high density, low permeability and high resistance to some forms of attack.

Normally HPC has water cement ratio between 0.35 to 0.40, achieved by addition of high range water reducing admixtures. Very high performance concrete is obtained by keeping water cement ratio below 0.35. All components of concrete have high quality. It also uses ultra fines, such as, silica fume, rice husk ash. The maximum nominal size of aggregates sizes are kept between 10-12 mm. Ultra-High Performance Concrete (UHPC) is a cementitious concrete material that has a minimum specified compressive strength of 150 MPa with assured level of durability, tensile strength and toughness requirements; fibres are generally included to achieve specified requirements. Slurry infiltrated fibre concrete (SIFCON) and slurry infiltrated (fibre) mat concrete (SIMCON) are some examples of the UHPC. Such a concrete has

50 times higher fracture energy than M30 grade concrete. Also they are lightweight, having half the weight and volume of NSC elements. They are used to have precast structural elements.

**Limitations of HPC**

A strict regime of quality control has to be ensured during production of this type of concrete. Unit production cost of the high performance concrete is generally higher compared to normal concrete as admixtures and high-quality special constituent materials are used. It needs trained and skilled manpower to manufactured and proper placement into the formwork of concrete elements.

### 5.2.4 Self-Compacting Concrete

Self-compacting or super-workable concrete was first developed in University of Tokyo, Japan in the year 1980. It is also regarded as a type of high-performance concrete. It can be placed in places of highly congested reinforcement and compacted under its own weight without any vibration. It has excellent deformability, and cohesiveness showing no segregation or bleeding. It consists of a higher amount of fine materials like fly ash, limestone filler. By using a synthetic high-range water reducing admixture (polycarboxylate ethers), the yield stress of the mix is lowered. Also, the viscosity of the mix is increased by addition of viscosity modifying admixtures (VMA). Such a mix is being increasingly used in bridges, tunnels, buildings.

There are three types of SCC, viz., powder type SCC, Stabilizer or VMA-type SCC and Combination type. They are chosen based on the construction requirements. Powder type SCC is made by increasing the powder content (finely ground fly ash, GGBS, stone powder) in the mix. It has reduced coarse aggregate content and increased high range water reducing (HRWR) admixtures. The VMA type SCC has fines content almost equivalent to conventionally vibrated concrete, but it viscosity modifying admixtures (naturally occurring cellulose, glenium stream 2, micro- and nano-silica) in place of HRWR admixtures.

**Materials Used for Self-Compacting Concrete**

Well graded, either round or cubical-shaped, aggregates are preferred for SCC with size to 20 mm. The fine aggregates used in SCC can be either natural or manufactured (M- Sand) with a uniform grade. The particles finer than 0.150 mm are generally considered as fines. To achieve optimum deformability as well as stability simultaneously, the fines content should be between 520 to 560 kg/m$^3$.

The mineral admixtures are selected based on the specific properties of the mix required. Mineral admixtures should be tested through laboratory experiments before the use. Addition of ground granulated blast-furnace slag (GGBS) enhances the rheological properties of the self-compacting concrete. The finer fly ash particles fill the internal concrete pores producing a dense impermeable matrix. Thus, it decreases permeability and increases the durability of structures. Silica fumes helps to increase the mechanical properties of the self-compacting concrete structure.

New generation superplasticizers (poly-carboxylate ethers or similar) are commonly used in SCC mix design. In order to improve the freeze and thaw resistance of the concrete structure, air entraining agents are used. To control the setting time, retarders are employed.

**Properties of self-compaction concrete**

Three properties of SCC in the fresh state are (i) Filling Ability Tests (ii) Passing Ability Tests (iii) Segregation Resistance Test. Filling ability is the fresh concrete property to flow into and fill the formwork easily and under self-weight. Hence it has to justify its name as self-compacting concrete. Passing ability refers to its property which enables it to pass through congested reinforcing bars without being blocked. To achieve this SCC normally uses maximum size of aggregate as 12.5 mm and percentage of overall aggregate content is lower than normal concrete (Fig. 5.1). Also SCC has to resistant to segregation during flowing and placing. Addition of VMA increases the segregation resistance.

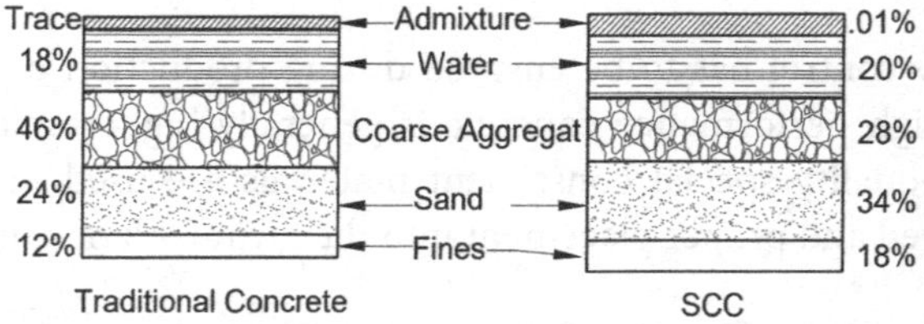


**Fig. 5.1:** Comparison of constituents of normal and self compacting concrete

The tests are conducted on self-compacting concrete to assess the above properties are satisfactory or not. Table 5.3 lists the most popular tests on it.

**Table 5.3:** Tests to assess properties of self-compacting concrete

| Property | Tests | Units for expressing test results | Range of values |
|---|---|---|---|
| Flowing Ability | V-funnel test | Sec | 8-12 |
| | $T_{50\ cm}$ slump flow test | Sec | 2-5 |
| | Orimet Test | Sec | 0-5 |
| Passing ability | J-ring test | mm | 0-10 |
| | L-Box test | $h_2/h_1$ | 0.8-1.0 |
| | U-box test | $(h_2-h_1)$ mm | 0-30 |
| | Fill Box-test | % | 90-100 |
| Segregation resistance | GTM screen ability test | % | 0-15 |
| | V-funnel as $T_{5\ min}$ test | Sec | 0 to +3 |

**Advantages of self-compaction concrete**

The main advantages of self-compacting concrete are: (i) The permeability of the concrete structure, when SCC is used, is decreased, (ii) The SCC construction is faster, and the problems associated with vibration and resulting noise production are eliminated, (iii) The concrete is placed with ease by itself and thus results in saving of labour cost, (iv) The overall durability and reliability of the concrete structure is high compared to normal concrete structures.

**Limitations of self-compaction concrete**

SCC construction faces the following limitations:

1. There is no globally accepted set of standard tests and mix design for SCC
2. The construction cost of SCC is lower by 10-15% than the conventional concrete.
3. The use of designed SCC mix require more number of trial batches and laboratory tests to ensure achievement of specified properties.
4. The procedure to monitor quality of production must be precise along with stringent ingredient material selection.

**Some major constructions using self-compaction concrete**

In India some major projects using SCC are Bandra-Worli sea link project, Mumbai; Delhi metro project, Delhi; Tarapur nuclear Power plant, Maharashtra; Kaiga Nuclear Power Project, Karnataka); Kota Atomic Power project, Rajasthan; The Signature Bridge on river Yamuna, New Delhi.

## 5.2.5 Light Weight Concrete

Lightweight concrete (LWC), especially one of its variant, Autoclaved aerated concrete (AAC) blocks have become a commonly used construction material nowadays. As per BS EN 206-1, lightweight concrete may be defined by as having an oven-dry density of between 800 kg/m³ and 2000 kg/m³ by replacing dense natural aggregates either wholly or partially with lightweight aggregates. The LWC reduces dead load of the structure, hence saves money, manpower and provide thermal insulation in certain cases.

Lightweight concrete can be classified according to its density of concrete. In terms of strength, three types of LWC are (i) low-strength concretes (0.5–3.5 MPa), (ii) moderate-strength concretes (3.5–15 MPa) and (iii) structural concretes (> 15 MPa). The density of these concretes ranges between 300–800 kg/m³, 800–1350 kg/m³ and 1350–1920 kg/m³ respectively.

The basic principle behind the making of lightweight concrete is by inducing the air in coarse aggregate as well in concrete. Several methods adopted are (i) conventional aggregates in the concrete can be replaced by cellular porous aggregates, also known as Lightweight aggregate concrete, (ii) The air bubbles can be introduced in concrete, also known as aerated concrete, (iii) During the preparation of concrete, when sand is omitted, is called no- fines concrete.

### *Types of Lightweight Concrete*

**Lightweight Aggregate Concrete**

Lightweight aggregate concrete can be obtained with density 25 to 40 % lower than normal weight concrete using (LWA). The shrinkage rate for lightweight aggregate concrete is 1.4 to 2 times higher compared to normal weight concrete (Clarke, 2002). Two major sources of light weight aggregates are described below:

- **Light weight aggregates from natural raw material**

  Light weight aggregates can be obtained by expansion (bloating) or agglomeration process applied to naturally occurring materials, viz., clay, shale, slate, perlite and exfoliated vermiculite, according to the specific need. The material is heated to fusion temperature, about 1400°C, making it in plastic state, where gas forms and get entrapped simultaneously. The sulphide and carbon compounds decompose and produce gases. Removal of carbon dioxide from carbonates and oxygen from $Fe_2O_3$ also may be another source of gases. The most common natural lightweight aggregate are Pumice, Scoria, Diatomite, Sawdust, Rice husk, and volcanic cinders.

  Pumice and diatomite are also naturally occurring aggregates. They possess variable properties, hence should be tested properly before using in the construction. Pumice is chemically inert with 75% silica content. In cold water environment, semi-consolidated sedimentary deposit is formed, known as diatomite.

- **Light weight aggregates from industrial by-products**

  The fly ash, from thermal power plants, is mixed with water and coal slurry, and then the mixture is fed into pelletizers (rotating pans) to form spherical pellets. The green pellets are sintered at 1400°C, to attain sufficient strength and thereafter, screened and graded. Foamed blast furnace slag is another by-product of iron industry produced by introducing steam into molten material. It is angular in shape, rough irregular glassy in texture and possess round shaped voids.

### No-Fines Concrete

In no-fines concrete, fine aggregates are generally omitted. The materials used consist on only cement, coarse aggregates and water. Use of only coarse aggregates results in larger voids in concrete, making it lightweight. It is recommended to use the coarse aggregates of same size (single sized aggregates) rather than well- graded aggregates. Due to this reason, the density of the concrete will be lesser because of voids. Density as low as 640 kg/m$^3$ can be achieved by using lighter coarse aggregates.

The strength of this concrete, in general, depends on the cement content in the concrete. In such concrete, shrinkage takes place rapidly than conventional concrete. This type of concrete has excellent architectural appearance.

### Aerated Concrete

Aerated concrete is made by introducing air or gas into a slurry composed of Portland cement or lime and finely crushed siliceous filler. While setting and hardening, a uniform cellular structure is formed. A common product of aerated concrete in India is Siporex. The ways to manufacture aerated concrete are (i) By forming gas through specifically designed chemical reaction within the mass during liquid or plastic state, (ii) By mixing preformed stable foam with the slurry, (iii) By using finely powdered metal (usually aluminium powder) with the slurry, it reacts with the calcium hydroxide from the hydration process giving out hydrogen gas. This hydrogen gas when contained in the slurry mix, gives the cellular structure.

Aerated or foamed concrete exhibits improved thermal insulation and they are self-compacting. This makes it ideal for use in difficult to reach spaces and sewer systems.

### Design Mix of Lightweight Concrete

- During the preparation of design mix of lightweight concrete, water- cement ratio of the concrete is determined by trial mixing. It is due to variable water absorption by aggregates.
- Pre-saturation of aggregates should be carried out to avoid excessive absorption of water. Concrete having saturated aggregates possess higher density. However, saturated aggregates are harmful in concrete prone to freezing & thawing action.
- Aggregates are coated with bitumen or water repellent coats to overcome the water absorption problem.

### Properties of Lightweight Concrete

Light weight concrete has the characteristics, such as low density, higher strength to density ratio. The tensile strength of aerated cellular concrete is 15-20% of the compressive strength. The thermal insulation, fire resistance, sound insulation reparability and overall economy is higher than normal weight. Aerated concrete is slightly alkaline. This low alkalinity and higher porosity makes it more prone to rusting compared to normal weight concrete.

### Advantages of Lightweight Concrete

Several merits have been described in the properties above. This type of concrete is easy to handle because of its lightweight. Its cost of transportation and handling is lower. It has improved the workability, and better resistance to freezing & thawing action. The light weight concrete utilizes industrial wastes such as fly ash, clinkers, slag and as such adds to sustainable development.

### Limitations of Lightweight Concrete

Lightweight concrete is generally very sensitive with water content in the mixture. It requires skilled labourers for proper workmanship. In some cases, the aggregates may float on the surface of cement mortar. Lightweight Concrete are porous hence lesser durable, and its mixing time is comparatively longer than conventional concrete.

**Applications of Lightweight Concrete**

It is used in the construction of roof slabs, and load bearing walls of small houses. It is also used in the construction of stairs. In tall buildings, this is used in the construction of partition walls. These are moulded in the form of slabs and used as thermal insulators inside the building.

## 5.3 COLD WEATHER CONCRETING

**Introduction**

Some parts of India experience cold climatic conditions. Cold weather conditions lead to delay in setting and hardening of concrete. If the ambient temperature falls below 0°C, mixing water can freeze to form ice lenses and adequate mixing may not be achieved. This section outlines effects of cold weather on concrete and precautionary measures that should be taken. The ideal temperature range of concrete for casting structural members is 15°C to 25°C. If the atmospheric temperature falls below 5°C, concreting is called cold weather concreting.

### 5.3.1 Effect of Cold Weather on Concrete

Cold weather affects concrete in a variety of ways. Some important effects are outlined below:

(i) Poor rate of strength development: Low temperature leads to slow rate of hydration of cement. This leads to delayed setting and hardening of concrete. This leads to poor rate of strength development in concrete.

(ii) Susceptibility to frost attack: As concrete remains plastic for longer time owing to delayed setting, it becomes prone to frost attack.

(iii) Slow construction: Due to delayed setting of concrete, removal of formwork may not be possible as scheduled by IS 456 (outlined in Section 4.2 of this book). The formwork cannot therefore be reused frequently enough, which leads to slower pace of construction.

(iv) Freezing of concrete at early stage: If ambient temperature goes below 0°C, free water in green concrete freezes. Apart from hindering the hydration process, it also leads to expansion of concrete volume as ice occupies more volume than water. This leads to improper compaction and thereby irreparable loss of strength and quality of concrete.

(v) Freezing and thawing: Due to variation of temperature across freezing point of water, concrete is subjected to freeze-thaw cycles. These cycles subject concrete to undesirable stresses, leading to poor durability of concrete. If freeze-thaw cycle occurs during the plastic stage of concrete, there can be loss of up to 50% in compressive strength of concrete.

If the ambient temperature is low (but above freezing point of water) at time of concreting as well as during and after hardening of concrete, there is no effect other than slow strength development. Though, the strength development is slow, the C-S-H gel structure developed at temperature around 10°C is superior to that obtained at usual temperature of 27°C.

If the ambient temperature is low (but above freezing point of water) at time of concreting but it falls below freezing point of water while concrete is still plastic, it leads to formation of large ice lenses in the concrete. This hampers the hydration process and also leaves behind cavities once these ice lenses melt. This leads to very poor structural integrity of the concrete mass and poor durability of the concrete structure.

If the ambient temperature is low (but above freezing point of water) at time of concreting, stays low till concrete hardens and attains reasonable strength and then falls below freezing point of water, most of the water has already been consumed in hydration and/or evaporation. As a result, only microscopic ice lenses are formed and structural integrity of the concrete mass remains largely unaffected. Therefore, freeze-thaw cycles at a later stage is less harmful than those during initial hardening of concrete.

If the ambient temperature is below freezing point of water at the time of concreting, one needs to ensure that water remains in liquid state during mixing and the green concrete does not get frozen. From the above discussion, it can be concluded that fresh concrete should not be subjected to freezing conditions until it attains a reasonable degree of hardness characterised by certain amount of strength (usually 5 to 7 MPa).

### 5.3.2 Precautions to be Taken While Concreting in Cold Weather Conditions

Certain precautions need to be taken while concreting in cold weather conditions to obtain good quality concrete mass and thereby durable concrete structures.

**Selection and treatment of ingredients of concrete:**

(i) **Cement:** In order to expedite the hydration process, Rapid Hardening Portland Cement (RHPC) should be used. Such cements are characterised by large proportion of $C_3S$ compared to $C_2S$. In case of extremely low ambient temperature, high alumina cement (cement with high $C_3A$ content) should be used.

(ii) **Preheating of ingredients:** Ingredients of concrete can be preheated so that concrete mix has a temperature suitable for hydration and setting. Heating of water is the easiest and most adopted strategy. However, mixing water should not have a temperature above 65°C, to prevent cement from undergoing flash set. If the ambient temperature is too low, heating of water alone cannot bring the mix to a suitable temperature range. In such cases, aggregates are also heated. While coarse aggregates are usually heated by injecting steam into the stock piles, fine aggregates are heated on plates being heated from underneath. Overheating of aggregates should be avoided. It should also be noted that cement should never be heated.

**Suitable concreting practices:**

(i) If the heat of hydration is prevented from being lost to the atmosphere, effect of low temperature on concrete can be compensated. The heat of hydration is conserved within the concrete mass by insulating the concrete with a membrane, saw dust or hessian cloth.

(ii) Formwork should not be stripped off for a considerable time to preserve the heat of hydration. Keeping formwork intact also maintains suitable temperature in the concrete mass.

(iii) The concrete mass can be heated electrically to maintain the temperature during hardening. Concrete temperature should be ensured above the freezing point of water till it achieves certain compressive strength (5 to 7 MPa). Heating mechanism should be designed carefully to avoid loss of mixing water due to evaporation. This can be met by covering the entire surface with vapour tight membranes.

(iv) Steam curing is preferred over moist curing in cold climatic regions. This is because there is hardly any loss of mixing water due to evaporation.

(v) Accelerating admixtures should be used to accelerate setting and hardening of concrete. This can reduce the time up to which necessary precautionary measures are to be taken.

(vi) Air entraining admixtures can be used to entrain millions of microscopic air bubbles in the concrete mass. Though slightly weaker in strength, air entrained concrete is resistant to freeze-thaw cycles compared to regular concrete, resulting into improved durability.

(vii) Wind shields should be placed around batching and mixing plants to ensure suitable temperature of the ingredients.

(viii) Upon placing the concrete, it should be immediately covered with membrane to prevent quick cooling action.

(ix) The subgrade should be cleared of ice, snow and frost and temperature of the subgrade should be increased if possible. This leads to good strength development in concrete and also good bond between concrete and subgrade.

(x) A record of daily ambient temperature should be maintained. Temperature of ingredients before mixing, and concrete upon mixing, at the time of placing and during early stages of hydration should also be recorded.

## 5.4 HOT WEATHER CONCRETING

**Introduction**

While states like Rajasthan has hot and arid climate, coastal states usually have hot and humid climatic conditions. High temperature leads to rapid hydration of cement and quick setting of concrete. In dry weather conditions, there is also a significant loss of mixing water due to evaporation. This section describes how hot weather affects concrete and the precautions that should be taken while concreting in such conditions. When concreting is done in a location with atmospheric temperature exceeding 40°C, it is called hot weather concreting.

### 5.4.1 Effect of Hot Weather on Concrete

The extent to which hot weather affects concrete depends on ambient temperature, relative humidity and properties of concrete. The important effects can be summarized as follows:

(i) **Loss of workability:** Green concrete tends to lose its workability due to evaporation of water. If evaporation is uncontrolled, concrete exhibits large voids leading to poor durability.

(ii) **High heat of hydration and associated cracking:** High temperature leads to rapid hydration of cement, which results in high heat of hydration. This leads to cracking of concrete, especially in case of mass concrete structures, such as dams and raft foundations.

(iii) **Poor C-S-H gel structure in concrete:** Though rapid hydration of cement leads to high early strength gain, the resulting C-S-H gel structure in concrete is of poor quality. This can result in marginal loss of long-term strength.

(iv) **Less time available for early stage operations:** Rapid hydration of cement and increased evaporation of water leads to early stiffening and setting of concrete. This leaves lesser time for workmen to perform concreting operations.

(v) **Increased plastic shrinkage and associated cracking:** Due to low relative humidity in hot and dry climate, the rate of evaporation of water from concrete surface is higher than the rate of movement of capillary water from interior to surface. This causes a moisture gradient in the concrete section, leading to increased plastic shrinkage. Increase in plastic shrinkage leads to excessive shrinkage cracks in concrete. This is prominent in case of thin structural members such as slabs.

(vi) **Difficult and expensive curing process:** Hot weather mandates huge demand of water for curing, making the curing process difficult and expensive. This is particularly true if Ordinary Portland Cement (OPC) of 53 grade is used.

(vii) **Poor bond between pavement and subgrade:** In hot weather, the subgrade layer below the concrete pavement tends to absorb water from the fresh concrete. This may lead to severe loss of water required for hydration and workability. This results in poor quality contact between pavement and subgrade.

These effects are detrimental to strength and durability of concrete, which may render structure not adequately functional throughout its design life.

### 5.4.2 Precautions to be Taken While Concreting in Hot Weather Conditions

In order to achieve good quality concrete in hot weather conditions, one needs to adhere to certain precautions.

**Selection of suitable ingredients of concrete:**

(i) **Cement:** In order to lower heat of hydration and thereby prevent excessive cracking of concrete, blended cements such as Portland Pozzolana Cement (PPC) and Portland Slag Cement (PSC) should be used. In case of very high temperatures, say around and above 50°C, Low Heat Portland Cement (LHPC) should be used. LHPC is usually characterised by large proportion of $C_2S$ compared to $C_3S$.

(ii) **Aggregates:** Cold water should be sprinkled over the stockpile of aggregates to keep them cool and their surfaces saturated. This will inhibit water absorption from the cement matrix, which can be harmful considering rapid evaporation. Further, aggregates should be stockpiled indoors.

(iii) **Water:** Temperature of mixing water affects concreting in hot weather more than that of any other ingredient. Cold mixing water with temperature around 5°C should be preferably used in hot weather concreting. If the ambient temperature is very high, crushed ice should also be added as part of mixing water. In such cases, complete melting of ice should be ensured to obtain a good quality mix.

**Practice of suitable early stage operations:**

(i) Different ingredients of concrete should be kept as cool as possible so as to produce concrete with temperature below 40°C. For mass concrete structures, the temperature of concrete should be restricted much below 40°C.

(ii) Formwork should be sprinkled with cold water to avoid water absorption by formwork material. Though metal formwork does not absorb water, timber formwork protects concrete from hot weather. Therefore, timber formwork with damp internal surfaces are preferred in hot weather conditions.

(iii) Any reinforcement projecting out of concrete and anchorage used for post-tensioning should be covered. Exposed steel can quickly increase the temperature of core concrete in its contact.

(iv) Water should be sprinkled on soil and subgrade before laying foundations and pavements to prevent water absorption by subgrade. A layer of lean concrete can also be helpful. However, concrete should be cast immediately after laying lean concrete layer to avoid formation of cold joint.

(v) Concrete is placed in comparatively thin layers to reduce the time interval between successive lifts. However, if these layers are extremely thin, they tend to lose mixing water quickly. Therefore, it is important to choose thickness of layers prudently.

(vi) Upon casting of concrete members, the exposed surface should be immediately covered with wet jute bags or hessian cloth. This will prevent excessive loss of water to evaporation.

(vii) Wet or moist curing should be initiated at the earliest possible time. Wetness in the cover (jute bags or hessian cloth) should be ensured till curing is commenced. For slabs, ponding is the most effective curing technique. Beams and columns should be covered with wet covers and water should be sprayed regularly.

(viii) In hot weather conditions, it is advisable to perform concreting operations in the evening so that green concrete is not exposed to very high day temperature.

(ix) A record of ambient temperature and relative humidity should be maintained. Temperature of concrete upon mixing, at the time of placing and during early stages of hydration should also be recorded.

## UNIT SUMMARY

Admixtures are used to improve specific properties of fresh and hardened concrete. Accelerating admixtures, retarding admixtures, water reducing admixtures, air entraining admixtures and super plasticizers have been described. Special types of concretes, their properties, advantages, limitations and their applications have been illustrated in details. Effects of cold and hot weather on concrete, and precautions to be taken while concreting in cold and hot weather conditions have been elaborated.

## EXERCISES

### Multiple Choice Questions

**1.** Which of the following statement(s) is/are true for an admixture used in concrete

(I) Improve impermeability
(II) Accelerate initial setting time
(III) Retards initial setting time
(IV) Increase the strength
(V) Increase durability

(a) I, II, IV, V (b) I, III, IV, V
(c) I, II, V (d) All statements are true

**2.** An accelerator shortens all except

(a) Setting time (b) Period of curing
(c) Period of removal of formwork (d) Strength of concrete

**3.** Identify the correct accelerator and retarder pair

(a) $CaCl_2$ and $CaSO_4$ (b) NaCl and $CaCl_2$
(c) NaOH and KOH (d) KOH and NaOH

4. **Addition of pozzolanic admixtures results in**
   (a) Improved workability
   (b) Reduction in heat of hydration
   (c) Increased resistance to sulphate attack
   (d) All of the above
5. **Which of the following can be used for waterproofing?**
   (a) Potash soaps
   (b) Butyl stearate
   (c) Petroleum waxes
   (d) All of the above
6. **Aerated concrete is produced by addition of**
   (a) Copper sulphate
   (b) Aluminium powder
   (c) Sodium silicate
   (d) Zinc sulphate
7. **Lightweight concrete has all the following beneficial characteristics except**
   (a) High strength-to-mass ratio
   (b) High thermal insulation
   (c) Reduced drying shrinkage
   (d) High sound insulation
8. **Lightweight aggregate are produced by**
   (a) Bloating clays with or without additives
   (b) Sintering fly ash
   (c) Using blast furnace slag
   (d) Any of the above
9. **Identify the true statement(s).**
   (a) Fresh fibre concrete has reduced workability and is less prone to segregation.
   (b) High modulus fibres improve both flexural and impact resistance simultaneously.
   (c) Low modulus fibres improve impact resistance of concrete.
   (d) All of the above
10. **Fibre reinforced concrete**
    (a) is used for precast products, airport runways, blast and impact resistant structures, tunnel lining and hydraulic structures
    (b) has superior crack resistance, improved ductility, high impact resistance and toughness
    (c) uses indented, crimped or bent fibres for improved bond
    (d) All of the above
11. **Lightweight aggregates weigh about**
    (a) 1000 kg/m
    (b) 2000 kg/m$^3$
    (c) 2500 kg/m$^3$
    (d) 4000 kg/m$^3$
12. **Select false statement**
    (a) Foam concrete can float on water and used for filling trenches
    (b) Fire resistance of autoclave aerated concrete is better than normal concrete
    (c) Sound insulation of lightweight concrete is better than normal concrete
    (d) None of them
13. **Workability of Self Compacting Concrete is measured using the ________**
    (a) Vicat's apparatus
    (b) Slump flow test
    (c) Slump test
    (d) Standard Consistency Test

**14.** Self–compacting concrete (SCC) is characterized by:

(a) High binder content
(b) High water–binder ratio
(c) Cementitious materials up to 30%
(d) Rough surface finish

**15.** Which of the following tests is best suited for measuring the viscosity of the self-compacting concrete?

(a) Slump cone test
(b) L-Box test
(c) J-Ring test
(d) V-Funnel test

**16.** Which of the following test is not suitable for measuring the passing ability of the Self Compacting Concrete?

(a) J-Ring test
(b) L-box test
(c) U-Box test
(d) Slump flow test

**17.** In Self Compacting Concrete, Slump flow test is mainly used to measure?

(a) Filling ability
(b) Passing ability
(c) Segregation resistance
(d) All of them

**18.** In the context of fibre reinforced composites (FRCs), consider the following statements:

Statement – 1: Aspect ratio of fibres used in matrix is chosen considering the maximum tensile and bond stresses.

Statement – 2: Method of mixing fibres in matrix plays critical role in fibres orientation in matrix.

(a) Both the statements are TRUE
(b) Statement-1 is TRUE and Statement-2 is FALSE
(c) Statement-1 is FALSE and Statement-2 is TRUE
(d) Both the statements are FALSE

**19.** Select true statement in the context of rheology of fresh concrete:

Statement – 1: Rheological behaviour of fresh concrete affects the ways it can be processed and placed.

Statement – 2: Rheology is the study of flow behaviour of materials exhibiting a time-dependent response to stress.

Statement – 3: Flow behaviours in fresh concretes can be obtained from direct measurements of torque and flow-rate in rheometers.

Statement – 4: Viscosity which is representative parameter for assessing the flow is defined as the ratio of stress to strain.

(a) Only 2 & 3
(b) Only 1, 2 & 3
(c) Only 2, 3 & 4
(d) All are correct

**20.** Pozzolana, used as an admixture in concrete, has the following advantages:

1. It improves workability with lesser amount of water.
2. It increases the heat of hydration and so lets the concrete set quickly.
3. It increases the resistance of concrete to attack by salts and sulphates.
4. It leaches out calcium hydroxide. Select the correct answer using the codes given below:

(a) 1, 2 and 3 only
(b) 1, 2 and 4 only
(c) 1, 3 and 4 only
(d) 2, 3 and 4 only

21. The most appropriate statement regarding use of super-plasticizers as admixture
    (a) Increases strength of concrete
    (b) Permits lower water cement ratio, thereby strength is increased
    (c) Reduces the setting time of concrete
    (d) Permits lower cement content, thereby strength is increased
22. In the context of self-compacting concrete (SCC), choose the true (T) / false (F) statements?
    (1) SCC is a flowing concrete mix that does not require external compaction effort and consolidates under its own weight.
    (2) The SCC is prepared in such a way that there is no segregation and at the same time there is enough fluidity for easy placement of the concrete.
    (3) The use of SCC can reduce the noise pollution in a construction site.
    (4) The amount of cement content is lower in SCC than normal concrete.
    (5) Use of SCC eases placement and hence saves time and manpower.
    (6) According to IS 10262, slump flow test can be used to measure the flowing ability of SCC and the recommended values for slump flow are 650 to 800 mm for SCC.
    (7) The filling ability or flowability of the concrete is defined as the ability of fresh concrete to flow into and fill all spaces within the formwork under application of adequate external vibrating effort.
    (8) The amount of coarse aggregate is lower in SCC compared to normal concrete.
    (9) Superplasticizers are used in SCC to reduce the water demand of concrete, or in other words, it helps in increasing the powder content at a given water content without compromising the workability of the mix.
    (10) The use of viscosity modifiers is done to reduce the viscosity of the fresh concrete paste and to make the concrete more flowable.

## Answers for Multiple Choice Questions

1. (d), 2. (d), 3. (a), 4. (d), 5. (d), 6. (b), 7. (c), 8. (d), 9. (d), 10. (d), 11. (a), 12. (d), 13. (b), 14. (b), 15. (d), 16. (d), 17. (a), 18. (a), 19. (b), 20. (c), 21. (b)

Q. No. 22

True statements – 1, 2, 3, 5, 6, 8 & 9

False statement – 4, 7 & 10

## Short and Long Answer Type Questions

1. What are the constituents of water reducing admixtures?
2. How do plasticizers and super-plasticizers improve workability of fresh concrete?
3. List examples of commonly used accelerating and set retarding admixtures.
4. Outline properties and applications of self-compacting concrete.
5. What are different methods to obtain lightweight concrete?
6. How are thermal and acoustic properties of lightweight concrete different from normal concrete?
7. What are the limitations of high performance concrete and self-compacting concrete?

**8.** Compare the properties of high strength concrete (HSC) and high performance concrete (HPC).

**9.** Mention some of the precautions to be followed in concreting for obtaining durable concrete in hot climatic regions.

**10.** Outline precautions to be adopted in cold weather concreting.

**11.** Enlist Indian states where cold weather concreting is essential.

## PRACTICAL

To be given as Unit VI

## KNOW MORE

**High strength concrete is different from high performance concrete. The former one does possess high strength but may not be durable. The latter one needs to be durable. High performance concrete satisfying *desired strength requirements is preferred over high strength concrete.***

## REFERENCES AND SUGGESTED READINGS


1. Gambhir, M.L., *Concrete Technology*, Tata McGraw Hill Publishing Co. Ltd., Delhi.
2. Shetty, M.S., Concrete Technology, S. Chand and Co. Pvt. Ltd., Ram Nagar, Delhi.
3. Santhakumar, A. R., *Concrete Technology*, Oxford University Press, New Delhi.
4. Neville, A. M. and Brooks, J.J., *Concrete Technology*, Pearson Education Pvt. Ltd.
5. Neville, A. M., *Concrete Technology*, Pearson Education Pvt. Ltd., New Delhi.
6. Sood, H., Kulkarni P. D., Mittal L. N., *Laboratory Manual in Concrete Technology*, CBS Publishers, New Delhi.
7. Clarke, J. (2002). *Structural Lightweight Aggregate Concrete*, Taylor & Francis e-Library, CRC Press, London.

# 6 Laboratory Tests on Concrete and its Ingredients

## UNIT SPECIFICS

Through this unit we have discussed the following aspects:

- The details and procedure of laboratory tests on cement, fine aggregates and coarse aggregates.
- Two commonly used laboratory tests to determine workability of fresh concrete.
- The procedure to prepare green concrete mix of a certain grade and assessment of compressive strength of hardened concrete at 7 and 28 days.
- The use and applications of non-destructive testing methods, viz., ultrasonic pulse velocity test and rebound hammer test.

The practical applications of the topics are discussed for generating further curiosity and creativity as well as improving problem solving capacity.

## RATIONALE

Knowing the properties of concrete and its ingredients is not enough to get competence in concrete technology. It is utmost important to have a first-hand experience on determination of these properties through laboratory experiments. This unit presents details of these laboratory tests on cement, fine aggregates, coarse aggregates, fresh concrete and hardened concrete. These experiments will enable students to determine properties of concrete and its constituents.

## PRE-REQUISITES

Understanding of topics from previous units, relevant to the experiment

## UNIT OUTCOMES

List of outcomes of this unit is as follows:

**U6-O1:** To understand the laboratory tests on cement, fine aggregates and coarse aggregates.

**U6-O2:** To learn about commonly used laboratory tests to determine workability of fresh concrete.

**U6-O3:** To prepare green concrete mix of required grade and assess compressive strength of hardened concrete at 7 and 28 days.

**U6-O4:** To understand the use and applications of non-destructive testing methods, viz., ultrasonic pulse velocity test and rebound hammer test.

| Unit-6 Outcomes | EXPECTED MAPPING WITH COURSE OUTCOMES (1- Weak Correlation; 2- Medium Correlation; 3- Strong Correlation) | | | | |
|---|---|---|---|---|---|
| | CO-1 | CO-2 | CO-3 | CO-4 | CO-5 |
| U6-O1 | 3 | 2 | 1 | 2 | 1 |
| U6-O2 | 1 | 2 | 3 | 3 | 3 |
| U6-O3 | 2 | 3 | 3 | 3 | 2 |
| U6-O4 | 1 | 3 | 3 | 3 | 1 |

## LIST OF EXPERIMENTS

1. To determine fineness of cement by sieving.
2. To determine specific gravity, standard consistency, initial and final Setting times of cement.
3. To determine compressive strength of cement.
4. To determine silt content in sand.
5. To determine bulking of sand.
6. To determine bulk density of fine and coarse aggregates.
7. To determine specific gravity and water absorption of fine and coarse aggregates.
8. To determine Fineness modulus of fine and coarse aggregate by sieve analysis.
9. To determine impact value of aggregate
10. To determine crushing value of aggregate.
11. To determine abrasion value of aggregate.
12. To determine elongation and flakiness index of coarse aggregates
13. To determine workability of concrete by slump cone test.
14. To determine workability of concrete by compaction factor test.
15. To prepare concrete mix of a particular grade and determine compressive strength of concrete for 7 and 28 days.
16. To demonstrate NDT equipment and related experiments.

## EXPERIMENT 1: FINENESS OF CEMENT BY SIEVING

**Objective:** To determine the fineness of a given sample of cement by sieving.

**Apparatus and Materials**

1. Digital weighing balance capable of weighing to the nearest 10 mg
2. IS Test Sieve 90 microns
3. Pan and lid for sieve assembly
4. Enamel tray
5. Bristle brush
6. Cement

## Theory

Concrete attains its strength mainly from the reaction of cement with water. This reaction, called hydration of cement, starts at the surface of the cement particles. Thus, larger the surface area available for reaction, greater is the rate of hydration. Finer particles have higher specific surface area per unit mass. Therefore, rapid development of concrete strength requires finer cement particles.

However, too fine cement is undesirable as the cost of grinding cement clinkers increases with fineness. Finer cement also requires more amount of gypsum to be added while grinding the clinkers, to prevent flash set. Moreover, finer cement deteriorates faster in presence of moisture and is more prone to shrinkage cracks. Standard consistency (amount of water required for making a standard paste) also increases with fineness. It is, therefore, required to have an optimal fineness of cement particles.

(a) (b)

**Fig. 6.1:** (a) IS sieve of size 90 microns with pan, (b) Digital weighing balance

## Procedure

1. Take 100 grams of cement on a standard IS sieve of size 90 microns. Break down any air-set cement lump without rubbing on the sieve.
2. Place the sieve carrying cement on the pan and cover it with its lid.
3. Holding the sieve assembly in both hands, gently sieve the sample continuously for 15 minutes by swirling, planetary and linear motions. If available, mechanical sieve shaker may be used.
4. At the end of sieving, weigh the residue left on the sieve. Divide weight of the residue by weight of cement sample to obtain percent weight retained on sieve.
5. Repeat the above steps and calculate fineness as the mean value for percent weight retained on sieve.
6. If the results for two samples differ by more than 1 percent absolute, repeat steps 1 to 4 for a third sample and then calculate fineness as the mean of the three values. For acceptability, as per IS 4031, this mean value should not exceed 10%.

## Observations and Calculations

| | Unit | Sample I | Sample II | Sample III |
|---|---|---|---|---|
| Weight of cement | grams | | | |
| Weight retained | grams | | | |

| | Unit | Sample I | Sample II | Sample III |
|---|---|---|---|---|
| Percent weight retained on sieve | % | | | |
| Mean percentage | % | | | |

**Results**

The mean fineness of given sample of cement is found to be ______ %.

**Conclusion**

Since the fineness of given cement sample is less/more than 10%, the given cement sample is acceptable/ unacceptable.

**Precautions**

1. Before use, sieve should be cleaned with the help of a bristle brush.
2. It is important to check the accuracy of the weighing machine before using.
3. Sieving must be carried out gently and continuously for 15 minutes at a stretch.

**References**

1. IS 4031 (Part I): Methods of physical tests for hydraulic cement: Determination of fineness by dry sieving. Bureau of Indian Standards, New Delhi.

## EXPERIMENT 2A: DETERMINATION OF SPECIFIC GRAVITY AND UNIT WEIGHT OF CEMENT

**Objective:** To determine specific gravity and unit weight of a given sample of cement.

**Apparatus and Materials**

1. Digital weighing balance capable of weighing to the nearest 0.2 mg
2. Digital weighing balance capable of weighing to the nearest 0.1 g
3. Le Chatelier's Flask
4. Container of known volume (typically 3 liters)
5. Cement
6. Kerosene / Naphtha

**Theory**

Specific gravity of a material is defined as the ratio of its density to that of a given reference material at the same temperature. The reference material is usually taken as water. Therefore, specific gravity can be understood as the ratio of mass of a material in a given volume to that of water in the same volume, both at the same temperature. Since, cement reacts with water, specific gravity of cement cannot be determined by introducing cement in water and measuring the displaced volume of water. Therefore, specific gravity of cement is determined using kerosene or naphtha, as outlined below in this experiment.

Since cement contains voids, total volume occupied by cement is different from that occupied by cement particles alone. At the same time, mass of these air voids is negligible compared to that of cement. Mass of a cement sample divided by its total volume (including voids) gives its unit weight.

Ordinary Portland Cement (OPC) has a specific gravity of around 3.15 and a unit weight of around 1.3. On the other hand, Portland Pozzolana Cement (PPC) has a specific gravity of around 2.9 and a unit weight of around 1.2. Therefore, depending on obtained values of specific gravity and unit weight, type of cement can also be ascertained.

(a) (b)

**Fig. 6.2:** (a) Le Chatelier's flask, (b) Cylinder of volume 3 litres

**Procedure**

*Specific gravity*

1. Fill the Le Chatelier's flask up to a level between 0 ml and 1 ml marks with kerosene oil. Record this reading as $V_1$.
2. Weigh the flask with kerosene, and record this weight as $W_1$.
3. Weigh 64 grams of cement and introduce it slowly in the flask, while avoiding choking at the neck. Once all the cement sample is introduced, weigh the flask with kerosene and cement as $W_2$.
4. After putting the stopper, gently roll the flask in an inclined position. This is done to free the cement from any air bubbles.
5. Immerse the flask in a constant-temperature water bath maintained at 27°C, so as to avoid variations greater than 0.2°C in the temperature of the liquid in the flask.
6. Take the reading of kerosene level on the flask as $V_2$. The difference between this level and initial level, i.e. ($V_2$ - $V_1$), gives displaced volume.
7. Calculate the specific gravity as expressed below.
8. Carry out the test (steps 1-7) twice, and report the average value. If the two values differ by more than 0.03, the test shall be performed for the third time.

*Unit weight*

1. Empty weight of a cylindrical container of known volume ($V$) is recorded as $W_3$.
2. The container is loosely filled with cement in three layers. After filling each layer, gently strike the container on a firm surface to compact the cement.
3. Weight of container with cement is measured and recorded as $W_4$.

**Observation Table**

| | |
|---|---|
| Weight of Le Chatelier's flask with kerosene, $W_1$ (in grams) | |
| Weight of Le Chatelier's flask with kerosene and cement, $W_2$ (in grams) | |
| Initial level of kerosene in Le Chatelier's flask, $V_1$ (in ml) | |
| Final level of kerosene in Le Chatelier's flask, $V_2$ (in ml) | |
| Weight of empty cylindrical container, $W_3$ (in grams) | |
| Weight of cylindrical container filled with cement, $W_4$ (in grams) | |
| Volume of cylindrical container, $V$ (in ml) | |

**Calculations**

Specific gravity of cement is calculated as:

$$Specific\ gravity = \frac{Weight\ of\ cement\ in\ grams}{Displaced\ volume\ in\ ml} = \frac{W_2 - W_1}{V_2 - V_1}$$

Unit weight of cement is calculated as:

$$Unit\ weight = \frac{Weight\ of\ cement}{Volume\ of\ container} = \frac{W_4 - W_3}{V}$$

**Results**

The specific gravity of given cement is ..........

The unit weight of given cement sample is ..........

**Conclusion**

Based on determined specific gravity and unit weight, the cement is OPC/PPC.

**Precautions**

1. The inside of Le Chatelier's flask should be dry and free from moisture before adding kerosene or naphtha.
2. Cement should be slowly and carefully introduced in Le Chatelier's flask, to avoid clogging at the neck of the flask.
3. Spilling and blowing of cement should be avoided as much as possible. The experiment for determining specific gravity should not be conducted in a windy environment.
4. The cylindrical container for finding unit weight of cement should be dry and clean before use.

**References**

1. IS 4031 (Part XI): Methods of physical tests for hydraulic cement: Determination of density. Bureau of Indian Standards, New Delhi.

## EXPERIMENT 2B: DETERMINATION OF STANDARD CONSISTENCY, INITIAL AND FINAL SETTING TIMES OF CEMENT

**Objective:** To determine standard consistency, initial setting time and final setting time of given sample of cement.

**Apparatus and Materials**

1. Vicat's apparatus (conforming to IS: 5513) with mould and glass plate.
   a. Plunger for standard consistency test (10 mm diameter)
   b. Needle for initial setting time (square section with side 1 mm)
   c. Needle for final setting time (an annular attachment at the end)
2. Weighing balance with accuracy of ±1 g
3. Gauging trowel (conforming to IS 10086)
4. Enamel trough
5. Standard spatula
6. Stop watch
7. Thermometer
8. Measuring cylinder – 500 ml
9. Cement

**Theory**

Standard consistency refers to a particular percentage of water by weight of cement to produce a standard cement paste. Vicat's apparatus is universally used to find the standard consistency.

With time, plastic cement paste attains sufficient hardness and rigidity. The elapsed time, from the addition of water, up to which the cement products remain in plastic condition is called initial setting time. It should not be less than 30 minutes. This setting time depends on the ambient temperature and relative humidity. The setting time decreases if the ambient temperature is high and relative humidity is low.

Gradually as time passes, the cement paste hardens. The time elapsed, from the time of mixing water, up to which the cement product completely loses its plasticity, is known as final setting time. It should be less than equal to 10 hours. The concrete is least vulnerable to external damages beyond final setting time.

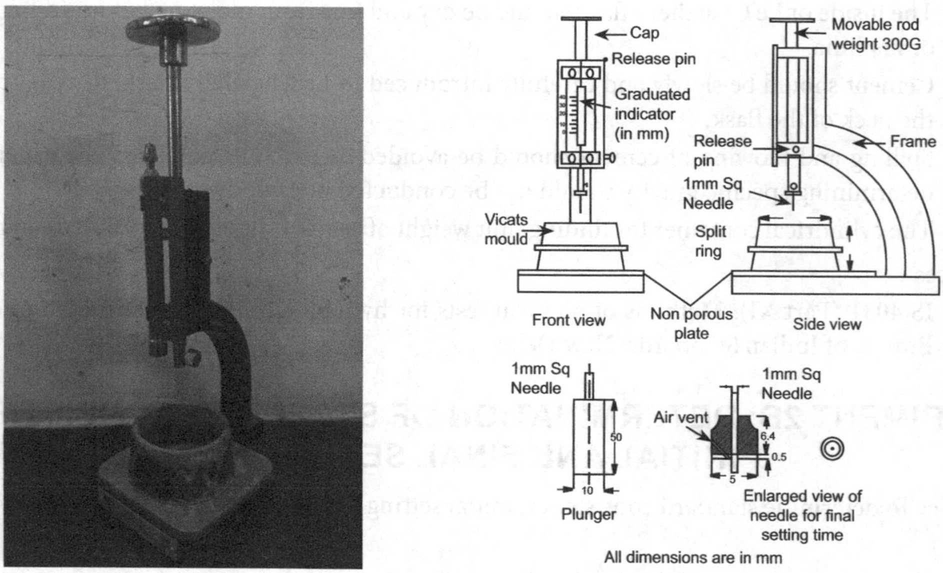


**Fig. 6.3:** Vicat's apparatus

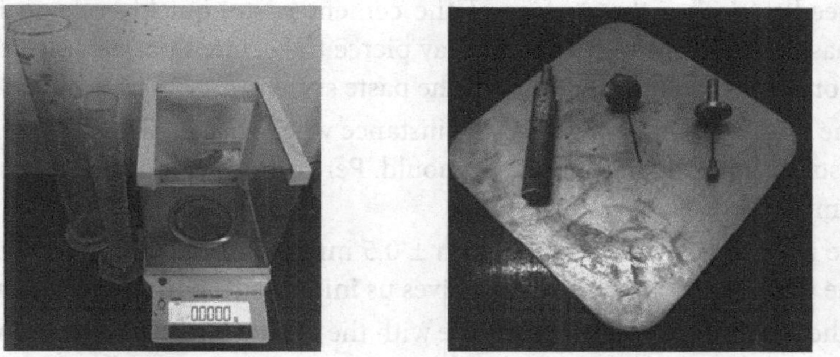

(a) (b)

**Fig. 6.4:** (a) Weighing balance and measuring cylinder, (b) Plunger and needles for standard consistency, initial setting time and final setting time (from left to right in bottom)

**Procedure**

*Standard Consistency*

1. Weigh 400 grams of cement and mix it with 30% of potable water (120 g or 120 ml). Complete gauging before any sign of setting occurs. The time of gauging should be strictly between 3 and 5 minutes. The gauging time shall be counted from the time of adding water to the dry cement until commencing to fill the mould.
2. Fill the mould completely with the cement paste and remove the excess paste by single stroke of the trowel making it level with the top of the mould. Shake the mould slightly to expel the air.
3. Place the mould, together with the glass plate, under the plunger attached to the Vicat's apparatus.
4. Lower the plunger to touch the surface of the cement paste, and calibrate the Vicat's apparatus to show zero reading when it touches the surface of test block.
5. As the plunger touches the cement surface, quickly release it to sink into the paste. This operation should be carried out immediately after filling the mould.
6. Note the penetration of plunger (10 mm dia) in cement paste. If the plunger penetrates by 33 to 35 mm from top of the paste, the paste is said to be of normal consistency. In other words, the plunger of Vicat's apparatus should stop between 5 to 7 mm from the bottom.
7. Make trial pastes with varying percentages of water till the above reading is obtained. The amount of water mixed, expressed as percentage by weight of the dry cement, gives the normal consistency (*P*).

*Initial setting time and final setting time*

1. Take 400 grams of cement. Prepare a neat cement paste using 0.85 times the water required for standard consistency (0.85P). Start the stopwatch at the instant when water is added to the cement.
2. Fill the Vicat's mould with the cement paste while resting on a glass plate. Remove the excess paste by single stroke of trowel, making the surface level with the top of the mould.
3. Place the mould, together with the glass plate, under the needle for initial setting time attached to Vicat's apparatus.
4. Lower the needle to gently touch the surface of the cement paste, and calibrate the Vicat's apparatus to show zero reading when it touches the surface.

5. As the needle touches the surface of the cement paste, quickly release it to penetrate the cement paste. At the start, the needle may pierce the cement paste completely. With time, the penetration depth is likely to reduce as the paste stiffens.
6. Repeat the procedure in Step 5 until the instance when the needle penetrates up to 5 mm ± 0.5 mm measured from the bottom of the mould. Perform these repeated trials at different points on the sample.
7. When the needle penetrates up to 5 mm ± 0.5 mm measured from the bottom of the mould, record the time in the stopwatch. This gives us initial setting time of the cement paste.
8. Replace the needle for initial setting time with the needle for final setting time. This needle has an annular attachment at the end.
9. Lower the needle to touch the surface of the cement paste, and then release it quickly. At the start, the needle may pierce the cement paste to an extent. With time, the penetration depth is likely to reduce as the paste hardens.
10. Repeat the procedure in Step 9 until the instance needle makes just a slight impression on the cement paste surface while its annular attachment fails to make any impression. Perform these repeated trials at different points on the sample.
11. When the final setting time needle makes a slight impression while its annular attachment is unable to make any impression on the cement paste, record the time in the stopwatch. This gives us the final setting time of the cement paste.
12. Report initial and final setting time to the nearest five minutes.

**Observation Table**

| | |
|---|---|
| Standard Consistency (in %) | |
| Initial Setting Time (in minutes) | |
| Final Setting Time (in minutes) | |

**Results**

The standard consistency of the given cement sample is found to be ____ %.

The initial setting time and final setting time for the given cement sample is ______ minutes and ______ minutes respectively.

**Conclusion**

Based on the values of initial and final setting times, the given cement sample is acceptable.

**Precautions**

1. The cement paste shall be prepared and kept at a temperature of 27°C ± 2°C (room temperature) and a relative humidity of at least 90%.
2. The Vicat's apparatus, its mould and needles should be cleaned after the test.

**References**

1. IS 4031 (Part V): Methods of physical tests for hydraulic cement: Determination of initial and final setting times. Bureau of Indian Standards, New Delhi.

## EXPERIMENT 3: COMPRESSIVE STRENGTH OF CEMENT

**Objective:** To determine compressive strength of given sample of cement.

**Apparatus and Materials**

1. Compression Testing Machine (CTM)
2. Standard vibration machine (conforming to IS 10080)
3. Cube moulds with side 70.6 mm – 6 nos.
4. Enamel trough
5. Gauging trowel
6. Digital weighing balance with an accuracy of ±1 g
7. Measuring cylinder with an accuracy of ±1 ml
8. Cement, Standard sand (conforming to IS 650) and Potable water

**Theory**

The compressive strength of cement depends on the chemical constituents of the cement. Different combinations of oxides form Bogue's compounds produce cements with different compressive strength. Each of these compounds has a specific contribution to the strength of cement. The strength is mainly contributed by tri-calcium silicate and di-calcium silicate. Tri-calcium aluminate and tetra-calcium alumino-ferrite have relatively low contributions to the strength of cement. Prior to use of cement in concrete construction, its strength should be properly assessed.

Depending upon the compressive strength of Ordinary Portland Cement (OPC), they are identified as OPC 53 grade, OPC 43 grade, and OPC 33 grade. Here, the grade indicates the compressive strength of cement cube after 28 days of curing in MPa.

**Fig. 6.5:** Moulds for preparing cement mortar cubes (each face with area 50 cm$^2$)

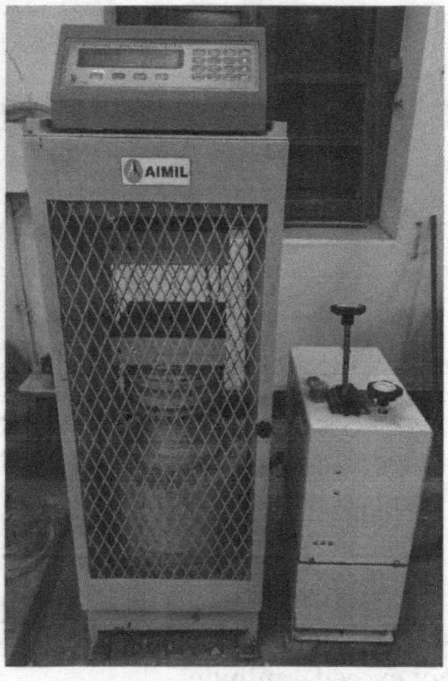

**Fig. 6.6:** Compression Testing Machine (CTM)

**Procedure**

1. Take 200 grams of given cement sample and 600 grams of standard sand (3 times of cement weight) in an enamel trough. Mix them dry with a trowel for one minute.
2. Weigh $p$% of water by weight of dry materials ( $p = \frac{P}{4} + 3$, where $P$ is the standard consistency in percentage) and mix it thoroughly with dry cement-sand mixture for 3 to 4 minutes, so as to obtain a mortar with uniform colour.
3. Apply grease/mould oil on the inner surfaces of six 70.6 mm side (50 $cm^2$ surface area) cube moulds, and fill them with the prepared mortar. Compact the filled mortar using standard vibration machine for 2 minutes.
4. Keep these cast cubes in atmosphere, at temperature of 27°C ± 2°C and relative humidity higher than 90% for 24 hours. Take these mortar cubes out of moulds, and keep them submerged in clean water.
5. Test three cubes at 3 days and three at 7 days, using compression testing machine with loading rate of 350 $kg/cm^2$/minute.
6. For each cube, calculate compressive strength by dividing maximum load by cross-sectional area (50 $cm^2$). Take the mean of the cube strengths to obtain compressive strength. If any of the cube strength differs from the mean strength by more than 10%, that cube strength value should be discarded. Report the compressive strength of cement to the nearest 0.5 MPa.

To satisfy Indian Standards, the observed compressive strength at crushing should not be less than the following values (in MPa).

| | OPC 33 (IS 269) | OPC 43 (IS 8112) | OPC 53 (IS 12269) |
|---|---|---|---|
| After 3 days | 16 | 23 | 27 |
| After 7 days | 22 | 33 | 37 |
| After 28 days | 33 | 43 | 53 |

**Observations and Calculations**

| Time of testing | Load in kN | | | Strength in N/mm² | | | Mean Strength (N/mm²) |
|---|---|---|---|---|---|---|---|
| | 1 | 2 | 3 | 1 | 2 | 3 | |
| 3 - days | | | | | | | |
| 7 - days | | | | | | | |

**Results**

Mean compressive strength of given cement sample is found to be ______ MPa and ______ MPa at 3 and 7 days respectively.

**Conclusion**

Depending on determined mean compressive strength and given grade of cement, the cement is acceptable/unacceptable.

**Precautions**

1. The time of mixing shall be not less than 3 minutes and the time taken to obtain a uniform colour should not exceed 4 minutes.

2. The water in which the cubes are submerged shall be renewed every 7 days, and shall be maintained at a temperature of 27 ± 2°C.

**References**

1. IS 4031 (Part VI): Methods of physical tests for hydraulic cement: Determination of compressive strength of hydraulic cement other than masonry cement. Bureau of Indian Standards, New Delhi.

## EXPERIMENT 4: DETERMINATION OF SILT CONTENT IN SAND

**Objective:** To determine silt content in fine aggregate by sedimentation method.

**Apparatus and Materials**

1. Watertight screw-topped glass jar with dimensions similar to 1 kg fruit-preserving jar
2. Device for rotating jar about its longitudinal axis at 80 ± 20 revolutions per minute, keeping it horizontal
3. *Sedimentation pipette with capacity of 25 ml*
4. 1000 ml measuring graduated cylinder (sedimentation tube)
5. Weighing scale of capacity more than 10 kg and accuracy of 1 gram
6. Weighing scale of capacity more than 250 grams and accuracy of 0.001 gram
7. Well-ventilated oven with temperature range 100-110°C
8. Solution containing 8 grams of sodium oxalate per litre of distilled water (100 ml of this solution to be taken and further diluted with distilled water to one litre)
9. Sand sample

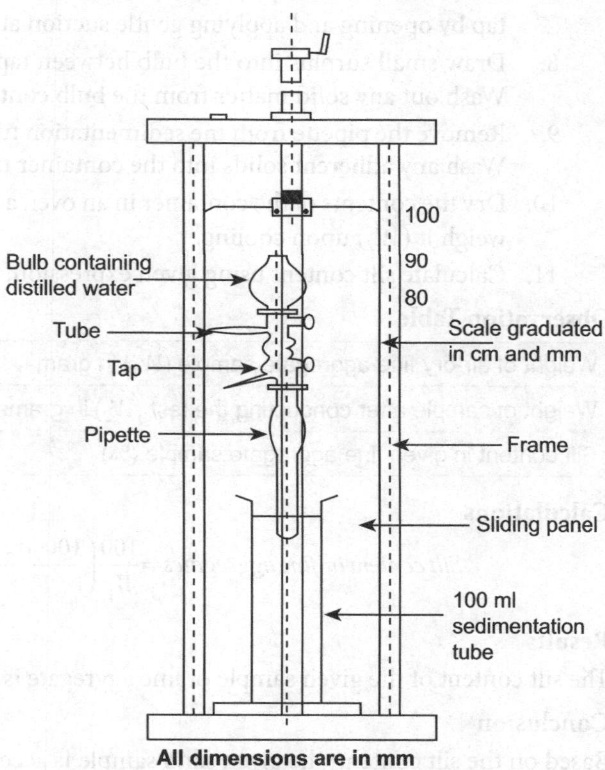


**Fig. 6.7:** Experimental set-up for determining silt content in sand

**Theory**

Sedimentation method is a gravimetric method for determining the clay, fine silt and fine dust, which includes particles up to 20 microns. Differences in the nature and density of materials or in the temperature at the time of testing may vary the separation point.

**Procedure**

1. Take approximately 300 grams of sand sample and record its weight accurately ($W_1$). The sand should be in the air-dry condition and pass through 4.75-mm IS sieve.

2. Place the sample in a screw-topped glass jar, together with 300 ml of the diluted sodium oxalate solution.
3. Securely fix the rubber washer and cap to ensure water tightness. Rotate the jar about its longitudinal axis at a speed of 80 ± 20 rpm for 15 minutes, while aligning this axis horizontal.
4. Pour the suspension into 1000 ml measuring cylinder (sedimentation tube) and wash the residue by gently swirling with successive 150 ml portions of sodium oxalate solution. Add the washings to the sedimentation tube to make the total volume up to 1000 ml.
5. Thoroughly mix the suspension in the sedimentation tube by inversion and place it right under the pipette (shown in Fig. 6.7).
6. Gently lower the pipette such that its tip gets immersed into the liquid to a depth of 100 mm.
7. Three minutes after placing the sedimentation tube in position, fill the pipette and the bore of tap by opening and applying gentle suction at.
8. Draw small surplus into the bulb between tap and tube, but this shall be allowed to run away. Wash out any solid matter from the bulb containing distilled water.
9. Remove the pipette from the sedimentation tube and run its contents into a weighed container. Wash any adherent solids into the container using distilled water from bulb through the tap.
10. Dry the contents of the container in an oven at 100 to 110°C, to constant weight. Take it out and weigh it ($W_2$) upon cooling.
11. Calculate silt content using given expression, and report it to the nearest 0.1%.

**Observation Table**

| | |
|---|---|
| Weight of air-dry fine aggregate sample ($W_1$) in grams | |
| Weight of sample after conducting the test ($W_2$) in grams | |
| Silt content in given fine aggregate sample (%) | |

**Calculations**

$$\textit{Silt content in fine aggregates} = \frac{100}{W_1}\left(\frac{1000W_2}{V} - 0.8\right)\%$$

**Results**

The silt content of the given sample of fine aggregate is found to be ______%.

**Conclusion**

Based on the silt content, the given sand sample is acceptable/unacceptable.

**Precautions**

1. Sedimentation assembly comprising of sedimentation tube and pipette should be handled carefully.
2. Dilution of sodium oxalate in water should be achieved accurately.

**References**

1. IS 2386 (Part II): Methods of test for aggregates for concrete: Estimation of deleterious materials and organic impurities. Bureau of Indian Standards, New Delhi.

## EXPERIMENT 5: DETERMINATION OF BULKING OF SAND

**Objective**: To observe bulking of fine aggregate in a field test and thereby determine the necessary adjustment for the bulking of fine aggregate.

**Apparatus and Materials**

1. Two containers
2. 250 ml measuring cylinder
3. Fine aggregates

**Theory**

River sand usually contains some amount of moisture. Free moisture forms a film around each particle, which keeps the neighbouring particles away from it, due to surface tension. If the moist sand is loosely filled in a container, it is likely to occupy a larger volume than it would occupy in dry condition. This increase in volume of sand due to moisture is called bulking of sand. If the sand is measured by loose volume, it is necessary to batch increased volume to obtain the required amount of sand. This correction depends on the extent of bulking.

Bulking of sand increases with the increase in moisture content up to a certain limit. Beyond this limit, the sand skeleton changes from flocculated to dispersed leading to a decrease in volume. Therefore, the sand sample attains its maximum volume at a certain moisture content, as shown in Fig. 6.8. This moisture content and associated volume increase is found by determining bulking of sand at different moisture contents.

This experiment outlines two commonly used procedures for determining bulking of sand for a given sample. Moisture content can then be determined to get one data point for the plot shown in Fig. 6.8. The test can be conducted for sand samples with different moisture content and grading, to obtain the plots in Fig. 6.8.

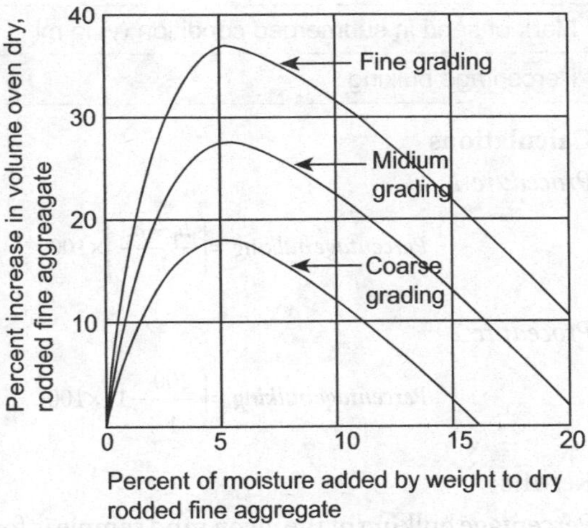


**Fig. 6.8:** Bulking of sand with variation in moisture content for different grading of sand

**Procedure**

*Procedure 1*

1. Put sand loosely into a container, until it is about two-thirds full.
2. Level the top surface of the sand and measure the height ($h_1$) by pushing a steel rule vertically down through the sand at the middle to the bottom.
3. Transfer the sand to another container ensuring no loss of material.
4. Fill half of the first container with water. Transfer back about half of the sand and rod it using a 6 mm diameter steel rod, so as to reduce its volume to a minimum.
5. Add the remaining sand and rod it in the same way. Level and smoothen the top surface of the inundated sand, and measure its depth ($h_2$) at the middle with the steel rule.
6. Calculate percentage of bulking using given expression, and report it to the nearest whole number.

*Procedure 2*

1. Pour damp sand (consolidated by shaking) into a 250 ml measuring cylinder, until it reaches 200 ml mark.
2. Fill the cylinder with water sufficient to submerge the sand completely, and stir it well. Sand surface will get lowered.
3. Record the mark ($y$) at the top surface of the sand in ml.
4. Calculate percentage bulking using given expression, and report it to the nearest whole number.

**Observation Tables**

*Procedure 1*

| | |
|---|---|
| Height of sand sample in the container ($h_1$) | |
| Height of inundated sand sample in the container ($h_2$) | |
| Percentage bulking | |

*Procedure 2*

| | |
|---|---|
| Mark of sand in submerged condition ($y$) in ml | |
| Percentage bulking | |

**Calculations**

*Procedure 1*

$$\textit{Percentage bulking} = \left(\frac{h_1 - h_2}{h_2}\right) \times 100$$

*Procedure 2*

$$\textit{Percentage bulking} = \left(\frac{200}{y} - 1\right) \times 100$$

**Results**

Percentage bulking of the given sand sample is found to be ________ % using procedure 1 and ________ % using procedure 2.

**Conclusion**

Based on the percentage bulking value, the given sand sample is of coarse/medium/fine grading. Further, moisture correction can be implemented based on determined bulking value.

**Precautions**

1. While transferring material from one container to another in procedure 1, there should be no loss of material.
2. Upon adding water to sand in the measuring cylinder in procedure 2, the contents should be stirred well to eliminate any air bubbles.

**References**

1. IS 2386 (Part III): Methods of test for aggregates for concrete: Specific gravity, density, voids, absorption and bulking. Bureau of Indian Standards, New Delhi.

# EXPERIMENT 6: BULK DENSITY OF FINE AND COARSE AGGREGATES

**Objective:** To determine bulk density of fine and coarse aggregates

**Apparatus and Materials**

1. Weighing balance sensitive up to 0.5% of the sample weight
2. Metal cylindrical measure with capacity 3 litres (for fine aggregates), 15 litres (for coarse aggregates up to 40 mm MSA) and 30 litres (for coarse aggregates larger than 40 mm MSA)
3. Steel tamping rod with diameter of 16 ± 1 mm, length of 600 ± 5 mm, with rounded ends
4. Shovel and Straight edge
5. Fine aggregates and coarse aggregates (CA10 and CA20)

**Theory**

Bulk density is the weight of aggregate required to fill a container of unit volume. This unit volume, therefore, consists of volume of solid material plus the volume of voids and is measured in kg/litre. Value of the bulk density of the aggregate depends upon shape, size distribution, specific gravity. More graded the aggregate, greater is the bulk density. Angular and flaky shape of the material reduce the bulk density. If this bulk density test is frequently conducted on the site, the appreciable change in the value of the bulk density at any one time helps to detect the change in grading or the shape of the material.

**Procedure**

Follow the given procedure for coarse as well as fine aggregates:

*Rodded bulk density*

1. Weigh the empty cylindrical measure ($W_1$) and record its volume ($V$).
2. Fill the cylindrical measure with thoroughly mixed aggregates in three layers. Tamp each layer with 25 strokes of the tamping rod.
3. Strike off the surplus aggregate using the tamping rod as a straight edge.
4. Record the weight of cylindrical measure with aggregates ($W_2$).
5. Calculate the net weight of the aggregate ($W_2$ - $W_1$) and thereby the rodded bulk density (in kg/litre) using given expression.

*Loose bulk density*

1. Weigh the empty cylindrical measure ($W_3$) and record its volume ($V$).
2. Fill the cylindrical measure with thoroughly mixed aggregates, using a shovel from a height not exceeding 50 mm from the top of the measure.
3. Level the aggregate surface using a straight edge.
4. Record the weight of cylindrical measure with aggregates ($W_4$).
5. Calculate the net weight of the aggregate ($W_4$ – $W_3$) and thereby the loose bulk density (in kg/litre) using given expression.

**Observation Table**

| | Coarse Aggregates | Fine Aggregates |
|---|---|---|
| Volume of cylindrical measure (litre) | | |
| Rodded bulk density (kg/litre) | | |

| | Coarse Aggregates | Fine Aggregates |
|---|---|---|
| Loose bulk density (kg/litre) | | |
| Condition of aggregate<br>(Oven dry / Saturated surface dry / Moist) | | |

**Calculations**

$$Rodded\ bulk\ density = \frac{W_2 - W_1}{V}$$

$$Loose\ bulk\ density = \frac{W_4 - W_3}{V}$$

**Results**

Rodded bulk density for coarse aggregate = __________ kg/litre
Loose bulk density for coarse aggregate = __________ kg/litre
Rodded bulk density for fine aggregate = __________ kg/litre
Loose bulk density for fine aggregate = __________ kg/litre

**Conclusion**

Based on the determined bulk density, the given aggregate sample is classified as light/medium/heavy weight aggregate.

**Precautions**

1. Moisture condition of aggregates at the time of test should be reported.
2. While filling the cylindrical measure to find loose bulk density, segregation of aggregate particles should be avoided.
3. The cylindrical measure should be calibrated periodically as per IS 2386 (Part III).

**References**

1. IS 2386 (Part III): Methods of test for aggregates for concrete: Specific gravity, density, voids, absorption and bulking. Bureau of Indian Standards, New Delhi.

## EXPERIMENT 7: DETERMINATION OF SPECIFIC GRAVITY AND WATER ABSORPTION OF FINE AND COARSE AGGREGATES

**Objective:** To determine water absorption of given samples of fine and coarse aggregates

**Apparatus and Materials**

1. Weighing balance of capacity more than 3 kg, and accuracy of ±0.5 g
2. Well-ventilated oven to maintain temperature of 100 to 110°C
3. Pycnometer
4. 1000-ml measuring cylinder
5. Funnel and filter papers
6. Shallow tray
7. Wire basket with perforations not more than 6.3 mm, and equipped with wire hangers
8. Airtight container of capacity similar to wire basket

9. Watertight container with sufficient volume to freely suspend the wire basket in it
10. Two dry soft absorbent clothes
11. Fine and coarse aggregates

**Theory**

Specific gravity of a material is defined as ratio of its density to that of water. Therefore, specific gravity can be understood as the ratio of mass of a material in a given volume to that of water in the same volume at the same temperature. Specific gravity of aggregates depends on the parent rock, the formation process and the attrition by water. Typical specific gravity for aggregates ranges between 2.60 and 2.80.

Water absorption of aggregates influences the amount of water available for hydration of cement and for provision of workability. For example, aggregates with very high water absorption capacity tend to absorb a lot of water resulting in less free water available in the concrete mix. This leads to reduced workability of the mix. Further, water absorption of aggregates also affects durability of concrete when it is exposed to freeze-thaw cycles and/or aggressive chemicals.

Water absorption of aggregate is obtained by measuring increase in weight of oven-dry sample when immersed in water for 24 hours. The increase in weight expressed as percent of weight of the oven-dry sample is called water absorption. While designing a concrete mix, corrective measures are adopted based on degree of water absorption of aggregates.

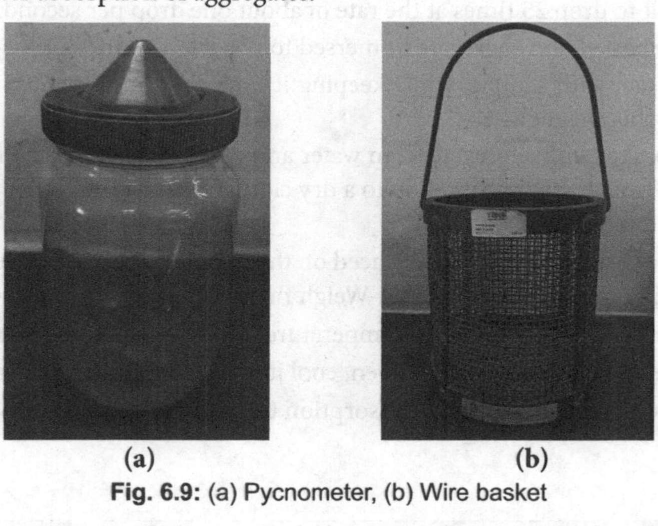

(a) (b)

**Fig. 6.9:** (a) Pycnometer, (b) Wire basket

**Procedure**

*Fine aggregates*

1. Take a sample of about 500 grams of fine aggregates in the tray and cover it with distilled water at a temperature of 22 to 32°C.
2. Remove entrapped air from the surface of the aggregate, by gently agitating with a rod. Keep the sample immersed for 24 ± 0.5 hours.
3. Drain out water from the sample, by decantation through a filter paper. Expose any aggregate retained on the filter paper to a gentle current of warm air to evaporate surface moisture, before adding it back to the sample. They should be stirred periodically to ensure uniform drying.
4. Weigh the saturated and surface dry sample ($W_1$).

5. Place the aggregate in the pycnometer, and fill it with distilled water. Remove any trapped air by rotating the pycnometer on its side, covering the hole in the apex of the cone with a finger. Wipe the outer surface of pycnometer and record its weight ($W_2$).
6. Empty all the contents of the pycnometer into the tray.
7. Refill the pycnometer with distilled water to the same level as before. Wipe the outer surface of pycnometer and weigh it ($W_3$).
8. Drain the water from the sample by decantation through a filter paper. Take back any material retained on the filter paper, to the sample. Place the sample in the oven at a temperature of 100 to 110°C for 24 ± 0.5 hours.
9. Carefully take the sample out of the oven, cool it in an air-tight container and weigh it ($W_4$).
10. Calculate specific gravity and water absorption using given expressions.

*Coarse aggregates*

1. Thoroughly wash the coarse aggregate sample to remove dust. Drain and place the sample in the wire basket.
2. Immerse the wire basket with aggregates in distilled water at a temperature of 22 to 32°C.
3. Remove the entrapped air from the sample by lifting the basket 25 mm above the base of tank and allowing it to drop 25 times at the rate of about one drop per second.
4. Keep the wire basket and aggregate immersed for 24 ± 0.5 hours.
5. Weigh the basket with sample, while keeping it immersed in water at a temperature of 22 to 32°C. Record this weight as $W_5$.
6. Remove the basket with aggregate from water and allow it to drain for a few minutes. Transfer the aggregate from the wire basket on to a dry cloth. Immerse the empty basket into water, jolt it 25 times and weigh it in water ($W_6$).
7. Gently dry the surfaces of aggregate placed on the dry cloth. Spread it out on another dry cloth and leave it, till it becomes surface dry. Weigh the surface dry aggregates ($W_7$).
8. Place the aggregates in the oven at a temperature of 100 to 110°C for 24 ± 0.5 hours.
9. Carefully take the sample out of the oven, cool it in an air-tight container and weigh it ($W_8$).
10. Calculate specific gravity and water absorption using given expressions.

**Observation Table**

*Fine aggregates*

| | |
|---|---|
| Weight of saturated surface dry aggregates ($W_1$) in grams | |
| Weight of pycnometer with aggregate and water ($W_2$) in grams | |
| Weight of pycnometer with water ($W_3$) in grams | |
| Weight of oven dry aggregates ($W_4$) in grams | |

*Coarse aggregates*

| | |
|---|---|
| Weight of basket with sample in water ($W_5$), in grams | |
| Weight of empty basket in water ($W_6$), in grams | |
| Weight of surface dry aggregate sample ($W_7$), in grams | |
| Weight of oven dry aggregate sample ($W_8$), in grams | |

**Calculations**

*Fine aggregates*

$$Specific\ gravity = \frac{W_4}{W_1 - (W_2 - W_3)}$$

$$Water\ absorption = \frac{(W_1 - W_4)}{W_4} X100$$

*Coarse aggregates*

$$pecific\ gravity = \frac{W_8}{W_7 - (W_5 - W_6)}$$

$$Water\ absorption = \frac{(W_7 - W_8)}{W_8} X100$$

**Results**

Specific gravity for fine aggregate = __________

Water absorption for fine aggregate = __________ %

Specific gravity for coarse aggregate = __________

Water absorption for coarse aggregate = __________ %

**Conclusion**

Based on the determined specific gravity, the given aggregate sample is classified as light/medium/heavy weight aggregate.

**Precautions**

The difference in the temperature of the water in the pycnometer while measuring $W_B$ and $W_C$ should not exceed 2°C.

**References**


1. S 2386 (Part III): Methods of test for aggregates for concrete: Specific gravity, density, voids, absorption and bulking. Bureau of Indian Standards, New Delhi.


## EXPERIMENT 8: DETERMINATION OF FINENESS MODULUS OF COARSE AND FINE AGGREGATE BY SIEVE ANALYSIS

**Objective:** To determine fineness modulus of coarse and fine aggregate and classify them

**Apparatus and Materials**

1. Sieves conforming to IS 460: 40 mm, 20 mm, 10 mm, 4.75 mm, 2.36 mm, 1.18 mm, 600 microns, 300 microns, 150 microns, Pan
2. Weighing balance
3. Tray and Trowel
4. Coarse and fine aggregates

**Theory**

While coarse aggregates have particle size more than 4.75 mm, particle size of fine aggregates is less than 4.75 mm. Fineness Modulus is a method of standardization of the grading of aggregate. It is only a numerical index of fineness. For a given sample of aggregate, sieve analysis is conducted to determine the particle size distribution, known as gradation. Fineness modulus is obtained by adding the percentage by weight of materials retained on each of the ten I.S. Sieves and dividing it by 100.

Typical range for fineness modulus of coarse aggregates is 5.5 to 8.0. Higher value of fineness modulus means sample with coarser particles. For all-in aggregates, fineness modulus varies in the range of 3.5 to 6.5.

Typical range for fineness modulus of fine aggregates is 2.3 to 3.2. Higher value of fineness modulus means coarser sand. Lower value of fineness modulus means finer sand. Based on fineness modulus, fine aggregates are classified as fine, medium and coarse sand.

| Type of sand | Fine sand | Medium sand | Coarse sand |
|---|---|---|---|
| Fineness modulus | 2.2 to 2.6 | 2.6 to 2.9 | 2.9 to 3.2 |

**Fig. 6.10:** Sieve assembly for fine and coarse aggregates

**Procedure**

1. Weigh air-dry samples of
   - 2 kg of coarse aggregate with nominal maximum size (MSA) of 20 mm (CA20)
   - 2 kg of coarse aggregate with nominal maximum size (MSA) of 10 mm (CA10)
   - 1 kg of fine aggregate
2. Prepare the sieve assembly using appropriate set of sieves starting with the largest at top. Ensure that the sieves are clean before use.
3. Place the aggregate sample in the top sieve.
4. Shake the sieve assembly using a sieve shaker or with hands. The shaking should give a varied motion, backwards and forwards, left to right, circular clockwise and anti-clockwise, and with frequent jarring, so that the material is kept moving over the sieve surface in frequently changing directions.
5. On completion of sieving, weigh the material retained on each sieve.
6. Calculate fineness modulus of coarse and fine aggregates using expression given below.

## Observations and Calculations

| I.S. Sieve | Coarse Aggregate | | | | | | Fine Aggregate | | |
|---|---|---|---|---|---|---|---|---|---|
| | 20 mm MSA (CA20) | | | 10 mm MSA (CA10) | | | | | |
| | Wt. Retained | Total wt. Retained | Cumulative percentage | Wt. Retained | Total wt. Retained | Cumulative percentage | Wt. Retained | Total wt. Retained | Cumulative percentage |
| 75mm | | | | | | | | | |
| 40mm | | | | | | | | | |
| 20 mm | | | | | | | | | |
| 10 mm | | | | | | | | | |
| 4.75 mm | | | | | | | | | |
| 2.36 mm | | | | | | | | | |
| 1.18 mm | | | | | | | | | |
| 600 μm | | | | | | | | | |
| 300 μm | | | | | | | | | |
| 150 μm | | | | | | | | | |
| Total: | | | | | | | | | |
| Fineness Modulus | | | | | | | | | |

$$Fineness\ modulus = \frac{Sum\ of\ cumulative\ percentage\ retained\ on\ each\ sieve}{100}$$

## Results

1. Fineness modulus of the given sample of coarse aggregate is _______.
2. Fineness modulus of the given sample of fine aggregate is _______. Therefore, the given sand sample can be classified as Coarse sand/ Medium sand/Fine sand.

## Conclusion

Based on the determined fineness modulus, the given sand sample is classified as coarse/medium/fine sand, and is acceptable/unacceptable.

Based on the determined fineness modulus, the given coarse aggregate sample is acceptable/unacceptable.

## Precautions

1. Material shall not be forced through the sieve by hand pressure. Lumps of fine material, if present, may be broken by gentle pressure with fingers against the side of the sieve.
2. If required, light brushing with a fine camel hair brush may be used on the 150-micron and 75-micron sieves to prevent aggregation of powder and blinding of apertures.
3. If deleterious materials such as clay, silt and organic matter are present in the aggregate sample, the sample should be thoroughly washed and then dried to air-dry condition.

## References

1. IS 2386 (Part 1): Methods of test for aggregates for concrete: Particle size and shape. Bureau of Indian Standards, New Delhi.

2. IS 383: Specification for coarse and fine aggregates from natural sources for concrete. Bureau of Indian Standards, New Delhi.
3. IS 460: Specification for test sieves. Bureau of Indian Standards, New Delhi.

## EXPERIMENT 9: DETERMINATION OF AGGREGATE IMPACT VALUE OF COARSE AGGREGATES

**Objective:** To determine the aggregate impact value of coarse aggregates.

**Apparatus and Materials**

1. An impact testing machine as shown in Fig. 6.11 and complying with the following:
   a. Total weight between 45 and 60 kg
   b. Metal base with diameter equal to or more than 300 mm, weighing between 22 and 30 kg, supported on rigid block with thickness of at least 450 mm
   c. Cylindrical steel cup with internal diameter 102 mm, depth 50 mm and thickness not less than 6.3 mm, that can be fastened to the base plate
2. Metal hammer weighing between 13.5 and 14.0 kg, with cylindrical end (100 mm diameter, 50 mm length, 2 mm chamfer at lower edge) concentric with the steel cup
3. Mechanism to raise the hammer and drop it freely between the vertical guides from a height of 380 mm
4. Indian Standard (IS) sieves of sizes 12.5 mm, 10 mm and 2.36 mm
5. Cylindrical measure with internal diameter of 75 mm and depth of 50 mm
6. Tamping Rod with diameter 10 mm and length 230 mm, having a rounded end
7. Weighing balance of capacity more than 500 g and accuracy of ± 0.1 g
8. Well-ventilated oven capable to maintain temperature of 100 to 110°C

**Theory**

The aggregate impact value gives a relative measure of the resistance of an aggregate to sudden shock or impact. It is different from resistance to a slowly applied compressive load. The aggregate impact value should be less than 30% for concrete for wearing surface applications such as roads, runways and other pavements. For any application other than wearing surfaces, aggregate impact value should be less than 45%.

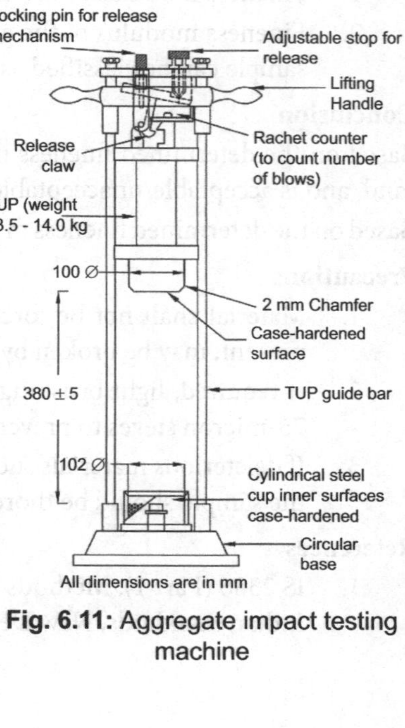


**Fig. 6.11:** Aggregate impact testing machine

**Procedure**

1. Take a sample of coarse aggregates, with all particles passing through 12.5 mm sieve and retaining on 10 mm sieve.
2. Dry the sample in an oven at 100 to 110°C for 4 hours, to achieve surface-dry condition. Take the sample out and cool it.
3. Weigh the empty cylindrical measure. Fill the cylindrical measure in three layers. Tamp each layer with 25 strokes from rounded end of the tamping

rod. Strike off the surplus aggregate using tamping rod as a straight edge. Weigh the cylindrical measure with aggregate. Calculate net weight of aggregate in the cylindrical measure ($W_1$) to the nearest gram.

4. Arrange different components of the impact machine as per IS 2386 (Part IV).
5. Transfer the aggregate sample to the cylindrical steel cup fixed to the base plate of impact machine. Compact the sample with 25 strokes of the tamping rod.
6. Raise the hammer such that its lower face is 380 mm above the upper surface of aggregate sample in the steel cup, and then drop it freely. Subject aggregate sample to a total of 15 such blows, with consecutive blows delivered at intervals of 1 second or more.
7. Remove crushed aggregate from the steel cup and sieve it using 2.36 mm sieve. Weigh the fraction passing through the sieve ($W_2$) to the nearest 0.1 gram, and the fraction retained on the sieve ($W_3$) to the nearest gram. If sum of $W_2$ and $W_3$ exceeds $W_1$ by more than 1 gram, discard the test result.
8. Repeat the test on another coarse aggregate sample, weighing $W_1$, taken from the same batch. Calculate aggregate impact value using given expression for both tests. Report mean of the two values, to the nearest whole number, as the aggregate impact value for the given sample of coarse aggregates.

**Observation Table**

| | Test 1 | Test 2 |
|---|---|---|
| Weight of surface dry sample ($W_1$) in grams | | |
| Weight of fraction passing through 2.36 mm sieve ($W_2$) in grams | | |
| Weight of fraction retained on 2.36 mm sieve ($W_3$) in grams | | |
| Aggregate impact value (%) | | |
| Mean aggregate impact value (%) | | |

**Calculations**

$$Aggregate\ impact\ value = \frac{W_2}{W_1} X100\%$$

**Results**

The aggregate impact value of the given sample of coarse aggregate is ________ %.

**Conclusion**

Select the correct statement:

- Since aggregate impact value is less than 30%, concrete made with this aggregate can be used for all applications.
- Since aggregate impact value is between 30 and 45%, concrete made with this aggregate can be used for any application other than wearing surfaces.
- Since aggregate impact value is more than 45%, concrete made with this aggregate cannot be used for any application.

**Precautions**

1. The components of impact machine should be carefully and accurately assembled such that the hammer guide columns ensure vertical free fall of the hammer.

2. The steel cup should be precisely and firmly fixed to the base plate of impact machine to receive adequate blows from the hammer.

**References**

1. IS 2386 (Part IV): Methods of test for aggregates for concrete: Mechanical properties. Bureau of Indian Standards, New Delhi.
2. IS 383: Specification for coarse and fine aggregates from natural sources for concrete. Bureau of Indian Standards, New Delhi.

# EXPERIMENT 10: DETERMINATION OF AGGREGATE CRUSHING VALUE OF COARSE AGGREGATES

**Objective:** To determine the aggregate crushing value of coarse aggregate

**Apparatus and Materials**

1. Compression testing machine with load capacity of 40 tonnes
2. Open-ended steel cylinder of diameter 150 mm, with plunger and base-plate as shown in Fig. 6.12
3. Tamping rod with diameter 16 mm and length 450 to 600 mm length, having a rounded end
4. Weighing balance of capacity 3 kg and accuracy of ± 1 g
5. Indian Standard (IS) sieves of sizes 12.5 mm, 10 mm and 2.36 mm
6. Cylindrical metal measure of diameter 115 mm and height 180 mm
7. Well-ventilated oven capable to maintain temperature of 100 to 110°C

**Theory**

The aggregate crushing values gives a relative measure of the resistance of aggregate to crushing under a gradually applied compressive load. If the aggregate crushing value is found to be 30 or higher, the result of this test may not be reliable. In such cases, one should determine the *ten percent fines value* instead of *aggregate crushing value.*

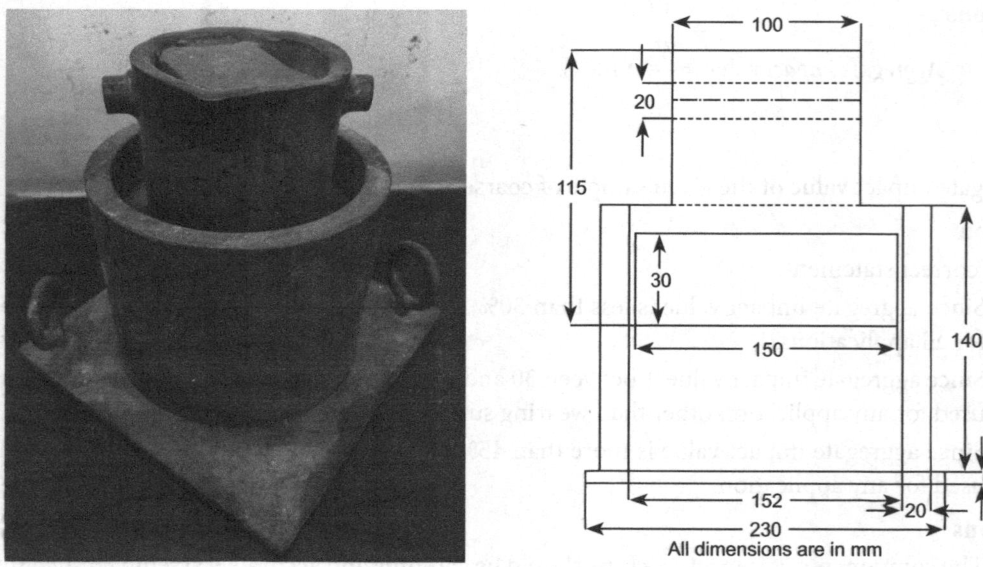


Fig. 6.12: Steel cylinder with plunger

**Procedure**

1. Take a sample of coarse aggregates, with all particles passing through 12.5 mm sieve and retaining on 10 mm sieve.
2. Dry the sample in an oven at 100 to 110°C for 4 hours, to achieve surface-dry condition. Take the sample out and cool it.
3. Weigh the empty cylindrical measure. Transfer the aggregate sample to the cylindrical measure in three layers. Tamp each layer 25 times with the tamping rod, and strike off surplus aggregate using a tamping rod or a straight edge. Weigh the cylindrical measure with aggregate. Calculate net weight of aggregate in the cylindrical measure ($W_1$) to the nearest gram.
4. Transfer the aggregate sample to the open-ended steel cylinder placed on the base plate, in three layers. Compact the sample with 25 strokes of the tamping rod. Level the top surface of the test sample.
5. Insert the plunger into the cylinder to rest horizontally on the levelled aggregate surface. Ensure that the plunger does not get struck in the cylinder.
6. Place the apparatus, with test sample and plunger, between the platens of the compression testing machine. Apply compressive load at a steadily increasing rate such that 40 tonnes (40 kN) of load is reached in 10 minutes, and then release the load.
7. Remove crushed aggregate from the steel cup and sieve it using 2.36 mm sieve. Weigh the fraction passing through the sieve ($W_2$) to the nearest 1 gram.
8. Repeat the test on another coarse aggregate sample, weighing $W_1$, taken from the same batch. Calculate aggregate crushing value using given expression for both tests. Report mean of the two values, to the nearest whole number, as the aggregate impact value for the given sample of coarse aggregates.

**Observation Table**

| | Test 1 | Test 2 |
|---|---|---|
| Weight of surface dry sample ($W_1$) in grams | | |
| Weight of fraction passing through 2.36 mm sieve ($W_2$) in grams | | |
| Aggregate crushing value (%) | | |
| Mean aggregate crushing value (%) | | |

**Calculations**

$$\textit{Aggregate crushing value} = \frac{W_2}{W_1} X100\%$$

**Results**

The aggregate crushing value of the given sample of coarse aggregate is ________ %.

**Conclusion**

Select the correct statement:

- Since aggregate crushing value is less than 30%, concrete made with this aggregate can be used for all applications.

- Since aggregate crushing value is between 30 and 45%, concrete made with this aggregate can be used for any application other than wearing surfaces.
- Since aggregate crushing value is more than 45%, concrete made with this aggregate cannot be used for any application.

**Precautions**

1. Assembly of base plate, cylinder and plunger should be aligned carefully so that plunger does not get stuck in the cylinder.
2. Care should be taken to avoid loss of fine particles during all the operations.

**References**

1. IS 2386 (Part IV): Methods of test for aggregates for concrete: Mechanical properties. Bureau of Indian Standards, New Delhi.
2. IS 383: Specification for coarse and fine aggregates from natural sources for concrete. Bureau of Indian Standards, New Delhi.

## EXPERIMENT 11: DETERMINATION OF AGGREGATE ABRASION VALUE OF COARSE AGGREGATES

**Objective:** To determine the abrasion value of coarse aggregates using Los Angeles test.

**Apparatus and Materials**

1. Los Angeles abrasion testing machine
2. Indian Standard sieve of size 1.70 mm
3. Abrasive charge: cast iron or steel spheres with diameter 48 mm and weight 390 to 445 grams; number of spheres depends on grading of the test sample
4. Well-ventilated oven capable to maintain temperature of 100 to 110°C

**Theory**

Abrasion resistance is the ability of a surface to resist being worn away by rubbing or friction. It is important in construction of floors, roads, or pavements. Abrasion resistance of concrete is primarily influenced by abrasion resistance of coarse aggregates, which is determined in laboratory by Los Angeles abrasion test machine. The principle of Los Angeles abrasion test is to produce abrasive action by use of standard steel balls (also called abrasive charge). These balls are mixed with aggregates and rotated in a drum for specific number of revolutions. The percentage wear of the aggregates due to rubbing with steel balls is determined and is known as Los Angeles Abrasion Value.

**Table 6.1:** Quantity of abrasive charge based on grading of aggregate sample

| Grading | Number of spheres | Weight of Charge (gm) |
|---|---|---|
| A | 12 | 5000 ± 25 |
| B | 11 | 4584 ± 25 |
| C | 8 | 3320 ± 20 |
| D | 6 | 2500 ± 15 |
| E | 12 | 5000 ± 25 |
| F | 12 | 5000 ± 25 |
| G | 12 | 5000 ± 25 |

(a) (b)

**Fig. 6.13:** (a) Los Angeles abrasion machine, (b) Abrasive charges

**Procedure**

1. Take a sample of clean aggregates and dry it in an oven at 105 to 110°C, to substantially constant weight. Record weight of aggregate sample ($W_1$) to the nearest gram.
2. Conduct sieve analysis on the test sample and grade it based on Table II of IS 2386. Determine the quantity of abrasive charge required for the test based on Table 6.1.
3. Place the test sample and the abrasive charge in the Los Angeles abrasion testing machine, and rotate the machine at a speed of 20 to 33 rpm. If aggregate sample corresponds to grading A, B, C or D, machine should be rotated for 500 revolutions. For aggregates with grading E, F or G, it should be rotated for 1000 revolutions.
4. Discharge the material from the machine and sieve it using a sieve coarser than 1.70 mm sieve. Sieve the finer portion using 1.70 mm sieve.
5. Wash the material coarser than 1.70 mm sieve and dry it in oven at 105 to 110°C, to substantially constant weight. Weigh it ($W_2$) to the nearest gram.
6. Calculate the difference between the initial weight and the final weight. Express it as a percentage of the initial weight of the test sample, to obtain aggregate abrasion value.

**Observation Table**

| | |
|---|---|
| Weight of oven dry sample ($W_1$) in grams | |
| Weight of fraction coarser than 1.70 mm sieve ($W_2$) in grams | |
| Aggregate abrasion value (%) | |
| Mean aggregate crushing value (%) | |

**Calculations**

$$Aggregate\,abrasion\,value = \frac{W_2}{W_1} X100\%$$

**Results**

The aggregate abrasion value of the given sample of coarse aggregate is found to be ____ %

**Conclusion**

Since aggregate abrasion value is less/more than 16%, these aggregates can/cannot be used to prepare concrete.

**Precautions**

1. Los Angeles abrasion testing machine should be driven and counter-balanced so as to maintain a substantially uniform peripheral speed. If an angle is used as the shelf, the machine should be rotated in such a direction that the charge is caught on the outside surface of the angle.
2. Care should be taken to avoid loss of fine particles during all the operations.

**References**

1. IS 2386 (Part IV): Methods of test for aggregates for concrete: Mechanical properties. Bureau of Indian Standards, New Delhi.
2. IS 383: Specification for coarse and fine aggregates from natural sources for concrete. Bureau of Indian Standards, New Delhi.

## EXPERIMENT 12: DETERMINATION OF FLAKINESS AND ELONGATION INDICES OF COARSE AGGREGATES

**Objective:** To determine flakiness index and elongation index of coarse aggregates

**Apparatus and Materials**

1. Weighing balance with an accuracy of 0.1% of weight of test sample
2. Thickness gauge shown in Fig. 6.14 (for flakiness index)
3. Length gauge shown in Fig. 6.15 (for elongation index)
4. Indian Standard sieves of size 63 mm, 50 mm, 40 mm, 31.5 mm, 25 mm, 20 mm, 16 mm, 12.5 mm, 10.5 mm and 6.3 mm, with pan and lid
5. Enamel tray and Scoop
6. Stopwatch
7. Coarse aggregate

**Theory**

Particle shape and surface texture influence the properties of freshly mixed concrete more than the properties of hardened concrete. Rough-textured, angular, and elongated particles require more water to produce workable concrete than smooth, rounded compact aggregate. Consequently, the cement content must also be increased to maintain the water-cement ratio. Generally, flat, and elongated particles are avoided or are limited to about 15 % by weight of the total aggregate. Presence of such undesirable particles is given by flakiness and elongation indices.

Flakiness index of coarse aggregate is the percentage by weight of particles in it whose least dimension (thickness) is less than three-fifth of their mean dimension. Elongation index of an aggregate is the percentage by weight of particles whose greatest dimension (length) is greater than nine-fifths times their mean dimension. Tests for flakiness and elongation indices presented here, are not applicable to particle sizes smaller than 6.3 mm. If flakiness index and/or elongation index of given coarse aggregate exceeds 35%, it should not be used to prepare concrete.

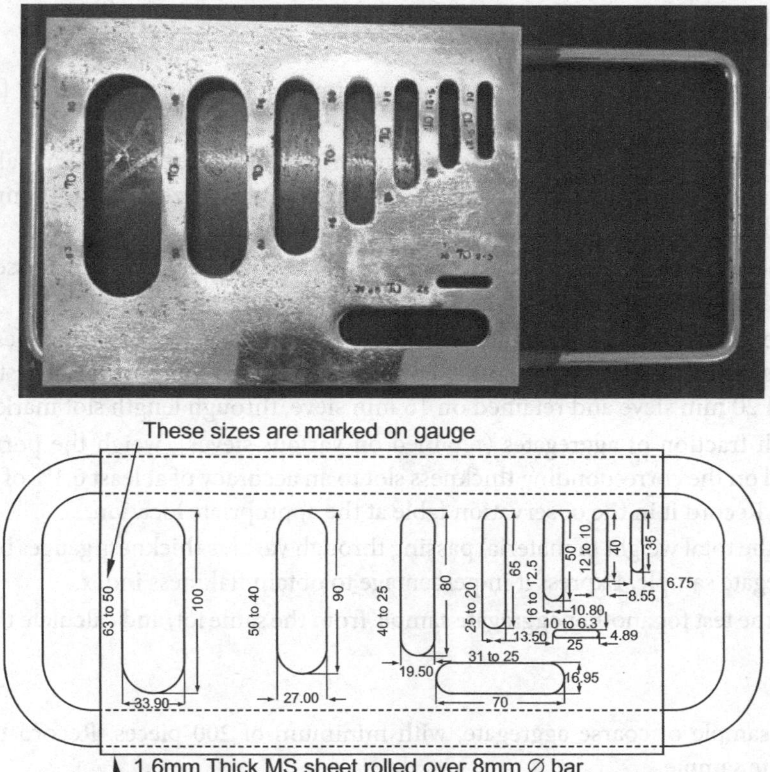


All dimensions are in mm

**Fig. 6.14:** Thickness gauge

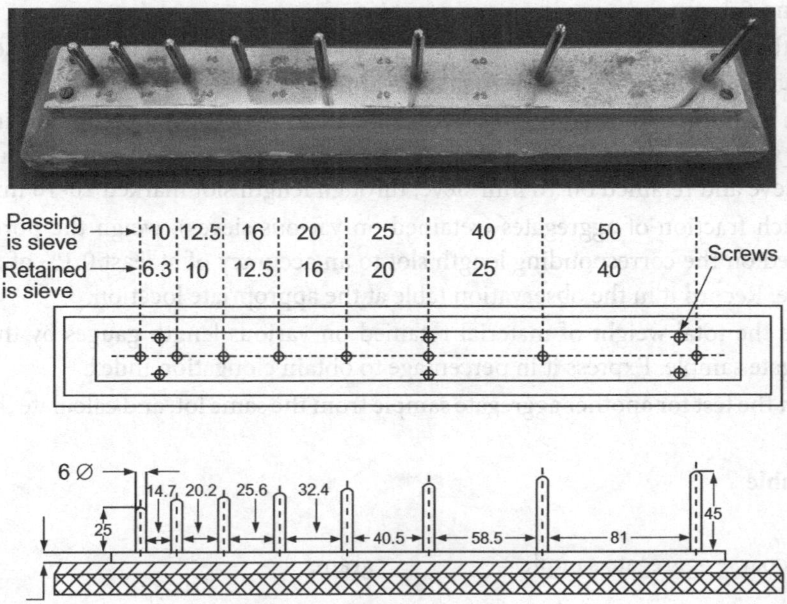


All dimensions are in mm

**Fig. 6.15:** Length gauge

**Procedure**

*Flakiness index:*

1. Take a sample of coarse aggregate, with minimum of 200 pieces. Record the weight of the aggregate sample.
2. Assemble the sieves depending on maximum size of aggregates (MSA), along with pan at bottom and lid at top. For instance, for CA20, use sieves of size 20 mm, 16 mm, 12.5 mm, 10.5 mm and 6.3 mm.
3. Place the aggregate sample on the top sieve, and sieve it through the sieve assembly by shaking it either manually or using a sieve shaker.
4. Gauge each fraction of aggregates (retained on various sieves) for thickness, using a metal thickness gauge shown in Fig. 6.14. For example, gauge the portion of test sample, passing through 20 mm sieve and retained on 16 mm sieve, through length slot marked 20-16 mm.
5. For each fraction of aggregates (retained on various sieves), weigh the portion of aggregate retained on the corresponding thickness slot to an accuracy of at least 0.1% of the weight of test sample. Record it in the observation table at the appropriate location.
6. Divide the total weight of material passing through various thickness gauges by the total weight of aggregate sample. Express it in percentage to obtain flakiness index.
7. Repeat the test for another aggregate sample from the same lot, and calculate the mean flakiness index.

*Elongation index:*

1. Take a sample of coarse aggregate, with minimum of 200 pieces. Record the weight of the aggregate sample.
2. Assemble the sieves depending on maximum size of aggregates (MSA), along with pan at bottom and lid at top. For instance, for CA20, use sieves of size 20 mm, 16 mm, 12.5 mm, 10.5 mm and 6.3 mm.
3. Place the aggregate sample on the top sieve, and sieve it through the sieve assembly by shaking it either manually or using a sieve shaker.
4. Gauge each fraction of aggregates (retained on various sieves) for length, using a metal length gauge shown in Fig. 6.15. For example, gauge the portion of test sample, passing through 20 mm sieve and retained on 16 mm sieve, through length slot marked 20-16 mm.
5. For each fraction of aggregates (retained on various sieves), weigh the portion of aggregate retained on the corresponding length slot to an accuracy of at least 0.1% of the weight of test sample. Record it in the observation table at the appropriate location.
6. Divide the total weight of material retained on various length gauges by the total weight of aggregate sample. Express it in percentage to obtain elongation index.
7. Repeat the test for another aggregate sample from the same lot, and calculate the mean flakiness index.

**Observation Table**

*Flakiness index:*

Total weight of coarse aggregate sample = ________ grams

| Size of Aggregate Thickness | | Size of corresponding thickness gauge (mm) | Weight of aggregate passing through thickness gauge | |
|---|---|---|---|---|
| Passing through IS Sieve | Retained on IS sieve | | Test 1 | Test 2 |
| 63 mm | 50 mm | 33.90 | | |
| 50 mm | 40 mm | 27.00 | | |
| 40 mm | 25 mm | 19.60 | | |
| 31.5 mm | 25 mm | 16.95 | | |
| 25 mm | 20 mm | 13.50 | | |
| 20 mm | 16 mm | 10.80 | | |
| 16 mm | 12 mm | 8.55 | | |
| 12.5 mm | 10 mm | 6.75 | | |
| 10 mm | 6.3 mm | 4.89 | | |
| | | Total | | |
| Flakiness Index | | | | |
| Mean Flakiness Index | | | | |

*Elongation index:*

Total weight of coarse aggregate sample = ________ grams

| Size of Aggregate Thickness | | Size of corresponding length gauge (mm) | Weight of aggregate retained on length gauge | |
|---|---|---|---|---|
| Passing through IS Sieve | Retained on IS sieve | | Test 1 | Test 2 |
| 63 mm | 50 mm | 101.7 | | |
| 50 mm | 40 mm | 81.0 | | |
| 40 mm | 25 mm | 58.5 | | |
| 31.5 mm | 25 mm | 50.9 | | |
| 25 mm | 20 mm | 40.5 | | |
| 20 mm | 16 mm | 32.4 | | |
| 16 mm | 12 mm | 25.6 | | |
| 12.5 mm | 10 mm | 20.2 | | |
| 10 mm | 6.3 mm | 14.7 | | |
| | | Total | | |
| Elongation Index | | | | |
| Mean Elongation Index | | | | |

**Calculations**

*Flakiness index:*

$$Flakiness\,index = \frac{Total\,weight\,passing\,through\,thickness\,gauge}{Total\,weight\,of\,aggregate\,sample} X100\%$$

*Elongation index:*

$$Elongation\,index = \frac{Total\,weight\,retained\,on\,length\,gauge}{Total\,weight\,of\,aggregate\,sample} X100\%$$

**Results**

1. The flakiness index of the given sample of coarse aggregate is __________ %.
2. The elongation index of the given sample of coarse aggregate is __________ %.

**Conclusion**

Based on determined values of flakiness and elongation indices, the given sample of coarse aggregate is acceptable/unacceptable.

**Precautions**

1. Weight of different fractions passing through thickness gauge and those retained on length gauge should be measured to an accuracy of 0.1% of the weight of test sample.
2. The test sample from the aggregate lot should be taken randomly. If required, aggregates in the lot should be mixed thoroughly.

**References**

1. IS 2386 (Part I): Methods of test for aggregates for concrete: Particle size and shape. Bureau of Indian Standards, New Delhi.
2. IS 383: Specification for coarse and fine aggregates from natural sources for concrete. Bureau of Indian Standards, New Delhi.

## EXPERIMENT 13: DETERMINATION OF WORKABILITY OF CONCRETE BY SLUMP CONE TEST

**Objective:** To determine workability of the concrete mix using slump cone test.

**Apparatus and Materials**

1. A metal mould, in the form of frustum a cone, having the following internal dimensions
   - Bottom Diameter 200 ± 2 mm
   - Top Diameter 100 ± 2 mm
   - Height 300 ± 2 mm
   - Minimum Thickness 1.6 mm
2. Steel tamping rod with diameter of 16 ± 1 mm, length of 600 ± 5 mm, with rounded ends
3. Flat and smooth base plate
4. Concrete mixer
5. Mixing tray and Trowel
6. Steel ruler with graduations at least up to 300 mm
7. Cement, Sand, Coarse aggregates and Potable water

**Theory**

Workability of concrete is a measure of ease in performing early stage concreting operations. It is a composite property which comprises of consistency and cohesiveness. Slump cone test is the most widely used test for measuring consistency. Higher slump value implies better consistency. This test is suitable for green concrete mixes with a range of consistency, corresponding to slump values between 10 mm and 210 mm. if the obtained slump value lies outside this range, the test results are not reliable and other methods of determining consistency of fresh concrete need to be used.

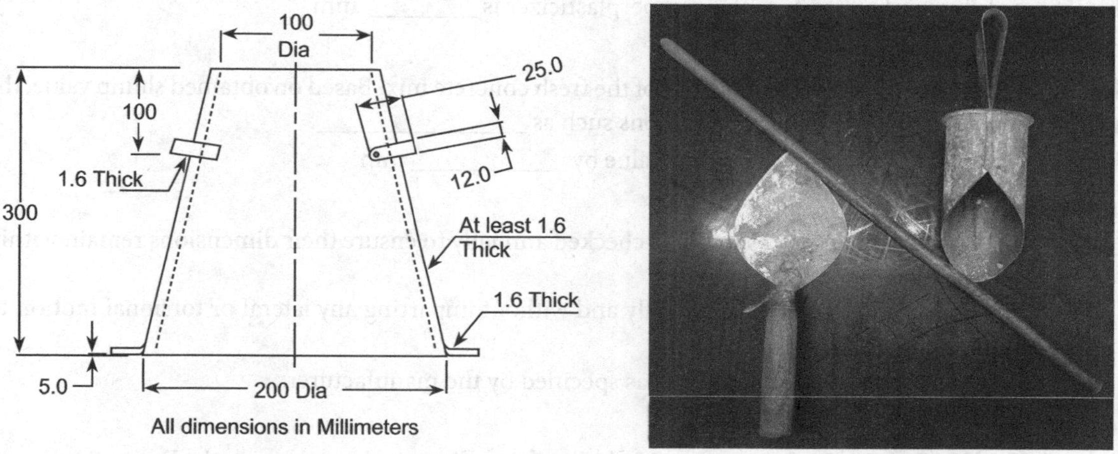


**Fig. 6.16:** Schematic diagram of slump cone, and Tamping rod, scoop and trowel

**Procedure**

1. Thoroughly clean and dampen the internal surface of the mould.
2. Place the mould on a flat and smooth base plate made of metal. The mould should be firmly held in place on the base plate and the base plate should be free from any extraneous shock and vibration.
3. Prepare the fresh concrete by mixing the ingredients in desired proportions, obtained from concrete mix design. Typically, take 4 kg of cement and appropriate quantities of other ingredients. For learning purpose in laboratory, consider a concrete mix with proportions 1 : 1.5 : 3 (cement : sand : coarse aggregate) and water-cement ratio of 0.50.
4. Fill the mould with freshly prepared concrete in three layers. Tamp each layer with 25 strokes of tamping rod. Apply these strokes in a uniformly distributed manner over the cross-section of the mould. Moreover, for second and third layers, these strokes should penetrate the underlying layer. For top layer, heap the concrete before tamping it.
5. Strike off the top layer and level it with trowel or tamping rod, to ensure that mould is exactly filled to the brim. Also, remove spilled concrete from the outer surface of the mould and the base plate.
6. Remove the mould by lifting it in a vertical direction slowly (in 5 ± 2 seconds), without applying any disturbance to the concrete in the mould. Complete the entire operation, from the start of filling concrete in mould to the removal of mould, within 3 minutes.
7. Removal of mould allows concrete to subside. Measure this subsidence to the nearest 5 mm, i.e., difference between height of the mould and highest point of the sample. This gives us the slump value of the fresh concrete mix.

8. Repeat the procedure with addition of superplasticizer to another freshly prepared concrete mix.

**Observations**

The observed slump using slump cone test is ________ mm without use of superplasticizer.
The observed slump using slump cone test is ________ mm with use of superplasticizer.

**Results**

The observed slump of concrete without superplasticizer is ________ mm.

**Conclusion**

This implies high/medium/low workability of the fresh concrete mix. Based on obtained slump value, the prepared concrete can be used for applications such as ______________.
Use of superplasticizer increase the slump value by ___________ mm.

**Precautions**

1. Mould and tamping rod should be checked annually to ensure their dimensions remain within specified tolerance limits.
2. Mould should be removed vertically and without imparting any lateral or torsional motion to the concrete.
3. Superplasticizer dosage should be as specified by the manufacturer.

**References**

1. IS 1199 (Part 2): Fresh concrete- Methods of sampling, testing and analysis: Determination of consistency of fresh concrete. Bureau of Indian Standards, New Delhi.

## EXPERIMENT 14: DETERMINATION OF WORKABILITY OF CONCRETE BY COMPACTION FACTOR TEST

**Objective:** To determine workability of the concrete mix using compaction factor test

**Apparatus and Materials**

1. Compaction factor test apparatus consisting of
   a. Two conical hoppers
   b. One cylindrical mould
2. Steel tamping rod with diameter of 16 ± 1 mm, length of 600 ± 5 mm, with rounded ends
3. Two ordinary trowels
4. Weighing balance of capacity up to 50 kg with an accuracy of ± 10 grams
5. Standard vibration machine (conforming to IS 10080)
6. Cement, Sand, Coarse aggregates and Potable water

**Theory**

Compaction factor test is a method to determine consistency of concrete. This test is applicable to concrete with nominal maximum size of aggregate up to 40 mm. Though this test is usually performed in a laboratory, it may also be used in field. This test is more precise and sensitive than slump cone test, and is particularly useful for dry concrete mixes (low workability). However, for very low workability (compaction factor less than 0.7), this test is not suitable. Compaction factor test gives behaviour of fresh concrete under the action of external forces.

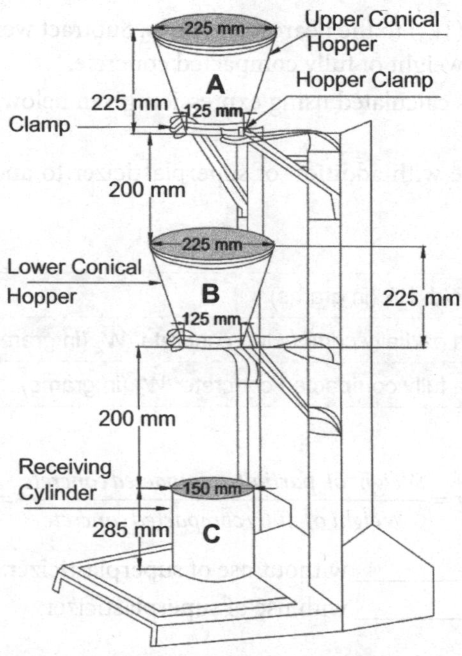


**Fig. 6.17:** Schematic diagram of compaction factor apparatus

**Procedure**

1. Dampen the inner surfaces of the hoppers and the cylinder.
2. Determine the weight of the cylindrical mould ($W_1$) without top plate and mount it on the base of the frame.
3. Prepare the fresh concrete by mixing the ingredients in desired proportions, obtained from concrete mix design. Typically, take 4 kg of cement and appropriate quantities of other ingredients. For learning purpose in laboratory, consider a concrete mix with proportions 1 : 1.5 : 3 (cement : sand : coarse aggregate) and water-cement ratio of 0.50.
4. Fill the upper hopper gently to the brim, keeping the trap door closed. Do not press the mix.
5. Open the trap door of upper hopper, preferably within two minutes of the mixing, allowing the sample to fall into the lower hopper.
6. After the concrete has come to rest, remove the top plate of the cylinder and open the trap door of the lower hopper. This allows the sample to fall into the cylinder.
7. If the concrete mixture does not easily fall from the hoppers, gently push the mixture with a rod.
8. Remove excess concrete from the cylinder using a trowel, and clean the outer surface of the cylinder. Perform this operation at a place free from shocks and vibrations.
9. Weigh the cylinder with concrete ($W_2$) to the nearest 50 grams. Subtract weight of empty cylinder from this weight to obtain the weight of partially compacted concrete.
10. Refill the cylinder with the same fresh concrete sample in layers approximately 5 cm deep. Vibrate these layers or ram them heavily so as to obtain full compaction. Strike off the excess concrete from top of the cylinder, and clean its outer surface. Weigh the cylinder with

compacted concrete ($W_3$) to the nearest 50 grams. Subtract weight of empty cylinder from this weight to obtain the weight of fully compacted concrete.

11. Compaction factor is calculated using expression given below, and is expressed to the nearest two decimal points.
12. Repeat the procedure with addition of superplasticizer to another freshly prepared concrete mix.

**Observation Table**

| | |
|---|---|
| Weight of empty cylindrical mould, $W_1$ (in grams) | |
| Weight of cylindrical mould with partially compacted concrete, $W_2$ (in grams) | |
| Weight of cylindrical mould with fully compacted concrete, $W_3$ (in grams) | |

**Calculations**

$$Compaction\ Factor = \frac{Weight\ of\ partially\ compacted\ concrete}{Weight\ of\ fully\ compacted\ concrete} = \frac{W_2 - W_1}{W_3 - W_1}$$

The compaction factor is ________ without use of superplasticizer.
The compaction factor is ________ with use of superplasticizer.

**Results**

The observed compaction factor of concrete without superplasticizer is ________.

**Conclusion**

This implies high/medium/low workability of the fresh concrete mix. Based on obtained compaction factor value, the prepared concrete can be used for applications such as ____________. Use of superplasticizer increase the compaction factor value by ____________.

**Precautions**

1. Mould and tamping rod should be checked annually to ensure their dimensions remain within specified tolerance limits.
2. While filling concrete in upper hopper, concrete should not be pressed/compacted.
3. Superplasticizer dosage should be as specified by the manufacturer.

**References**

1. IS 1199 (Part II): Fresh concrete- Methods of sampling, testing and analysis: Determination of consistency of fresh concrete. Bureau of Indian Standards, New Delhi.

## EXPERIMENT 15: MIX DESIGN FOR A PARTICULAR GRADE OF CONCRETE AND DETERMINATION OF ITS 7-DAYS AND 28-DAYS COMPRESSIVE STRENGTH

**Objective:** To prepare concrete mix of a particular grade and determine compressive strength of concrete for 7 and 28 days

**Apparatus and Materials**

1. Cube moulds with side 70.6 mm – 6 nos.
2. Tray and Trowel

3. Digital weighing balance with an accuracy of ±1 g
4. Measuring cylinder with an accuracy of ±1 ml
5. Concrete mixer- Drum or pan type
6. Standard slump cone
7. Steel tamping rod with diameter of 16 ± 1 mm, length of 600 ± 5 mm, with rounded ends
8. Measuring scale
9. Standard vibration machine (conforming to IS 10080)
10. Compression Testing Machine (CTM)
11. Cement, Sand, Coarse aggregates (CA10 and CA20), Potable water, Admixtures

**Theory**

oncrete comprises of ingredients such as cement, water, sand, coarse aggregates and admixtures. All these ingredients are mixed in certain proportions to obtain concrete of desired quality. This process of selecting suitable ingredients in right proportions to produce concrete of desired quality is called concrete mix design.

The standard procedure to ascertain compressive strength of concrete is to cast a set of 6 cubes. Generally, three cubes are tested at 7 days and 28 days each. Usually 7 days strength is about 60-70% of 28-days strength.

**Fig. 6.18:** Moulds for preparing concrete cubes (150 mm side)

**Procedure**

*Mix design:*

1. Obtain proportions of concrete ingredients (per cubic metre of concrete) as per mix design procedure detailed in Unit III.

*Determination of compressive strength:*

1. Calculate quantities of ingredients, viz., cement, sand, CA10, CA20 and water, so as to obtain approximately 72 kg of concrete.
2. Weigh the required quantities of all ingredients and mix them thoroughly in a concrete mixer until uniform colour of concrete mix is obtained. Mixing time is not less than 2 minutes after all the ingredients are fed into the mixer.
3. Clean all the six cube moulds and apply mould oil on their inner surfaces.
4. Workability of fresh concrete mix is determined using slump cone test (Experiment 13).
5. Fill concrete in cube moulds in three layers of 50 mm. Ram each layer thoroughly by hand using tamping rod (35 strokes per layer) or compact each layer using standard vibration machine.
6. Store concrete filled moulds for 24 hours, at a place free from shocks and vibrations, with temperature of 27 ± 2 °C and relative humidity of at least 90% (moist gunny bags may be used for this purpose).
7. Remove concrete cubes from moulds and place them submerged in potable water (at temperature of 24 to 30 °C) for curing.
8. Take three cubes out of curing tank at 7 days and wipe off surface water to make them saturated surface dry.
9. Measure dimensions of cube specimens and their weight.

10. Place the cubes between both platens of the compression testing machine and apply compression at a rate of approximately 140 kg/sq.cm/minute. Record the maximum load applied and note the crack features at failure.
11. Perform steps 8 to 10 for the remaining three cubes at 28 days.

**Observations and Calculations**

| Mix design for concrete grade M___ and target slump _____ mm | | | | | | |
|---|---|---|---|---|---|---|
| **Ingredients** | **Water** | **Cement** | **Sand** | **CA10** | **CA20** | **Admixture** |
| Quantity (kg/m$^3$) | | | | | | |
| Ratio (per unit weight of cement) | | | | | | |
| Quantity (kg per 72 kg of concrete) | | | | | | |

| Weight of cube specimen | | | | | |
|---|---|---|---|---|---|
| **Time** | **Specimen 1** | **Specimen 2** | **Specimen 3** | **Average Weight (Kg.)** | **Remarks** |
| 7 days | | | | | |
| 28 days | | | | | |

| Result of cube strength | | | | | | |
|---|---|---|---|---|---|---|
| **Time** | **Load in kN** | | | **Average load in kN** | **Average Stress in N/mm$^2$** | **Remarks** |
| | **Specimen 1** | **Specimen 2** | **Specimen 3** | | | |
| 7 days | | | | | | |
| 28 days | | | | | | |

Observations on failure pattern: ______________________________

**Results**

The average compressive strength of concrete is found to be ______ N/mm$^2$ at 7 days and ______ N/mm$^2$ at 28 days.

**Conclusion**

Based on determined compressive strength of concrete, the obtained concrete is acceptable/unacceptable.

**Precautions**

1. Carefully measure ingredients, especially quantity of water.
2. Optimal mixing of ingredients is advised. Over mixing may lead to segregation and bleeding.
3. Temperature of curing water should be monitored. In case of cold weather, water heaters should be used to maintain adequate temperature of water in the curing tank.

4. While testing under compression, cube surfaces should have uniform contact with platens of the CTM.
5. Time (7 days and 28 days) should be measured from the time of adding water during preparation of concrete mix.

**References**

1. IS 516 (Part I, Section I): Hardened concrete - Methods of test - Testing of strength of hardened concrete - Compressive, flexural and split tensile strength. Bureau of Indian Standards, New Delhi.

## EXPERIMENT 16: DEMONSTRATION OF NON-DESTRUCTIVE TESTING (NDT) EQUIPMENT

**Objective:** To demonstrate working principles, uses and application of non-destructive test equipment

**Apparatus and Materials**

1. Ultrasonic Pulse Velocity (UPV) meter with accessories
2. Rebound Schmidt Hammer with accessories

**Theory**

Testing of concrete cubes in the compression testing machines is destructive, as cubes fail after cracking and test specimens are completely destroyed. Therefore, several non-destructive testing (NDT) methods have been devised to assess the strength of the in-situ structural concrete members, without causing any permanent damages. Two popular NDT methods are: (i) Ultrasonic Pulse velocity method, and (ii) Rebound hammer method. These methods are widely used for assessing the concrete strength and uniformity. While, the ultrasonic pulse velocity method gives a measure of uniformity of the concrete mass, the rebound hammer test estimates surface hardness of the concrete. Working principles of UPV meter and rebound hammer are detailed in Unit 3.

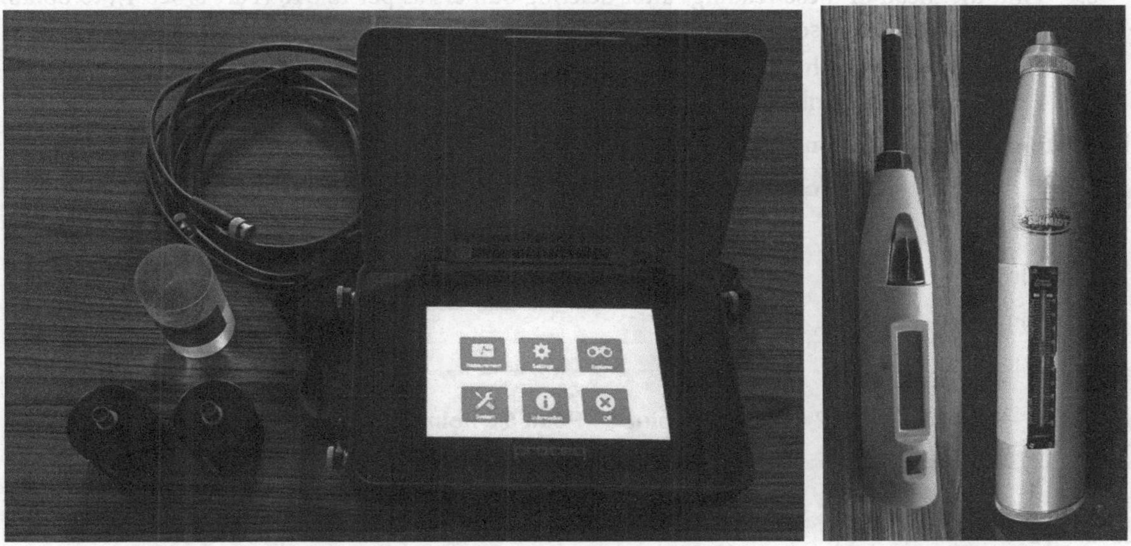

(a) (b)

**Fig. 6.19:** (a) Ultrasonic Pulse Velocity (UPV) meter, (b) Rebound hammer

**Procedure**

*Ultrasonic Pulse Velocity (UPV) test*

1. Calibrate the ultrasonic pulse velocity (UPV) meter by testing against the standard calibration bar.
2. Clean and smoothen the test surfaces using a grinding stone. If opposite faces of a concrete member are accessible, take one test surface on either face. This is called direct measurement. If opposite faces are not accessible but orthogonal faces are accessible, take one test surface on either orthogonal face. This is called semi-direct measurement. If only one face is accessible, take both test surfaces on the same face of concrete member, at a certain spacing. This is called indirect measurement.
3. Apply acoustical couplants like grease or petroleum jelly on the prepared test surfaces.
4. Place transducers on the prepared test surfaces.
5. Select the right options depending on the nature of measurement (direct / semi-direct / indirect). Feed the path length.
6. Record the ultrasonic pulse velocity and estimate quality of concrete based on Table I of IS 516 Part V Section I.

*Rebound hammer test*

1. Confirm the rebound hammer is calibrated by testing against the testing anvil.
2. Clean and smoothen the test surface using a grinding stone.
3. Release the plunger before use and then strongly press it, keeping normal to the concrete surface. Upon pressing, lock the plunger in its position.
4. Note the reading on the display window of the hammer. This reading is the rebound number.
5. Repeat above steps at a minimum of six points. Select points of impact at least 25 mm away from any edge or shape discontinuity.
6. Find the mean of these readings after deleting outliers as per IS 516 (Part 5/Sec 4), to obtain rebound number (also called rebound index).
7. Compressive strength can then be found employing a calibration graph of compressive strength versus Rebound number, usually provided by manufacturer.

**Observations and Calculations**

| | Ultrasonic pulse velocity (km/s) | Quality of concrete |
|---|---|---|
| Location 1 | | |
| Location 2 | | |
| Location 3 | | |

| | Point 1 | Point 2 | Point 3 | Point 4 | Point 5 | Point 6 | Mean Rebound Number | Estimated compressive strength (MPa) |
|---|---|---|---|---|---|---|---|---|
| Location 1 | | | | | | | | |
| Location 2 | | | | | | | | |
| Location 3 | | | | | | | | |

**Results**

Ultrasonic pulse velocity at the tested location is found to be _______ km/s.

Rebound number at the tested location is found to be _______.

**Conclusion**

Based on ultrasonic pulse velocity value, the concrete quality is excellent / good / doubtful / poor.

Based on rebound number, the compressive strength is estimated as ______ MPa, using calibration chart provided by manufacturer of the rebound hammer.

**Precautions**

1. Ultrasonic pulse velocity test should be conducted on a clean, dry and smooth surface.
2. Couplant should be applied adequately on the test surface to ensure good contact between transducer and test surface, so as to achieve reliable results.
3. The point of impact, in case of rebound hammer test, should be at least 25 mm away from any edge or shape discontinuity.
4. The rebound hammer should be used such that impact is normal to the concrete surface. This may require additional care while using rebound hammer on the soffit of a concrete member.
5. Rebound hammer should be used on a clean, dry and smooth surface.

**References**

1. IS 516 (Part V, Section I): Hardened concrete - Methods of test – Non-destructive testing of concrete: Ultrasonic pulse velocity testing. Bureau of Indian Standards, New Delhi.
2. IS 516 (Part V, Section IV): Hardened concrete - Methods of test – Non-destructive testing of concrete: Rebound hammer test. Bureau of Indian Standards, New Delhi.
3. IS 13311 (Part I): Non-destructive testing of concrete- Methods of Test: Ultrasonic pulse velocity testing. Bureau of Indian Standards, New Delhi.
4. IS 13311 (Part II): Non-destructive testing of concrete- Methods of Test: Rebound hammer. Bureau of Indian Standards, New Delhi.

## UNIT SUMMARY

- This unit provides detailed laboratory procedures to assess properties of concrete and its ingredients.
- Fineness, specific gravity, standard consistency, initial and final setting times and compressive strength of cement are determined using laboratory experiments based on Indian Standard.
- Experiments to determine bulk density, water absorption and fineness modulus of fine and coarse aggregates are described. Procedure to assess silt content in sand and bulking of sand have been provided. Tests to determine strength indicators of coarse aggregates, such as impact value, crushing value and abrasion value, are presented. Experiments on parameters related to shape of coarse aggregates, viz., elongation and flakiness indices, are also described.
- Laboratory tests to find workability of fresh concrete and compressive strength of hardened concrete are also detailed. Use and applications of non-destructive tests on hardened concrete are briefly presented.

# CO AND PO ATTAINMENT TABLE

Course outcomes (COs) for this course can be mapped with the programme outcomes (POs) after the completion of the course and a correlation can be made for the attainment of POs to analyze the gap. After proper analysis of the gap in the attainment of POs necessary measures can be taken to overcome the gaps.

**Table for CO and PO attainment**

| Course Outcomes | ATTAINMENT OF PROGRAMME OUTCOMES (1- Weak Correlation; 2- Medium Correlation; 3- Strong Correlation) | | | | | | |
|---|---|---|---|---|---|---|---|
| | PO-1 | PO-2 | PO-3 | PO-4 | PO-5 | PO-6 | PO-7 |
| CO-1 | | | | | | | |
| CO-2 | | | | | | | |
| CO-3 | | | | | | | |
| CO-4 | | | | | | | |
| CO-5 | | | | | | | |

The data filled in the above table can be used for gap analysis.

# INDEX

## T



## U



## V



## W

Dynamic QR Code for the book